Praise for *Educational Oases in the Desert*

"The book is well-written … [Sciarcon's] detailed and concentrated account adds a valuable piece to the history of Jewish women in this period."

— *Association of Jewish Libraries Reviews*

"While the pedagogical empire created by the AIU has received broad treatment before, this book narrows its focus to a specific time period and locale, allowing for a more nuanced look at the interplay between girls' schools, issues such as gender and education, and concepts of Westernization, cultural transplants, and agents of change."

— *H-Net Reviews (H-Judaic)*

"In addition to immersing the reader in the fascinating world of turn-of-the-century Ottoman Iraq, this book contributes to the growing body of scholarship about Jewish girls' education, the AIU, and female education in the Ottoman Empire during this period."

— *Reading Religion*

Educational Oases in the Desert

JONATHAN SCIARCON

EDUCATIONAL OASES IN THE DESERT

The Alliance Israélite Universelle's Girls' Schools in Ottoman Iraq, 1895–1915

SUNY PRESS

Cover image: The Alliance Israélite Universelle Girls' School in Baghdad, late nineteenth century

Published by State University of New York Press, Albany

Printed in the United States of America

For information, contact State University of New York Press, Albany, NY
www.sunypress.edu

Production, Jenn Bennett
Marketing, Fran Keneston

Library of Congress Cataloging-in-Publication Data

Names: Sciarcon, Jonathan, author.
Title: Educational oases in the desert : the Alliance israélite universelle's girls' schools in Ottoman Iraq, 1895–1915 / Jonathan Sciarcon.
Description: Albany, NY : State University of New York Press, 2017. | Includes bibliographical references and index.
Identifiers: LCCN 2016035405 (print) | LCCN 2016059181 (ebook) | ISBN 9781438465852 (hardcover : alk. paper) | 9781438465845 (pbk : alk. paper) ISBN 9781438465869 (e-book)
Subjects: LCSH: Alliance israélite universelle. | Girls' schools—Iraq—History. | Girls—Education—Iraq. | Jewish day schools—Iraq—History.
Classification: LCC LC2410.3 .S35 2017 (print) | LCC LC2410.3 (ebook) | DDC 371.82209567—dc23
LC record available at https://lccn.loc.gov/2016035405

10 9 8 7 6 5 4 3 2 1

CONTENTS

LIST OF TABLES

ACKNOWLEDGMENTS

I am pleased to have the opportunity to thank the people and institutions whose assistance made this book possible. My graduate school mentor Nancy Gallagher introduced me to the Alliance Israélite Universelle and the study of Iraqi Jewry during my time at the University of California, Santa Barbara. Her support has been essential to my professional work as a researcher and educator.

I am profoundly grateful to Jean-Claude Kuperminc for granting me access to the Alliance Israélite Universelle's archive in Paris in 2013. The archive's staff was kind, helpful, and efficient in assisting me. I would also like to thank Vardit Samuels and her colleagues at Harvard University's Widener Library's Judaica Division for allowing me to use Harvard's microfilmed Alliance archive in 2010 and 2012. Although I did not ultimately use the material I consulted there, I am grateful to Sarah Maspero and her colleagues in Archives and Special Collections at the University of Southampton's Hartley Library for allowing me to consult the Anglo-Jewish Association's archives. Sarah did, however, inform me that the organization's nineteenth- and early twentieth-century archival files are available online through Hartley Library's website. I did make use of these files. Finally, I would like to thank the staff of the British National Archives for their assistance in both 2011 and 2013.

My research has been funded by two main sources. The University of Denver provided me with initial research funds upon my arrival as a faculty member in 2010, which allowed me to conduct preliminary research in London and in Cambridge, Massachusetts. I later received a Faculty Research Fund grant from the university's division of Arts, Humanities, and Social Sciences, which allowed me to conduct my research in Paris and Southampton.

I had the good fortune to work with excellent scholars at the University of California, Santa Barbara, especially R. Stephen Humphreys, Salim Yaqub, Hal Drake, and John W.I. Lee. During my time in Santa Barbara I also benefitted greatly from the support of friends. These include Monica Orozco, Nancy McLoughlin, Patrick Shapland, and, especially, the late Tom Sizgorich. Tom was a great friend and mentor to many younger scholars in Santa Barbara, Albuquerque, and Irvine, and his kindness will continue to enrich his friends' lives for many years to come. I also owe a debt of intellectual gratitude to my excellent undergraduate professors at the University of Delaware: Mark J. Miller in the Department of Political Science, and Daniel F. Callahan in the Department of History.

In 2010 I arrived at the University of Denver to teach in the Department of History and the Center for Judaic Studies. I cannot overstate how supportive my colleagues in Denver have been. Ingrid Tague, Susan Schulten, and Sarah Pessin have been extraordinary chairs and have aided my growth as a scholar and a teacher. I would also like to thank the following current and past University of Denver colleagues for their friendship and support during the writing process: Peter Hanson, Elizabeth Karlsgodt, Carol Helstosky, Mike Gibbs, Rafael Ioris, Elizabeth Escobedo, William Philpott, Adam Rovner, Jodie Kreider, Joyce Goodfriend, Nicholas Rockwell, Alison Schofield, Sari Havis, Jeanne Abrams, Hilary Smith, Bonnie Clark, Danny Postel, Nader Hashemi, Joshua Wilson, Tracy Mott, and Seth Masket. I owe a profound debt of gratitude to my University of Denver colleague and friend Andrea Stanton. Andrea provided valuable feedback on two of this book's chapters and pointed me toward important scholarly works on the general history of women's education in the modern Middle East. I am also grateful to the following staff members in the Department of History and the Center for Judaic Studies for their help over the years: Yasmaine Ford, Meaghan Boland Burns, Jeff Quinlisk, Adam Westbrook, and Patricia Guerra.

I would like to express my profound gratitude to Rafael Chaiken, Assistant Acquisitions Editor at SUNY Press, for championing this book and guiding me through its publication. Additionally, I want to thank Jenn Bennett, Production Editor at SUNY Press, for helping shepherd this book through the production process.

I would like to thank several close friends for their support throughout the writing process: Mike Norman, Leslie Raeder Norman, T.J. Tremblay, Jessica Tremblay, Jason Forgy, Christa Forgy, Jared Katzman, Rebecca Sallee Hanson, and Justin Abramson. Michelle Mussafi helped develop this book's title. Blake

Wyman, Michelle Segura, Jeniese Cathay, and Cynthia Chan Monson all provided childcare for my son so I could spend additional time writing. I cannot thank them enough for their help. I would also like to thank Steve Suval and Gail Suval for their support and love.

I am fortunate to have wonderful and supportive parents in Robin Sciarcon and Beniamino Sciarcon. They have encouraged my intellectual interests at every point in my life, and I cannot thank them enough for all they have done, and continue to do, for me. One person who has certainly made a significant impact on my life over the past two years is my son Phineas. I treasure his presence in my life and hope to be as strong a role model for him as my parents were for me.

Finally, this book could not have been written without the love and encouragement of my wife and partner, Laura Sciarcon. Laura accompanied me on trips to Boston, London, Paris, and Southampton, and has supported my work on this project over the past six years. Laura, you have enriched my life in ways I cannot begin to explain. Plus, you managed to get me Larry David's autograph for my thirty-fourth birthday. This book is for you. I love you.

INTRODUCTION

On November 14, 1911, a large crowd, which included foreign dignitaries and high-ranking Ottoman officials, assembled in the Jewish quarter of Baghdad to attend a ceremony marking the opening of a new, state-of-the-art, permanent home for the Alliance Israélite Universelle's (AIU) Laura Kadoorie School for Girls. Nissim Albala, the director of the AIU's Albert Sassoon School for Boys in Baghdad, and husband of Marie Albala, the director at the Laura Kadoorie School, delivered a celebratory speech in which he discussed the latter institution's goals. In making his case for the importance of female education, he noted:

> The woman, guardian and mistress of the family, holds between her hands the education of children and, consequently, the future of the family and the nation. It is therefore important to prepare her for this difficult task by strengthening her heart and enlightening her mind.[1]

In these two sentences Albala succinctly summed up his organization's main rationale for establishing girls' schools. Girls needed to be educated so they could grow into women capable of raising cultivated children, managing a household, and acting as a true life partner for a husband. Neither Albala nor the AIU was unique in making such an argument in 1911, as female education had long been championed throughout parts of Europe, North America, and the Middle East by the early twentieth century. However, the AIU was instrumental in spreading this type of sentiment throughout the Jewish communities of Ottoman Iraq in the late nineteenth and early twentieth centuries.[2]

Background

The AIU's establishment of a girls' school in Baghdad in early 1895 marked the arrival of formal Jewish female primary education in the non-Mediterranean Ottoman Arab world. Over the next two decades, the Girls' School in Baghdad significantly expanded in size, scope, and reputation, cementing itself as one of the most prestigious Jewish institutions in the city. As a result of this school's success and the AIU's desire to increase its influence in the region, three more girls' schools—Mosul (1911), Hilla (1912), and Basra (1913)—were founded in the Ottoman provinces that would later constitute the modern state of Iraq in the late Ottoman period.

Although these schools made important contributions to these communities, and in fact the AIU continued to operate schools in British-administered Iraq and independent Iraq until 1951, they have been almost totally ignored in academic scholarship.[3] This lack of attention is likely a result of the Zionist movement having eclipsed other international Jewish organizations such as the AIU, in the mid-twentieth century, leading to the creation of the state of Israel in 1948. This period also witnessed the mass departure of the vast majority of Iraq's Jewish community between 1949 and 1952 and the slow death of the community that remained over the next half-century.

This is not to say that Iraqi Jewish history in general has been totally ignored by scholars of Middle Eastern and Jewish history. From the 1960s through the early 1990s Israeli historians, often having been born in Iraq, wrote both religious and political histories of these communities, focusing primarily on the Baghdadi community. They did so both to ensure the survival of modern Iraqi Jewish heritage and memory and also to try to explain why Jewish life there had come to an end.[4] Several scholars even devoted significant works to studying the history of religious and secular education in these communities in the nineteenth and twentieth centuries, though these works were often far more descriptive than analytical.[5]

Only one scholar in this period, Maurice Sawdayee, devoted a book-length monograph to the AIU's activities. Although Sawdayee's *The Baghdad Connection* made a significant contribution to the field of Iraqi Jewish History, it has key limitations. First, it makes almost no attempt to analyze statements made by AIU teachers and representatives and instead relates these writers' beliefs and prejudices as if they were indisputable facts. Second, it covers the AIU's nearly ninety-year history in Baghdad in a broad manner and rarely discusses key developments or issues in any detail. Third, Sawdayee's work relies heavily on the Anglo-Jewish Association's (AJA) Annual Reports (AJAR) and the annual Bulletin de l'Alliance Israélite Universelle's (BAIU) reports on the AIU's activities in Baghdad. The AJA was an AIU sister organization founded in London in 1871. These sources provide important statistical information on AIU schools and occasionally include insightful reports or reproduced letters from AIU teachers and representatives, but they are no substitute for the AIU's correspondence archive. The files in this archive include all extant letters written by AIU teachers and representatives, as well as occasional letters by local community members, local government representatives, and local representatives of European governments. Fourth, Sawdayee's work devotes very little attention to the AIU Girls' School in Baghdad or the organization's general goals for female education. Thus, it is not surprising that in the mid 1990s, Zvi Yehuda, a scholar who has written several articles on the AIU's activities in Iraq, with a specific emphasis on the city of Hilla, noted that the AIU's activities in Iraq are still awaiting basic research.[6]

Over the past quarter-century, Iraqi Jewish history and culture has increasingly received attention from historians and scholars of comparative literature. Several of these works have been interdisciplinary and have focused on issues of Arab Jewish identity and Iraqi Jewish attempts to adapt to and gain acceptance in Iraqi nationalist discourse from the 1920s through the 1940s.[7] These innovative studies have helped put scholars of Iraqi Jewish history and culture in dialogue with scholars who have broader interests in the fields of modern Middle Eastern History, Jewish History, and Identity Studies. Much of this recent scholarship has, however, focused on the Hashemite period (1921–1958) and, with some notable exceptions, said little about the late Ottoman period, women's history, or secular education.[8]

Aim, Scope, and Methodology

This book aims to fill part of this scholarly gap, and also to build on the works of previous scholars of Iraqi Jewish education, such as Sawdayee and Yosef Meir, by focusing on the AIU's project of female education in the Ottoman provinces of Baghdad, Basra, and Mosul from 1895 to 1915. In 1914 and 1915, the Ottoman entry into World War I forced the AIU to close all of its schools in Iraq with the exception of Basra, which the British immediately occupied at the start of the war. In focusing on the AIU's girls' schools in these provinces in this period, this book marks the first such monograph-length study on this topic and also only the second book devoted to the study of the AIU in this region.

Furthermore, it is the most in-depth study to date on specific AIU girls' schools in any period and geographic location.

The vast majority of this study is devoted to the AIU Girls' School in Baghdad, renamed the Laura Kadoorie School for Girls in 1910, while the final chapter discusses the girls' schools opened in Mosul, Hilla, and Basra toward the end of the Ottoman period. In addition to providing an institutional history of these schools in the Ottoman period, this study also aims to discuss and analyze the lives of the women and, to a lesser extent, their subordinates, who ran these schools. These women acted not only as administrators and teachers in the school but also, as this study will show, as models of French Jewish–inspired AIU modernity for their students and as intercultural liaisons on behalf of the AIU in the communities where they lived and worked.

Writing the histories of AIU schools in the Ottoman provinces of Baghdad, Basra, and Mosul presents certain methodological and source challenges. Unlike other parts of the Ottoman Empire or the Arab world, these areas lacked a vibrant and consistent Jewish print culture in this period, although a strong Jewish print culture developed in Baghdad in the 1920s.[9] Furthermore, little indigenous contemporary secular source material exists from this period, and while many Iraqi Jews later wrote memoirs in Arabic, Hebrew, English, and French, almost all were born after 1900, often well after, and nearly all were men. Thus, memoirs are not helpful in analyzing these schools' histories.

Ottoman archives likely have files that discuss these schools, but as I do not read Ottoman Turkish I have not been able to access them. While the British and French had active consulates in Baghdad and often wrote about general events in the city, neither paid significant or consistent attention to the region's Jewish communities or its educational institutions. Fortunately, the AIU's teachers and representatives maintained an active correspondence with the organization's Central Committee in Paris. Although male directors of boys' schools were required to write more frequent letters than their female counterparts at girls' schools, the latter usually penned monthly letters and bimonthly reports about their schools and communities. They also often wrote additional letters discussing their personal lives and interactions with students and students' families.

Therefore, this study relies extensively, though not exclusively, on the correspondence of AIU female directors and, to a lesser extent, on the letters of female teachers who worked under them. It also relies partly on the letters of the male directors and teachers working in the AIU's boys' schools in the cities under discussion. These letters, all housed in the AIU's correspondence archive, are occasionally supplemented by reports from the BAIU, AJAR, the

Archives of the Anglo-Jewish Association, the London Jewish Chronicle, and the British Foreign Office.

While the letters of AIU teachers and agents are a veritable treasure for scholars of late nineteenth- and early twentieth-century Ottoman Iraqi Jewish History, they do have their limitations. Most notably, the letters only rarely give voice to the students who studied at these institutions. Although the teachers and agents occasionally penned long reports on local customs, life-cycle events, and the state of local communities, these reports likely tell us almost as much about their respective authors' prejudices as they do about the subjects they purport to explain.[10] In this way they are similar to the travel literature and missionary field reports written by European and American visitors to these regions during this period.[11] Furthermore, when teachers fell ill, traveled, or, in the case of female teachers, gave birth to children, they often ceased writing letters for long periods of time, creating sizeable gaps in their correspondence records. In some cases, especially when it was a female director who took a leave, these gaps can be filled in by information in the letters of other teachers in the school or at its sister or brother school. It is, however, worth noting that these letters contain invaluable information, and are often the only sources, on the inner workings of the institutions they describe. They also are often the only window scholars have into the lives of teachers, students, and families in the communities where the schools were located. As such they may be the most valuable primary extant primary sources for scholars dealing with certain communities in the study of Ottoman and Middle Eastern Jewish women's history.

In addition to the methodological challenges posed by relying on AIU correspondence, this study faces the challenge of having little direct historiography on the organization's schools in Baghdad, Mosul, Hilla, and Basra to respond to. Thus, besides its analytical aims, this study is also recuperative in that it is bringing unknown information and stories to light. As a result of these challenges I have tried to situate this work within the broader fields of Ottoman Jewish History and Middle Eastern Women's History. I have done so with a focus on comparing these schools' histories with both AIU and non-AIU girls' schools, with the latter including Muslim, Jewish, and Christian schools, in the Ottoman Empire and non-Ottoman Arab world.

The AIU and Female Education

The AIU was founded in Paris in 1860 by notable French Jews who—inspired by the Damascus Affair of 1840, which saw Damascene Jews accused of a blood libel, and the Mortara Affair of 1858, in which a Jewish boy in the Papal States was taken away from his family and forcibly converted to Catholicism—aimed to work to morally and educationally uplift, or regenerate, what they perceived to be backward and less fortunate Jewish communities in eastern Europe, the Middle East, and North Africa.[12] Over the next half-century, the AIU established an extensive network of boys' and girls' primary schools, as well as vocational workshops, throughout Ottoman and non-Ottoman southeastern Europe, Anatolia, the Ottoman Arab provinces, Egypt, Morocco, Tunisia, French-controlled Algeria, and Iran.[13] These schools were often the first secular educational institutions to appear in these communities. Furthermore, they often ranked among the most prestigious secular schools, including state-run schools, in these cities.

It is worth noting that the AIU was one of many Jewish organizations in this period dedicated to international Jewish solidarity, education, welfare, and relief.[14] Other notable organizations with similar goals during this period included the AJA, founded in London in 1871 by British members of the AIU, and the Hilfsverein der deutschen Juden, founded in Germany in 1901.[15] Additionally, philanthropic Jews such as Moses Montefiore and members of the Rothschild family spent vast sums of money and engaged in international lobbying on behalf of various Jewish communities around the world, especially in Ottoman Palestine.[16] Finally, the Zionist movement also emerged during this period, though its nationalist goals conflicted with the internationalist yet assimilationist goals of the aforementioned Jewish organizations.[17] Although it faced competition from these other groups, the AIU was clearly the most internationally active and successful of the nineteenth- and early twentieth-century international Jewish organizations.

Despite its international work and the fact that the majority of its monetary support came from European Jews living outside of France, the AIU operated as a relatively centralized French Jewish–dominated organization.[18] The main decision-making body within the AIU was its Central Committee, located in Paris and dominated by French Jews.[19] It was the Central Committee that decided whether or not to open schools, which teachers would be sent to specific schools, and, in most cases, which subjects were to be taught in such schools.[20] The Central Committee received regular reports from the male and female directors of its boys' and girls' schools, and less regular reports from AIU-trained instructors. Its members also corresponded with members of the various regional committees that operated in cities where AIU schools existed. All correspondence that reached the Central Committee was addressed to the AIU's Secretary-General, who promptly answered each letter.[21] The most famous and long-serving Secretary-General in this period was Jacques Bigart, who held the position from 1892 to 1934. Thus, the Secretary-General acted as the main intermediary between AIU instructors and the Central Committee.

During its formative years, the AIU focused its efforts on establishing boys' schools, the first of which was opened in Tetuan, Morocco, in 1862. Within a decade of its founding, the organization had established a network of boys' schools from Morocco through the Ottoman Empire, including its Arab, Anatolian, and European provinces.[22] These schools were not always successful and sometimes met with communal opposition because of their focus on secular subjects, though the AIU did not ignore religious education or Hebrew language instruction. However, most schools survived and eventually prospered.

As the establishment of early AIU schools in the Ottoman Empire coincided with the height of the latter's Tanzimat period, which included widespread educational reforms, they often received the support and encouragement of Ottoman officials.[23] While the Ottoman government during this period was often skeptical of foreign schools because of the arrival and expansion of various Christian missionary school networks in the empire over the course of the mid- to late nineteenth century, most Ottoman officials viewed the AIU schools positively.[24] This was because the AIU's main goal was to help local Jews better assimilate into Ottoman society, and although its schools welcomed Muslims and Christians, they in no way attempted to convert these students to Judaism. The missionary schools, on the other hand, were viewed as attempting to convert Muslims to Christianity or as advancing the imperial or nationalist goals of the countries from which the missionaries hailed.[25]

While AIU leaders initially focused on establishing boys' schools, in 1865 the organization's first president, Adolphe Crémieux, perhaps the most politically influential French Jew in the mid-nineteenth century, gave a speech to the AIU general assembly calling for the creation of girls' schools.[26] This speech was motivated by Crémieux's belief that women socialized and educated their children and also provided emotional and intellectual support for their husbands.[27] Therefore, he saw girls' education as essential to the AIU's project of regeneration, as only educated mothers and wives could bring about cultural transformations among what he perceived to be the backward Jewish communities where the AIU operated.

In the twelve years following Crémieux's speech, the AIU opened eleven girls' schools, two of which were located in Morocco, two in Bulgaria, and seven in the Ottoman Empire's western Anatolian and southeastern European provinces.[28] Over the next quarter-century, the AIU expanded its network of girls' schools into the Ottoman Empire's Arab provinces, Egypt, and also Iran. As was the case for the boys' schools, the girls' schools were often the first such formal educational institutions in the Jewish communities in which they were established.

This, however, was not always the case. For example, the Jews of Alexandria, Egypt, had established a short-lived community-run school for girls in 1840, more than a half-century prior to the AIU's arrival in the city.[29] Additionally, the AIU schools were not the only foreign-run Jewish schools. In Ottoman, Palestine Christian missionaries had set up institutions for Jewish girls in the early to mid–nineteenth century, and in 1854 an agent of the British branch of the Rothschild family founded the first Jewish-run school for Jewish girls in Jerusalem.[30] This institution was renamed the Evelina de Rothschild School in 1868, and in 1894 it was transferred to the control of the AJA. Meanwhile, the first foreign school for indigenous Algerian Jewish girls in French-controlled Algeria was founded in 1836.[31] What was significant about the AIU was not just that it introduced formal female Jewish education in many communities but that it established a tri-continental educational network that ensured that its institutions followed similar curriculums and, mostly, adhered to the organization's high standards.

The AIU's goals for female students were in many ways similar to those of the missionary schools that operated in the Ottoman Empire and Iran, especially American and British Protestant groups. Building on Enlightenment-era debates over proper female education and the articulation of a specific ideology of domesticity in nineteenth-century western and central European societies, as well as in the United States, both the AIU and missionary societies viewed women as key agents in the quest to transform indigenous societies.[32] Indeed, based on this perception of the importance of "getting" women, by the late nineteenth century Protestant missionary groups had come to focus more effort on the establishment of female schools rather than male schools in the Ottoman Empire and Iran.[33]

It is worth noting that one key difference between the AIU and various missionary societies is that the former was not looking to convert non-Jews to Judaism or even to radically transform the practice of Judaism among religious Jews. Rather, the goals were to help Jewish men and women modernize and assimilate into their home societies. Girls were viewed as central to this secular mission through their future roles as wives and mothers.[34] In contrast, the ultimate goal of most missionaries, even if it was not often achieved, was to educate and convert girls so that they would raise proper Christian children and perhaps even encourage their non-Christian husbands to convert.[35] The AIU was working to improve existing communities, whereas missionaries were in a sense working to create new Christian societies out of the Muslim, Christian, and Jewish communities they encountered.

Still, in terms of their practical work with indigenous women, the AIU and missionary societies had more commonalities than differences. Both groups based their initial educational programs on their own, similar, gendered understandings of what constituted a proper educated woman. Unlike boys' education, which was meant to prepare male students for a lifetime of activity in the public sphere, girls' education was linked to notions of domesticity. It was, therefore, meant to prepare women to be proper mothers, wives, homemakers, and household managers.[36] Thus, girls spent less time than boys studying subjects such as math, science, history, and geography but instead learned handicraft skills such as sewing, embroidery, and ironing, and sometimes also studied the culinary arts.[37] These organizations also worked to teach girls proper manners and focused much of their attention on female propriety, hygiene, and morality.[38]

One area where the French Jewish AIU differed, at least slightly, from the most non-French Protestant missionary societies operating in the Ottoman Empire and Iran was with regard to its link to the so-called French "civilizing mission." The civilizing mission is most often associated with having provided cover, and ideological support, for French colonialism by holding that it was republican France's duty to spread civilization to primitive peoples around the world, especially in various parts of Africa.[39] Although the AIU was not associated with French colonialism, at least outside of North Africa, and did not force its way into Jewish communities through violence or intimidation, its members and leaders believed that they were bringing a specifically French form of civilization and modernity to their co-religionists in southeastern Europe, the Middle East, and North Africa.[40] Thus, even when local communities preferred that English or a local language be used as the primary language of instruction in AIU schools, the Central Committee always insisted that French play this role.

The historiography of the AIU's work in the field of female education is limited and difficult to categorize. Some scholars have written articles or chapters on individual schools or on female education in specific cities, while others have focused more narrowly on the lives, work, and letters of female AIU teachers.[41] Others have tried to focus on both the schools and their teachers.[42] With the notable exceptions of Joy Land's important doctoral dissertation on female teachers in late nineteenth- and early twentieth-century Tunisia and Frances Malino's forthcoming book on the lives and work of an intergenerational family of female AIU teachers from North Africa, no book-length study has yet been devoted to topics related to AIU female education.[43]

Besides being limited in number, though the field is certainly growing, studies on AIU girls' schools and AIU female teachers have focused mainly on North Africa, western Anatolia, and southeastern Europe. While some studies have briefly touched on the AIU's general program in the Ottoman Empire's Arab hinterland, scholars have not utilized the AIU's correspondence archive to examine these schools or their teachers in any detail.[44] This study contributes to the field of AIU studies by providing an analytical recuperative history of this organization's girls' schools in late Ottoman Iraq. In doing so, this book opens the field to new explorations in the study of AIU girls' schools and female instructors in the non-Mediterranean Ottoman Arab world while also broadening our understanding of the organization's general project of female education.

This book also makes a key contribution to the field of modern Middle Eastern Women's History and its subfield of Iraqi Women's History. The field of Middle Eastern Women's History has grown exponentially and matured over the past thirty years. During this period, scholars have moved from writing groundbreaking recuperative histories of various women's movements and communities and using class as an analytical lens through which to view social and cultural change to employing gender and postcolonial analyses to the study of women's roles in both the public and private spheres.[45] Much of this scholarship has, naturally, focused on the relationship between women and the state in the context of Islam, nationalism, colonialism, civil war, and occupation. It should also not be surprising that much of this scholarship has focused on women in either the most populous Middle Eastern countries such as Egypt, Iran, and Turkey or the most easily accessible ones such as Morocco, Tunisia, Israel, the West Bank and Gaza, Lebanon, and, until recently, Syria.

One country that has been largely ignored is Iraq. While some scholars have focused on the impact of recent wars on Iraqi women, very little scholarship in any language exists on women's history in the Ottoman provinces of Baghdad, Basra, and Mosul that later came to constitute the modern state of Iraq after World War I.[46] Thus, in addition to this book's contributions to Iraqi Jewish History, Ottoman Jewish Women's History, and Middle Eastern Jewish Women's History, by focusing on the AIU's girls' schools in these provinces during this period this study contributes to the field of Iraqi Women's History.

It also highlights the AIU's contribution to the early stages of formal female education in these provinces and its role in establishing the first women's society in Baghdadi history.

Teachers' Perceptions of Local Communities

Although the AIU's teachers were committed to improving the lives of their students and the communities in which they lived, these teachers often had no qualms about expressing negative opinions about the individuals and communities they served. Often such comments were directed at local rabbis, who were derided for their prejudice, ignorance, and resistance to change when they opposed AIU initiatives.[47] When discussing the AIU's teachers' critique of traditional Judaism, Aron Rodrigue writes:

> The Judaism practiced by Sephardi and Eastern Jewry was believed to have "degenerated" because of persecution and ignorance. The whole program of "regeneration" was predicated upon a sometimes violent critique of traditional Jewish society and popular culture. The railing against the superstition of the local Jews and the fanaticism and obscurantism of the rabbis was a constant theme in the letters of the Alliance teacher. To some extent this was natural, since the raison d'être of the teacher was to erect an alternative educational system to the one headed by the rabbinate. The dismantlement of the latter system was a corollary of the work of the Alliance. The rabbis and the teachers were rivals in the quest to mold the minds and souls of future generations, and the critique of local Jewish culture was part and parcel of the kulturkampf between essentially secular and religious value systems. It comes as no surprise that the teachers frequently referred to themselves as "missionaires laïques."[48]

Still, Rodrigue notes elsewhere that the AIU's goal was not to erase the communities' religious character.[49] Rather, the goals were help the communities maintain a spiritual attachment to Judaism while internalizing perceived Western notions of secular education, propriety, self-confidence, and international solidarity.

One frequent criticism of Jewish communities in the Ottoman world was that they refused to provide the necessary funds for the operation of AIU schools even though the organization never established schools in cities without first receiving an invitation to do so from prominent members of the local community.[50] There is a wide range of possible explanations for the refusal of members of local communities to provide adequate financial support for these institutions. Some may have been unable to do so even if they wanted their community to benefit from an AIU presence, while others may have preferred to direct limited communal funds to community-run religious schools. In some cases, outright resistance might have been directed toward AIU schools. Regardless of the reason, the organization's teachers sometimes viewed members of Jewish communities as taking advantage of the AIU's generosity.

In addition to discussing specific issues AIU teachers were also tasked with providing narrative snapshots of the communities in which they worked for their superiors in Paris. Rodrigue contends that these teachers' descriptions of local customs and their framing of communities as being "frozen in time" mirrored those found in nineteenth- and early twentieth-century European travel literature.[51] Interestingly, Frances Malino notes that this European, and specifically French, point of view toward local communities was learned and internalized by AIU students from North Africa, the Ottoman Arab provinces, and southeastern Europe, who were chosen to study in Paris and become the next generation of AIU teachers.[52] Teachers often reserved special condemnation both for women's roles in Jewish communities in which they worked and the actions of women themselves.[53] While often promoting a separate-spheres ideology, which saw a woman's place as in the domestic sphere and a man's place as in public, AIU teachers consistently called for an end to local patriarchal cultures that kept women confined to the home, uneducated, and sometimes forced into unsuitable marriages.

Finally, teachers, especially directors, often acted in a political capacity owing to their connection to an organization headquartered in a wealthy and influential country.[54] When necessary, AIU teachers would try, often successfully, to use their connections with local consuls, not necessarily French ones, to convince the Ottoman government to redress whatever problems members of Jewish communities were facing. In this way these teachers often earned the respect, gratitude, and trust of local Jews who had once viewed their organization with suspicion.

Ottoman Educational Reforms and Impact

As mentioned previously, the AIU's establishment in 1860 and the subsequent expansion of its educational network in the late nineteenth century took place during a period of Ottoman political, economic, and social reforms. Education was central to these reforms. While the Ottoman government had begun establishing quasi-secular schools for military purposes in the late eighteenth and early nineteenth centuries, its leaders did not attempt to introduce state-run primary or secondary schools until 1839.[55] It was not until 1869, however, that the state formulated a coherent, empire-wide educational program, and even then the program remained largely unimplemented until the 1880s.[56]

Ottoman educational reforms during this period were linked to Ottoman elites' notions of modernity. These predominantly Sunni Muslim elites aimed to increase the scope and authority of the central government over nearly all aspects of provincial life, create a well-trained and efficient bureaucracy, improve overall economic performance in order to increase governmental revenue, and ensure the loyalty of all Ottoman subjects and citizens.[57] By accomplishing these goals Ottoman elites hoped their empire would be able to successfully resist and compete with advanced European states.

Starting in 1869, and picking up steam during the Hamidian period (1876–1908), the Ottoman government attempted to vastly increase the number of primary and secondary schools, especially in provinces located outside of western and central Anatolia. Up until this point, primary education had been the near exclusive purview of religious communities in Ottoman cities and towns.[58] Additionally, as previously mentioned, many foreign schools, especially Christian missionary institutions, had also been established in provincial cities to cater to non-Muslim communities and had often attracted Muslim students. Thus, the construction of an empire-wide primary and secondary public school system can be seen as an Ottoman attempt to counter foreign influence throughout the empire and increase its citizens' interactions with the central government.[59]

Along with establishing its educational network, the Ottoman government attempted to crack down on foreign schools. It did so by placing such institutions, from 1869 onward, under the jurisdiction of the Ministry of Public Education (MPE), which had been established in 1857. This allowed the MPE to send inspectors to visit these institutions and to ensure that these institutions were formally registered with the government. It is worth noting, however, that the scholar Benjamin Fortna has shown that the MPE clearly was often unable to get foreign schools to abide by all governmental regulations. For example, an 1893 Ottoman governmental document mentions the existence of 392 foreign schools, of which 341 did not have official permission to exist.[60] While the Ottoman government was more concerned with Christian missionary schools than ones operated by the AIU, this book will highlight several incidents that saw governmental officials challenge the legal right to exist of AIU schools in Baghdad, Mosul, and Basra.

Although the Ottoman government aimed to bring primary schools to all parts of the empire from 1869 onward, its ability to do so was constrained by a lack of financial resources. As a result, the government tasked local communities with raising most of the funds for such institutions, thus ensuring that progress would be uneven throughout the provinces.[61] Rural towns, especially, often lacked primary schools, as most of these communities lacked the financial resources to support such institutions.[62]

Early Ottoman public educational programs also largely excluded girls. While the empire's first public primary school for girls was opened in 1858 in Istanbul, similar institutions would not appear in many provinces for another twenty-five to fifty-five years.[63] This lag occurred even though women's education had become a topic of conversation in the Ottoman press and among elites.[64] Thus, even more than for boys, foreign- and community-run schools for girls often enjoyed a significant head start compared to Ottoman schools. In fact, throughout the empire, the government did not even begin focusing on training female instructors to work at schools until the early 1870s.[65] As a result of the uneven nature of spread of Ottoman public education, foreign schools, although often viewed as suspect, not only continued to play major roles in the empire, especially its provinces, after 1869, but they actually grew in importance during this period.

Public Education and Population in Ottoman Baghdad

As the largest and most important city in the Ottoman Iraqi provinces, Baghdad has received the most scholarly attention of any city in this region.[66] Baghdad was a multicultural city that housed significant Shiite, Sunni, Jewish, and Christian populations. It was also home to numerous foreign residents attached to foreign consulates, businesses, and, to a lesser extent, schools that were located in the city.[67] As of 1908, one writer estimated the total indigenous urban population of Baghdad to be around 150,000, of which 50,000 were Shi'i, 40,000 were Sunni, 53,000 were Jewish, and 7,000 were Christian.[68]

The Tanzimat reforms, which started in 1839, did not reach Baghdad until the 1840s and remained largely unimplemented until the governorship of Midhat Pasha from 1869 to 1872. Even then, many parts of the Ottoman Iraqi provinces remained untouched for some time. From the 1860s through the outbreak of World War I, the Ottoman government's focuses in the Iraqi provinces were on standardizing provincial administration and boundaries, establishing educational institutions, strengthening the Sixth Army, settling tribes, responding to the rise of British power in the Persian Gulf, and dealing with the so-called "Shi'i problem."[69]

It was Midhat Pasha who, after having his provincial administration borrow money from a local Muslim charitable holding, established the first public school for boys in 1869.[70] This was, however, not the first modern boys' school in the city, as the AIU Boys' School had opened in 1864. It also was not the first public boys' school in the region, as one appears to have been established in Mosul in or around 1864.[71] In addition to founding primary schools, Midhat Pasha also opened a technical school in 1870, which marked the arrival of state-sponsored vocational training in the city.[72] While boys' schools continued to be established in the provinces over the next twenty-five years, the first public girls' school in the region was established only in 1896, in Mosul.[73] The first public girls' school in Baghdad, which appears to have been a middle school, was opened in 1898 or 1899.[74] It appears that the girls who attended this school had received education at home or through local, non–government-supported religious schools.

Although foreign schools both existed and prospered in Baghdad, they do not seem to have garnered the amount of negative attention that such institutions did in other parts of the Ottoman Arab world. Perhaps this was because the AIU, which was a Jewish institution dedicated to the mission of helping Jews better integrate into Ottoman society, was the most conspicuous of these institutions in the late nineteenth century, whereas Christian missionary schools were more active in cities near the Mediterranean. Another possible reason was that the main fear for Ottoman authorities in Baghdad was not foreign but rather Shiite influence. Historians of both Ottoman education and Ottoman Iraq have noted that the central government invested significant resources in the 1890s and the first decade of the twentieth century in trying to use education as a tool for socializing Ottoman Iraqi Shia into normative Ottoman political culture.[75] In any case, several cities and towns in Ottoman Iraq, and especially the city of Baghdad, would prove to be fertile ground for the AIU from 1864 to 1914.

Main Arguments

The main argument that guides this work is that both male and female AIU teachers in Ottoman Iraq, like their colleagues in other areas, viewed female education through a gendered lens linked to their understandings of an ideal modern society. Women played key roles in this modern society as the primary educators of children and were viewed as a society's most important agents of socialization. As I show in Chapter 1, male teachers in the AIU Boys' School in Baghdad concluded that their work in the classroom would never succeed in creating polished, Westernized men as long as Baghdadi Jewish girls and women remained uneducated. Thus, several male teachers became the chief advocates of the establishment of a girls' school in the city in the 1880s and 1890s.

Building on the work of Susan G. Miller, one of the main themes of this work is the influence of the female directors of the AIU girls' in schools in Ottoman Iraq on the schools' students. I show, especially in Chapters 1 and 2, how the directors acted not only as educators but also as models of modernity who tried to impart new moral and aesthetic norms onto students. These students would, theoretically, then internalize and adopt these norms, ensuring that lessons learned in the classroom would transfer into the protected domestic sphere. In this way Jewish girls would not only grow up to be educated women but would also come to adopt a worldview that differed from that of their own mothers, which they would then pass down to both sons and daughters. Furthermore, academically and morally educated women would either be able to provide moral reinforcement for husbands who were graduates of the AIU boys' schools or work to transform husbands who lacked formal education into modern men. Thus, from the perspective of AIU administrators, moral and educated women were essential prerequisites for the moral and cultural regeneration of Jewish communities in this region.

In this work I also advance arguments related to the work of individual directors and teachers. Perhaps most notably, I show how different teachers aimed to use the schools' curriculums to achieve certain pedagogical and social goals. I also examine the methods teachers used to attract or retain community support for their schools. It is worth noting that the AIU's girls' schools in Ottoman Iraq did not have uniform experiences with regard to communal support or popularity.

Chapter Outline

Chapter 1 begins by providing general background information on the Jewish community and Jewish education in late Ottoman Iraq. It then proceeds to discuss the arrival, reception, and development of the AIU Boys' School in Baghdad from 1864 through the early 1890s. This chapter then shows how successive directors and teachers at the Boys' School in the late 1880s and early to mid-1890s came to view the establishment of an AIU Girls' school in the Baghdad as a necessary complement to the organization's project of creating modern Baghdadi Jewish men. The final half of this chapter looks at Rachel

Danon's role as director and teacher in establishing and running the Girls' School in 1895.

Chapter 2 examines the Girls' School's rapid expansion under Danon's leadership from 1896 to 1899 as well as obstacles both the school and Danon faced during this time period. Notably, this chapter highlights how Danon acted as a model of what she perceived to be European modernity to her students in her focus on transforming them into proper schoolgirls.

Chapter 3 details Oro Sémach's tenure as director of the Girls' School from 1899 to 1904. It focuses on key changes she made to the school's curriculum and goals, including the establishment of a lending library and the creation of the first female society in Baghdadi history, as well as her attempts to both find a permanent home for her school and to increase the size of the school's academic staff. An important theme in this chapter is the impact of disease on teacher and student morale and the school's progress as Baghdad suffered through a major outbreak of the Bubonic plague in 1901and 1902 and a devastating cholera epidemic in 1904. This chapter also discusses early interactions between the wealthy, philanthropic Kadoorie family, which was originally from Baghdad but had settled in India and China in the nineteenth century, and the AIU.

Chapter 4 tells the story of the Girls' School from 1905 through the end of the Ottoman period in 1915, at which point the archival record for this period ends. Marie Albala directed the school through most of this decade. During this period the school finally received a permanent home, thanks to the financial support of the Kadoorie family, and was renamed the Laura Kadoorie School for Girls. This period also witnessed a major focus on expanding the school's vocational program and integrating it within the school itself.

Chapter 5 moves beyond Baghdad to examine the histories of AIU Girls' School in the Ottoman Iraqi cities of Mosul, Hilla, and Basra from 1911 to 1915. These schools were not founded until the very end of the Ottoman period and, like the Girls' School in Baghdad, have received little scholarly attention. This chapter highlights how the AIU, in some cases, struggled to capitalize on the success of the Baghdad Girls' Schools when setting up schools in smaller Ottoman Iraqi cities with less wealthy Jewish communities. Finally, because of the lack of scholarship on AIU activities in Ottoman Iraq, this chapter also makes contributions to the study of the boys' schools in these cities.

1

PIONEERING FEMALE JEWISH EDUCATION

The AIU in Baghdad, 1864–1895

The AIU identified Baghdad, which contained the largest Jewish population in the eastern Arab world at the time, as the key center for a future boys' school in the early 1860s.[1] In fact, Baghdad received the AIU's third school with the opening of the Boys' School in late 1864. This followed the establishment of a boys' school in Tetuan, Morocco, in 1862 and one in Damascus in 1864. However, Baghdad would not receive a girls' school until 1895. This was well after similar schools had been established in other key cities closer to the imperial center, such as Salonica, Izmir, and Istanbul. It was, however, around the same time that such schools were established in Ottoman Tripoli and British-ruled Alexandria.

Although upon the Baghdad Girls' School's opening, the Boys' School had existed for over three decades, the former institution still faced local opposition to girls' education, especially from fathers who did not want to pay tuition for their daughters and mothers who viewed their daughters' education as unnecessary. Furthermore, the Girls' School's first director, Rachel Danon, was tasked with determining how to place students with varying levels of education and ability into suitable groups so that both they and the school could function efficiently. She also had to attend closely to budgetary issues to ensure the school would remain somewhat financially secure, even if the school could count on generous support from both the Central Committee in Paris and the AJA's Executive Committee in London.

In addition to her administrative role as director, Danon also acted as a quasi-diplomatic liaison on behalf of the school in the Jewish community, positioning herself as a modern, educated, cultivated Jewish woman to both her students and their families. Her goals were thus varied as she aimed to establish an enduring school while also setting in motion what she and the Central Committee believed to be a modernization process for Jewish girls.

Yet, while Danon focused on grooming educated and modern girls, the wider goals the school was established to achieve were not limited to female education. In fact, over the course of the late 1880s and early 1890s, the male faculty at the city's Boys' School had concluded that in order to effect lasting social change among the Baghdadi Jewish community, boys' education was insufficient. These educators believed the AIU needed to place at least equal emphasis on the education of Jewish girls, as they were the future wives of graduates of the Boys' School and the mothers of future students of both the AIU's schools and of members of the Baghdadi Jewish community. Only by including girls could the AIU achieve its goal of regenerating the Jewish community in Baghdad.

Therefore, while this chapter discusses and analyzes key aspects of the Girls' School's first year of existence, it also draws from the BAIU, AJAR, *The Jewish Chronicle*, and general AIU correspondence to provide a general background of the AIU's activities in Baghdad. The chapter also discusses the role that Saul Somekh, the director of the Boys' school from 1888 to 1893, played in laying the foundation for the Girls' School. Additionally, it is my hope that by focusing much of this chapter on the events of 1895, scholars of both Jewish and Middle Eastern girls' education will be made aware of the richness and depth of information contained in just one year of correspondence of female teachers at AIU institutions. Indeed, while the lion's share of this chapter's evidence is drawn from the letters of Rachel Danon, I do not attempt to discuss and analyze everything Danon wrote in 1895. Rather, I have focused on information and anecdotes that she related in these letters that shed light on the school's establishment and functioning; her goals as a director, teacher, role model, and cultural emissary; and issues that would recur in future years. One key theme that has been omitted from this chapter, as Danon's letters from 1895 almost solely ignore the issue, is that of the personal life and struggles of a female director in a foreign country. While not discussed here, this is a recurring theme in later chapters.

The Jewish Community in Late Ottoman Baghdad

Since many of its members traced their histories to the pre-Islamic period, the Baghdadi Jewish community was believed by many to predate all other communities in the city. If one were to separate Sunni from Shiite Muslims, then the Jewish community was also the city's largest. One scholar estimates the Jewish population in Baghdad in 1904 as exceeding 63,000, although it is impossible to assert exactly how many Jews lived in the city at any given time in the late Ottoman period.[2] What is beyond dispute is that the Jewish population in the city during this period accounted for between 30 and 40 percent of the city's total population.

According to a 1910 British report, the Jewish community in Baghdad was the second largest community in the empire, behind Salonica, and, in general, a prosperous one.[3] The report's author claimed that about 5 percent of the community was wealthy, while 30 percent were middle class, 60 percent were poor, and the remaining 5 percent so destitute that they subsisted through begging.[4] According to the same report, Jews enjoyed a near monopoly over much of the city's trade.[5] One contemporary scholar notes that Jewish traders were so successful that the city's trade came to a near standstill on the Jewish Sabbath.[6] It appears that the main competition for Jewish traders came not from indigenous Muslims and Christians but rather from British agents operating in the region.[7] However, it must be mentioned that some Jews, like the famous Sassoon family, gained British citizenship and set up firms both in the United Kingdom and in India and Hong Kong. As will be seen, these wealthy Jewish families, whether living in or outside of Baghdad, often funded educational initiatives, including those undertaken by the AIU, during this period.

Religious leaders also played a key role in late Ottoman Baghdadi Jewish society, though Yaron Harel has shown how rabbinical power was often constrained by members of the wealthy, secular Jewish elite during this period.[8] Interestingly, as a result of struggles between the Baghdadi Jewish-moneyed elite and local rabbis, the Chief Rabbi in the community, who was often not a native of the city, often wielded minimal power and was viewed as both subordinate to secular interests and inferior to other local rabbis in terms of religious knowledge and authority.[9] By the 1880s, the position of Chief Rabbi had been largely undermined by secular and religious challengers, with the leadership of the city's AIU Boys' School among the former group.[10] Harel notes that this decline coincided with the rise of a new secular, wealthy elite who favored the introduction of modern education.[11] It is likely that conflicts within the religious establishment and between religious and secular groups during this period aided the AIU's work and subsequent expansion in Baghdad and throughout Ottoman Iraq. However, rabbis, as will be seen, still wielded significant power in certain instances.

Finally, it is important to mention that while the AIU ultimately established the first modern Jewish school in Baghdad in 1864, the latter's establishment did not mark the arrival of European notions of modernity. As both Lital Levy and Orit Bashkin have recently shown, Baghdadi Jews, starting in the early 1860s, took part in the broader Haskalah, or Jewish enlightenment, via correspondence with their Indian, Middle Eastern, and European coreligionists, and the intermittent use of print culture.[12] Indeed, during this period, members of the Baghdadi Jewish intelligentsia internalized European orientalist notions of "Eastern" backwardness and, when discussing what they perceived to be less fortunate Jewish communities in neighboring regions, recast themselves as bearers of modernity in contrast with their backward coreligionists in these cities.[13] Thus, it would be inaccurate to claim that the AIU was solely responsible for large-scale social changes that took place in the city in the late Ottoman period. It would also be inaccurate to assert that the organization implanted European ideals over a community that had previously enjoyed little contact with the outside world, even if this is how AIU writers sometimes portrayed the situation.

Overview of Jewish Education in Late Ottoman Baghdad

Scholars of Jewish education in nineteenth-century Baghdad appear to be in unanimous agreement that the establishment of the AIU Boys' School in 1864 marked the arrival of a Jewish educational institution that focused primarily on secular subjects.[14] In this sense it can be said to mark the beginning of "modern" education in the city. In the decades prior to the AIU's arrival, most Jewish boys received their education in either a Talmud Torah or a heder.[15] Hayyim Cohen mentions that there were numerous heders in the nineteenth century but only one Talmud Torah, which opened in 1832.[16] Furthermore, he states that the two institutions followed a similar curriculum and that the major difference between them was that heders were co-educational, though few girls attended, whereas Talmud Torahs were open only to boys.[17]

Both heders and Talmud Torahs focused on preparing students for later religious study and consisted mainly of learning the Hebrew language and of rote memorization of Jewish religious texts, though other subjects were sometimes included. Cohen's description of these schools, and their teachers' pedagogical techniques, is not positive:

> In most cases, one of the rooms in the teacher's house served as the heder, while in the hot summer months, his courtyard was used. The room was bare, the pupils sitting on mats, or sometimes on simple benches without

> backseats. There was no blackboard or any furniture in the room, but the teacher's punishment cane was most prominent.
>
> Children from the age of 3–4 up to 12–13 attended the heder together, without any classification as to age or knowledge. The teacher called up each child in turn, taught him a letter of the Hebrew alphabet, or a word, or a sentence according to the child's knowledge, and if he had reached the stage of writing, he would write letters or sentences in the child's copybook, and the child was obliged to copy these lines according to the teacher's example. A child who did not read well or write beautifully was punished by blows or by having to rewrite the material. Since there were often more than 50 pupils, not infrequently it happened that each of them was called before the teacher not more than once a day. While one child was being taught the others would be up to mischief: the teacher's helper who was supposed to supervise them was not very effective.
>
> The child in the heder started his schooling by learning the Hebrew alphabet, then words and sentences, until he was able to read fluently from the Holy Scriptures, with different tunes for the different books of the Bible. At a more advanced stage, if his studies were not interrupted, the child also learned to translate certain chapters of the Bible, and only after that, also writing and even arithmetic. Older children would study the writing of commercial letters in Arabic but with Hebrew characters. They were not taught Hebrew as a spoken language. Even the translation they learned was in an old Arabic dialect which they did not always understand. In the heder no Talmud or religious rules were taught....
>
> The children in the heder did not learn very much, since they studied for a few years only, and were taught by a teacher who not only had no pedagogic training but whose own knowledge was scanty. The salary he received was low and he had to engage in some other occupation—as the cantor or the ritual slaughterer, for example—sometimes during the instruction hours.[18]

There is no reason to doubt Cohen's general criticisms, but the quality of instruction must have varied from school to school.

As a result of the lack of modern schools during this period, untrained religious teachers enjoyed a virtual monopoly over formal Jewish primary education. It must be noted that in the mid-nineteenth century missionaries also became active in Baghdad and occasionally attempted to recruit Jewish students by offering modern education.[19] However, they do not seem to have made a major impact on the community. Thus, rather than missionary or governmental schools, which were discussed in the Introduction, in Baghdad it was the AIU schools that posed the first major challenge to religious teachers' control over formal education for Jewish boys.

Unlike Jewish boys' education, Jewish girls' education in mid– to late nineteenth-century Baghdad was almost entirely informal. Girls, especially those born to middle- and upper-class families, were raised to learn how to maintain a Jewish household and raise families and were not expected to have a consistent, visible role in public society.[20] While it does appear, based on the reports of AIU teachers, that by the 1880s young girls occasionally received formal religious education alongside young boys in heders, girls primarily depended on their mothers, or other women in their families, for their education.[21] Upon approaching puberty, most girls, and certainly nearly all girls from middle- and upper-class families, were confined to their parents' homes to protect their reputations prior to marriage. Furthermore, as in other Jewish communities in the Arab world, many Jewish girls in Baghdad married at very young ages, sometimes as young as eight or nine.[22]

Even though the AIU had established a Boys' School in 1864 and the Ottoman government began establishing public institutions for boys' education, formal education for girls remained largely ignored by both the community and the AIU for the next three decades. The establishment of an AIU Girls' School in Baghdad seems to have been briefly considered in the early 1880s by the organization's representatives but was apparently sidelined by rabbinical opposition.[23] As will be seen, a vocational workshop for girls was opened briefly in either late 1885 or early 1886 but closed shortly thereafter. The idea of a dedicated girls' school was seriously entertained by the AIU only in the 1890s. It was at this point that the Boys' School's faculty members came to believe that in order to transform men, women needed to be transformed as well. In a sense, these educators came to view girls' education as even more important than boys' education because the former significantly influenced the latter through all stages of life, first as mothers and sisters and later as wives. Based on recent scholarship dealing with both colonial and nationalist education in the nineteenth and early twentieth centuries, this line of thinking appears to have been quite common among foreign male and female educators in the Arab world during this period.[24]

The AIU Boys' School in Baghdad

Although several studies have discussed aspects of the AIU Boys' School's founding and its trajectory, no study has attempted a detailed history of either the Boys' School's early or later years.[25] In this section I aim to present a brief overview of the school's early history to highlight certain developments that later affected the Girls' School. I also discuss general AIU goals that in some ways affected students and teachers in both schools.

The AIU established its first Boys' School on December 10, 1864.[26] Although the school's enrollment grew over its first year, from forty-three to seventy-five, the school's first director, Salomon Nerson, soon left after a falling-out with the head of the local AIU Committee. During his brief tenure, Nerson had also struggled to convince local rabbis to endorse the school's goals.[27] Such problems were typical of new schools in Jewish communities during this period. For example, Aron Rodrigue has shown that the modern Hasköy School established by the Jewish community in Istanbul in 1864 faced intense rabbinical opposition, resulting in the institution being placed under an edict of excommunication.[28] According to a letter from 1866 penned by the Boys' School's recently hired Arabic and English teacher, John Muattar, its enrollment had declined by half by the beginning of 1866, and the school would have fallen apart if not for Isaac Lurion, the head of the local AIU Committee.[29] Muattar also lamented the fact that locals did not want their children studying multiple languages at the same time as they assumed that these students were not capable of successfully doing so.[30] It is worth noting that while the language of instruction in the Boys' School was French, increasing British influence in this area necessitated that English also be taught.[31] Arabic was also taught, as it was the main vernacular language in the region. Ottoman Turkish, the instruction of which was later made compulsory in all schools by the Ottoman government, was taught as well because it was the empire's administrative language. Finally, as in all AIU institutions, Hebrew was also a part of the curriculum.

While some religious authorities supported the school's founding, others vehemently opposed its existence. The French Consul in Baghdad, responding to a letter sent to him by the students at the Boys' School, informed the Central Committee in Paris that local rabbis were railing against the school and threatening its progress.[32] He contended that the rabbis had come to feel threatened by the prospect of students receiving instruction in secular subjects.[33] Although the consul viewed these men as "stupidly fanatical," their opposition is understandable in the context of both the changing nature of Ottoman rule throughout the empire and the arrival of a foreign institution, albeit an avowedly Jewish one, aiming to alter local Jewish society.[34] This was because increasing Ottoman state centralization, including attempts to re-order Ottoman Jewish society through the appointment of an imperial Chief Rabbi to whom all other rabbis would be subordinate, and the efforts of foreign organizations to set up secular schools threatened local rabbinical authority throughout the Jewish communities of the Ottoman Arab world.[35] It appears from the students' letter, however, that the local rabbis who opposed the school had very little actual power. Their main weapon was slander, as they unjustly accused the students of atheism.[36] This certainly would have aroused suspicion among certain segments of the population, but with a centralizing government in favor of educating Ottoman boys and key members of the community willing to support the school, the rabbis seem to have made little headway. While the Girls' School would later receive support from some religious figures and evoke the ire of others, neither the Boys' nor the Girls' School appears to have ever faced an existential threat from rabbinical opposition. However, as will be discussed, rabbinical opposition clearly hindered the initial establishment of a girls' school.

In addition to varying levels of opposition, the school's staff and students faced the challenge of a lack of a suitable building. The school was located in a cramped area in the middle of the city's Jewish quarter and lacked windows and gardens.[37] Fortunately, Albert Sassoon, a Jewish philanthropist who had roots in Baghdad but who lived in British India, donated funds for the organization to erect a new building, which opened in 1873.[38] From this point forward the institution was known as the Albert Sassoon School. Over two decades later, the AIU's new Girls' School in Baghdad would also face serious problems with regard to its first home.

Another key development that occurred during the 1870s was the founding of the AJA in London in 1871. In addition to setting up its own schools, this organization worked closely with the AIU and came to play a key supportive role in Baghdad. Besides providing grants to the AIU Boys' School, from the late 1870s, the members of the AJA's Executive Committee in London took it upon themselves to find and pay the salary of the school's English teacher. This greatly aided the AIU both logistically and financially, though it also allowed the AJA influence over the Boys' School. This led to debates over whether French or English should be given precedence in primary education.[39] The AJA would later champion the creation of the Girls' School and provide it with significant and consistent financial support.

Unlike the first three decades of the later Girls' School's existence, the Boys' School experienced wild fluctuations in enrollment from the 1860s through the early 1880s. In the 1860s this fluctuation seems to have been a result of both the first director's abrupt and premature departure in early 1866 and local opposition, or at least ambivalence, to the new school. Over the course of the early to mid-1870s, likely as a result of both the opening of a new building and of support from the newly created AJA, the school began admitting more students, many of whom did not pay tuition. By 1875, the student body had grown to nearly 300, though it appears that only between 150 to 200 students showed up on any given day. Enrollment then dropped precipitously over the next half decade, so that by 1882 the school counted only 125 students, nearly evenly divided between paying and nonpaying students.[40] The school then witnessed a dramatic increase over the next several years, and by 1886 once again had over 200 students, most of whom were nonpaying.[41] By 1895, the year the Girls' School opened, the Boys' School's enrollment totaled 210, consisting of 116 paying students and 94 nonpaying students.[42] The Boys' School's enrollment fluctuations and frequent shifts in the ratio of paying to nonpaying students may have convinced the Girls' School's first director to take a firm stand on the issue of tuition and to opt for a slow-growth strategy with regard to enrollment.

While at times the Boys' School seems to have struggled to attract paying students and to win the support of various segments of the community, it was very successful in gaining the support of the Ottoman government and the representatives of foreign governments in Baghdad. Ottoman Governor Midhat Pasha, who has often been praised by scholars for his role in promoting secular education in Baghdad, occasionally visited the school during his time in office and was pleased with his personal review of its students.[43] He also apparently established a strong relationship with the AIU's local committee and intervened on behalf of the city's Jews on at least one occasion.[44] Indeed, as Paul Dumont has shown, one of the organization's key accomplishments in late Ottoman Baghdad was having its representatives relay local concerns to the central Ottoman government. Gaining the ears of local consuls whose governments had influence in Istanbul allowed these teachers and representatives to serve as intermediaries between the local population and the Ottoman government in Istanbul when community members felt threatened by members of the local non-Jewish community and even the local government.[45] Thus, it is not surprising that French and British consuls also occasionally visited the school, quizzed the students on various topics, and expressed their support for the school's activities. On at least one occasion, the French and British consuls visited the school together to jointly quiz the children in French and English.[46]

Furthermore, while the school was established specifically to educate Jewish boys, it also sometimes admitted the children of prominent Muslims and Christians in the city. This helped the school to build a strong reputation, and gain support, beyond Jewish circles. Indeed, in 1924, Yusuf Rizk-Allah Ghanimah, an Iraqi Christian who attended the Boys' School from 1898 to 1902, penned a history of the Jews in Iraq partly because of the positive views he developed toward the Baghdadi Jewish community as a child.[47]

Finally, the school's goals were both to prepare boys for gainful employment and also to create modern, educated men who would be well prepared, from the AIU's members' perspectives, to lead their community and families out of ignorance and into a new world. For the AIU, modernity implied a separation of synagogue and state, the casting aside of superstitions in favor of rational analysis, a focus on secular subjects such as science, history, geography, and languages, the abandonment of traditional forms of dress in favor of "European" styles, and the adoption of new forms of hygiene.[48] Thus, the AIU Boys' School's faculty hoped to alter the ways boys acted both inside and outside the classroom. Yet, while boys were important to the AIU's goals, it soon became apparent to the institution's male teachers that in order to bring about societal change the organization would have to focus equally on the community's girls.

Before moving beyond the Boys' School to focus on girls' education, it is worth mentioning that while it experienced its share of difficulties in its first three decades, the Boys' School also trained a cadre of young men who would come to play significant roles in not only the Baghdadi Jewish community but also in Ottoman and, later, Iraqi national life. One of these boys, and certainly the most prominent Jew in late Ottoman Baghdadi and later Iraqi history, was Sassoon Heskel. Heskel was born in 1860 and attended the Boys' School in the 1870s before leaving to join his uncle, Saleh Daniel, who was Baghdad's Jewish representative in the first Ottoman Parliament prior to its suspension in 1878, to live and study in Istanbul in 1877.[49] Heskel later became an Ottoman Parliament member as well, following the CUP revolution of 1908–1909, and subsequently became Iraq's first Minister of Finance.[50] In this latter capacity he was the country's first and only Jewish cabinet member. Thus, it is fair to say that the Boys' School made a great impact not just on the Baghdadi Jewish community but on both Ottoman and later national Iraqi political history.

A Failed Attempt at Girls' Education

Certain influential members of Baghdad's Jewish community had desired a girls' school for some time, though it is uncertain to what extent the AIU's Central Committee in Paris thought such an undertaking to be worthwhile. For example, in 1874, Isaac Lurion, the European-born head of the AIU's local committee in Baghdad, formally requested that the Central Committee consider establishing such an institution.[51] The Central Committee discussed the issue but concluded that it would be too difficult to find a suitable candidate to direct the school.[52] The idea of establishing a girls' school came up several times over the next two decades. It seems to have been discussed in 1883, as the AJA's annual report for

1882–1883 included a brief note signaling the organization's desire to work with the AIU to build such a school.[53] The BAIU from the same year indicated that the AIU hoped to establish girls' schools in multiple cities, including Baghdad.[54]

Finally, in June 1885, Jacques Louria, the director of the Boys' School, announced a plan to create a girls' workshop alongside the new Vocational School the AIU was building for lower-class boys. In this announcement, Louria wrote, "A workshop for girls will be created in which we will instruct 20 girls in needlework. We will also provide them with some indispensible instruction in subjects such as Hebrew, Arithmetic, and Arabic.... This workshop will be the point of departure for the creation of a Girls' School."[55] Several months later, Louria noted that he was optimistic about the workshop because rabbinical opposition to the idea of girls' education appeared to have decreased in recent years.[56]

Unfortunately for Louria, he underestimated the extent of this opposition. In March 1886 he wrote to the Central Committee to inform them that some rabbis were so angered by the opening of the workshop, which counted thirty students, that they had begun trying to prevent Jews from sending their children there.[57] Some were even considering excommunicating members of the community who did so.[58] It is worth noting that some rabbis who disapproved of girls' education were supportive of the Boys' School. For instance, in April 1886, Louria informed the Central Committee that a local rabbi wanted to help raise money for the AIU Boys' School but was completely opposed to the girls' workshop.[59]

As a result of such strong opposition, the workshop closed at some point, either in the late spring or early summer of 1886. In August, Silas Sassoon, a Baghdadi Jew from India who was visiting his native city at the time, penned a letter to Louria, begging him to recommit the AIU to the girls' workshop.[60] He even promised to provide the institution with seventy-five francs per month if it was reopened.[61] According to Louria, Sassoon was preaching to the converted, but the former believed the latter was ignoring obvious rabbinical and even communal opposition to the workshop as well as the general prospect of formal girls' education.[62] The workshop remained closed, and the issue appears to have disappeared from the AIU's agenda over the next several years.

Saul Somekh and the Planning of the Girls' School

It was Saul Somekh, himself a native Baghdadi Jew, who, as director of the Boys' School in the late 1880s and early 1890s, appears to have been instrumental in advocating for and convincing the AIU's leadership in Paris to at least seriously consider undertaking the project of setting up such a school for girls. Somekh, who had previously worked in AIU Boys' Schools in Jaffa, Tunis, Aleppo, and Istanbul, along with his colleague Morris Cohen, the Boys' School's British English teacher, who had been recruited for the school by the AJA more than a decade earlier, both deplored what they considered to be the lowly social condition of Baghdadi Jewish women and hoped to improve their situation. The Jewish woman in Baghdad, according to Somekh, was, "very hardworking; her social condition very unfortunate, she knows only a life of work and hardship."[63] Improving women's lives only for the sake of women, however, was not the goal of these men.

Although as director, Somekh wielded more influence than his colleague, it was Cohen who, in 1895, in a letter written to the AJA just after the Girls' School had opened, most clearly articulated some of the key reasons why the AIU and the local Baghdadi Jewish community stood to benefit from educating women. This letter, titled, "SUPERSTITION AMONG THE JEWS IN BAGDAD," devoted its first four paragraphs to highlighting perceived communal problems linked to women's ignorance:

> In reviewing the social condition of the Jews of Baghdad, the greatest drawback to improvement is found to be the ignorance and superstition of the women. Their prejudicial influence acts continually upon all with whom they come in contact. The ridiculous notions which they acquire in childhood cling to them through life, and are finally transmitted to all the members of their respective families. The consequences of their erroneous notions are met with at every step, and their conduct, which naturally adapts itself to their absurd ideas, strikes the mind of an educated person with the profoundest astonishment.
>
> From the cradle to the grave they wade through a maze of superstitious and unmeaning practices to which they attach the utmost importance, while they invariably disregard the commonest precepts which are observed in civilized countries for the preservation of health or the improvement of the heart and mind. Is it to be wondered at, then, that our efforts to improve the masses have not met with sufficient visible success? The good we do at the Boys' School, on the one hand, is undermined by detrimental home influence, and more particularly female influence, on the other hand. We have a double task to perform. We have not only to eradicate deeply-rooted erroneous ideas imbibed from infancy and supply their place with modern and diametrically opposed principles, but

> we have to make way against the silent and powerful contrary influence continually acting at home upon minds hardly released from its grasp. While we expect our pupils to have some civilizing influence upon their own families, our own task is rendered doubly hard by the opposition that every home offers to the introduction of any ideas at variance with those which have for ages been currency, and which have the sanction and open support of the entire community. As a matter of fact, it is indeed hard to find a single person, man, woman, or child, who does not look upon the ideas and practices which we term superstitions as the most reasonable and most natural in the world. Indeed, it may be asked, why should they view them in any other light? Who has ever dared to raise his voice against them, and show that they are wrong? Who would have the courage to tell them that the richest, most respected, and the most important men in the Jewish community of Bagdad, as well as all the spiritual leaders, are on the very same low level in matters of superstition as the women themselves? It is, however, sad to have to state that such is really the case, and still more melancholy to see how indifferent the community is to education and how difficult it is to persuade them of its beneficial results.
>
> As we cannot penetrate into the sanctuary of the family circle, there must be many ideas and practices which escape our knowledge altogether, and cannot be brought within the sphere of our action, and we must hope that our pupils, on growing up, may be able to exert that civilising influence which we are at present unable to communicate to all.
>
> In order that this may be carried on with efficiency, it is absolutely necessary and may be considered of primary importance that the female portion of the community should be able to understand and appreciate what is required of them. It has often been said that "men are what women make them." But without any instruction, can they be expected to set any value upon what we term improvement? Unless they are trained to our ways of thinking, how can we expect them to adopt our modes of action? If no effort is made to eradicate their prejudices and correct their errors, how can we expect them to share our views?[64]

Cohen's letter is insightful for scholars of Women's History and also Gender Studies, as he places the blame for the Jewish community's lack of social progress on the moral failings of women, which he contends were transmitted intergenerationally to both sons and daughters through the cloistered domestic space of the household.[65] Thus, regardless of how well the AIU educated boys, the community would continue to experience slow social change since the organization lacked the ability to both provide its students with their initial socialization and to reinforce AIU ideals at home. Implicit in his argument was the common nineteenth-century Victorian-gendered understanding of women as masters of the domestic sphere, responsible for socializing children in ways that would influence them for their entire lives.[66]

Educating girls, therefore, would not only improve the lives of girls and women, but would, in modern Keynesian parlance, have a multiplier effect. It would ensure that educated men would have their values reinforced in the private, domestic sphere, by educated partners. Similar to what Afsaneh Najmabadi has pointed out with regard to changing perceptions of women's roles as wives by advocates of girls' education in late nineteenth-century Iran, the AIU aimed to educate girls partly in order to create wives suitable for companionate marriages with its Boys' School graduates.[67] More important, however, proper education for girls would ensure that children of both sexes would be raised by mothers who had been socialized to reject superstition in favor of rational analysis and who could pass that type of thinking on to their children and help guide the Jewish community into the modern period. This would not only transform Baghdadi Jewish society but would guarantee that it would not revert back to what Cohen clearly believed to be its irrational past (and present). To put it another way, Cohen viewed women, in their roles as mothers, as intergenerational conduits for civilization. Furthermore, in their roles as wives, they had the ability to either reinforce or alter their husbands' social values. As other historians of nineteenth- and early twentieth-century female education have argued, many advocates for women's education in this period assumed that providing women with education would be a way of ensuring that men's thinking and actions would be permanently altered for the better.[68] In other words, drawing from Elizabeth Antebi's work, the goal was to change the woman to change the man.[69]

While Cohen portrayed Baghdadi Jewish society as static and dominated by irrational thought, Somekh clearly believed that this community had experienced some positive change in the recent past. In a letter from May 19, 1890, Somekh claimed that the community was ready for a school for girls. However, he warned that although many fathers had expressed the desire to educate their daughters, the AIU should not count on total financial support for girls' education from Baghdadi Jewish families.[70] Interestingly, in the same letter Somekh declared that the rabbis were supportive of the creation of a girls' school, though he expanded on this in a later letter, dated April 16, 1891. In this piece of correspondence, Somekh, apparently responding to fears of rabbinical opposition relayed to him by the AIU's Central Committee in Paris, stated that older rabbis were opposed to any kind of progress but assured his superiors that they had no moral authority over the minds of their community members.[71] Perhaps more important, he asserted that they were, "viewed very badly by the community, which has come to detest them."[72] Although he does not link the decline in rabbinical prestige to rabbinical struggles with the AIU, Yaron Harel argues that rabbinical authority in Baghdad began to wane in the 1870s and 1880s as a result of increased secularization among Baghdadi Jews and intra-rabbinical disputes exacerbated by the Tanzimat reforms.[73]

Still, it is difficult to analyze the veracity of Somekh's specific statements about the decline in rabbinical authority. There are at least two plausible theories regarding his argument, though neither may be true. The first is simply that he was telling what he believed to be the unadulterated truth; the second is that he was exaggerating in order to convince his superiors to construct the school. Irrespective of the "truth" of Somekh's assertions regarding rabbis, the fact that he was a native Baghdadi Jew, born in the city in 1858, may have influenced members of the Central Committee to view him as credible source about the community, above and beyond his role as the director of the Albert Sassoon School. Furthermore, while Somekh, in his letters, was careful to avoid coming across as considering the school's future founding as a *fait accompli*, possibly because he did not want to overstep the bounds of collegiality in his letters to his superiors, it is clear that he was attempting to make the case for such an undertaking.

Alongside championing the opening of a girls' school, Somekh also was also a staunch advocate for a local Jewish teenage girl he believed could one day direct a girls' school, potentially even one in Baghdad. Somekh's correspondence includes multiple letters that present the case for Dola Levy, who was fourteen years old when Somekh first mentioned her to the AIU in early 1890.[74] While Somekh's letters discussed Levy's abilities and accomplishments as well as her parents' views regarding her own education, they went into very little detail regarding anything else related to her family. According to his first letter, Levy was an intelligent girl from an honorable family, which was capable of paying for the cost of her travels from Baghdad to Paris for training, and would make a fine future director for a girls' school in Baghdad.[75] This was an important statement since, although not a formal policy at this point, the AIU preferred to not send directors and teachers to work in schools located in their home communities.

In a subsequent letter Somekh mentioned that although girls did not normally frequent the AIU Boys' School in Baghdad because of conservative communal mores that prohibited boys and girls from socializing with one another, Levy had been allowed to do so until her parents removed her, apparently once she neared puberty.[76] As a student, she had learned how to speak, read, and write French, and had retained these skills even after being removed from the school.[77] He also praised Levy's family for being conversant with European culture and described her father as the city's leading accountant.[78] Somekh also noted that Levy was healthy and that although she would clearly arrive in Paris well behind other girls her age in terms of academics she possessed the ability to catch up.[79] His comment about Levy's need to catch up with other students was clearly a reference to Baghdad's lack of a girls' school. Finally, again striking a compromising tone, he informed his superiors that her parents were not wedded to the idea of her returning to her native city and would consent to the AIU assigning her to where she would be most needed following her training in Paris.[80]

Somekh's correspondence with the Central Committee regarding Levy's potential candidacy sheds significant light on both the social condition of upper-class Jewish girls in Baghdad and on his own goals as an advocate for female education. Although Levy's parents were supportive of her education, and even hoped that she would one day become a teacher herself, which would entail a life in the public spotlight, the fact that they removed her from school at the age of either eleven or twelve highlights the importance that Jewish families attached to their daughters' reputations.[81] It is uncertain exactly how old Levy was when she left school, as Somekh mentioned only that she had left the school just prior to his arrival in 1888.[82] Additionally, although he later stated that her family approved of Levy working in other cities, it appears that Somekh at first hoped that the organization would consider preparing Levy to run a future school in Baghdad.[83] This may explain why Somekh devoted so much space to describing Levy's father's economic and social position in the city. Besides merely assuring the AIU's Parisian leadership of Levy's family's irreproachable morality, support, and ability to finance their daughter's education, Somekh was also likely highlighting the family's prominent place in the local community. This might have been to portray Levy as the ideal candidate to assuage local concerns about female education and mitigate criticism of the opening of a girls' school.

It is worth noting that Levy was eventually admitted to the AIU's training program but was ultimately sent to work in Damascus, and not her native city, in 1896, over one year after the girls' school in Baghdad opened. Thus, it seems from this brief case study that the Central Committee's members respected Somekh's opinions enough to seriously consider his proposals but also appear to have believed that future AIU-trained directors and female teachers destined for Baghdad should not be natives of the city.

By early 1891, after floating the idea for a girls' school and linking his advocacy for Levy's admission to the AIU female teachers' program in Paris to it, Somekh's arguments seem to have gained receptive ears in Paris. Not only did the Central Committee allow Somekh to expand the AIU's apprenticeship program in Baghdad to include young girls whose families wanted them to learn employable skills such as dressmaking and embroidery, but the AIU's Secretary-General also asked Somekh his opinion about the chances for success of a girls' school.[84] At the same time he tasked Somekh with creating a provisional budget for such an institution's first year of operation.[85]

As previously discussed, Somekh responded affirmatively to the question about the chances of the school's success. Regarding the budget, he painted a rather negative picture. Somekh's letter, dated April 16, 1891, stated that money was the main obstacle to the founding of a girls' school. In this letter Somekh predicted that it would cost approximately 3,540 francs per year to run the school and that the organization could expect only 900 francs in tuition from approximately thirty paying students.[86] His budget assumed that sixty students would be nonpaying, bringing the total enrollment to ninety, which, at least initially, would mean that it was smaller than the Boys' School. He attempted to forestall criticism for his projected 2,640 franc deficit by assuring the Central Committee that the AJA, which he pointed out had long championed the creation of a girls' school, would offset half of it.[87]

Besides the deficit, Somekh's chief concern appears to have been attracting a capable female director to lead the school. After stating that an annual salary of 1,800 to 2,000 francs would be adequate to attract a qualified candidate to a dreadful location such as Baghdad, Somekh devoted much of the remainder of the letter to advising the Central Committee as to the route a female teacher should take from Western Europe to Baghdad.[88] He advised a sea journey, which, assuming Marseilles, France, as the departure point, and Basra as the end point, would take eighteen days, including a stop in Bombay, India.[89] Upon arriving in Basra, the teacher could take either a British or Ottoman ship up the Tigris and arrive in Baghdad within the day.[90]

In addition to crafting a provisional budget and dispensing advice as to how best to attract and transport a future director for the school, Somekh's letter also spelled out his vision for how the school's curriculum should be structured. He asserted that the students should be divided into three main tracks and that the initial focus should be on teaching them French and Hebrew.[91] Interestingly, he strongly advised against the instruction of Arabic, as the general language of instruction in the school would be French, and he believed it would be nearly impossible to find a suitable female Arabic teacher in Baghdad.[92] Somekh's omission of Arabic is important to note since the vast majority of Baghdadi Jewish families at this time would have spoken Judeo-Arabic in their homes. By focusing on French and Hebrew, rather than Arabic, Somekh's desired program would have potentially rendered Jewish girls unable to gain employment or potentially even to access the social and cultural spheres outside of either the local Jewish community or the elite French-speaking community in the city.

Indeed, such a focus would have worked against integrating Jewish girls into general Baghdadi society. This issue was not as important for Jewish boys, as Jewish men had long conducted their personal and financial business in the public sphere, allowing them to mix with their non-Jewish counterparts. However, Jewish women in the urban Ottoman Arab world had historically had fewer interactions with non-Jewish women, and certainly with non-Jewish men, because of dominant cultural taboos related to women traveling outside of the house.[93]

Although Somekh had hoped to pre-empt criticism of his proposed budget, he apparently met with some resistance from the Central Committee. In a letter from mid-June, 1891, Somekh defended his budget by disparaging the local Jewish community:

> Your observations on this question are perfectly just but, given the moral state of our co-religionists in Baghdad, it would be fanciful to appeal to their sense of self-sacrifice. They have the means but not the willingness, they are lacking in generosity. You asked me for a budget and I drew one up using the most exacting methods. I assessed that local resources could cover 900 francs in tuition and do not believe that we can count on a higher amount of revenue.[94]

Indeed, Somekh proceeded to declare Baghdadi Jews to be egotistical, exploitative, and willing to benefit monetarily from the resources and work of international philanthropists while refusing to contribute to their own community.[95] Implicit in this letter was the notion that Baghdadi Jews, even after more than a quarter-century of AIU influence, still required external actors to work actively on their behalves to force change upon them.

Unfortunately, Somekh, who left Baghdad in early 1893, did not take up the issue of the Girls' School again. Instead he left it to his successor, Joseph Danon, who had arrived just prior to Somekh's departure, to deal with the issue. Danon, who had previously worked as a teacher in AIU schools in Sofia and Tunis and, most recently, as a director in Sousse, Tunisia, arrived with his wife Rachel, who had previously taught in the Girls' School in Tunis. While Somekh did not remain in Baghdad long enough to see the opening of the Girls' School, he was instrumental in advocating for girls' education in general and was the person who first influenced the AIU's Paris leadership to seriously consider opening such an institution. He also accurately predicted some problems the school would face in the future, including the recruitment of able teachers, the issue of families refusing to pay for their daughters' educations, and the challenge of finding adequate language teachers.

After spending a year getting situated in Baghdad, Danon began building on Somekh's advocacy by also championing the creation of a girls' school. Most notably, he penned a letter to Paris in June 1894 arguing that the graduates of the Boys' School required educated companions to ensure that they would retain the moral values they had adopted while studying under AIU supervision.[96] Again, this idea of companionate marriage was gaining ground in both foreign- and indigenous-run schools in the Ottoman Empire and Middle East in this period. For example, in British-occupied Egypt, children were taught that the family unit had at its center educated husbands and wives whose bonds were based on love.[97] Danon also noted that the AIU's work over the previous three decades had helped to prepare the community for the creation of such a school and that he did not expect much resistance to it.[98] This letter proved decisive, and his superiors soon consented to the establishment of a girls' school in Baghdad.

Rachel Danon and the Opening of the Girls' School

In March 1893, around the time of her twenty-second birthday, Rachel Danon arrived with her husband Joseph in Baghdad so that the latter could take up his new position as director of the Albert Sassoon School. After the Central Committee agreed, in mid 1894, to establish a girls' school in Baghdad, it tasked Rachel Danon with acting as the institution's first director and ordered her to begin ordering materials and enrolling students.[99] This was not an easy task as Danon had never previously served in this capacity, and the Baghdadi Jewish community had never had a formal school for girls, with the exception of the short-lived AIU-run vocational workshop that had closed in 1886.

It is worth noting that although her husband was an older and more experienced teacher, Rachel Danon, in her role as director, was not merely a figurehead put in place so that Joseph could exert supreme influence over both schools. Rather, the two worked as colleagues, even though Rachel's salary was less than half of Joseph's, and were responsible for leading their respective schools. In certain instances, however, such as when they communicated with the Ottoman government, Joseph would take the lead. One early example of this was with regard to registering the school with the Ottoman government. Joseph engaged in some legal trickery in order to fast-track the school's approval by Ottoman authorities, who required the school be registered in the name of an Ottoman citizen. Since Rachel had been born and raised in France and held that country's citizenship, Joseph registered the new school under the name of an unnamed Ottoman woman.[100]

In spite of her husband's struggles to get the school registered, during this time Rachel's focus remained on organizing the school. Her initial letter mentioned that since local customs dictate that the Girls' School should have only female teachers, and because the local rabbi under consideration to teach Hebrew struggled with the language's script, she would try to find a local female Hebrew teacher.[101] While she feared that this might prove difficult because of the dearth of qualified Jewish female teachers in Baghdad, she expressed her confidence that the Central Committee would provide her with proper teachers if necessary.[102] In this letter Danon also requested that the Central Committee provide her with various teaching materials, including song books and physical training manuals as well as various training manuals for the girls who were apprenticing outside of the school.[103] The idea that girls' schools should have an exclusive or nearly exclusive female teaching staff was apparently widespread in the Arab world's Jewish communities and extended to institutions beyond the AIU's network. The Evelina de Rothschild School in Jerusalem, for example, adhered to similar principles during this period.[104]

Before discussing the AIU Girls' School's opening it is worth mentioning that this institution was only the second school for girls in the city. The first such institution was a Catholic school for girls, which had been founded by a Carmelite priest in 1868 and then transferred to the authority of French Catholic nuns in 1880.[105] While an Armenian girls' school had been founded in the 1850s, it is unclear whether this institution was still in existence in the 1880s. In fact, a British consular report from 1885 listed the Catholic Girls' School run by the French Sisters of Charity as the only girls' school in the city.[106] A small Armenian school with two teachers and a seamstress was included in the report, indicating that girls likely attended the school, but this may have been a co-educational institution.[107] In any case, the report noted that the Armenian school was far behind the others in terms of quality.[108]

Danon must have already made great progress prior to penning her first letter to Bigart, as the school opened its doors barely a month later, on Tuesday, January 22, 1895. From Danon's initial letter following the school's opening, it seems that Somekh's previous estimates, from 1891, for initial enrollment at the Girls' School had been too optimistic. The latter had predicted that the school would attract thirty paying students, but in reality only a total of twenty-five students were even enrolled in the school the day it opened.[109] In fact, as late as December 1894, the AJA, which normally received its information about Baghdad from AIU sources, believed that the school would open its doors with one hundred students, including eighty tuition-paying students.[110] Danon attributed the low enrollment to the prejudices of fathers who continued to believe that women were inferior to men and so refused to pay for their daughters' educations.[111] She also stated her preference to enroll a lower number of students rather than allow girls from middle-class families to enroll without paying tuition.[112] It thus appears that while they accepted Somekh's general recommendation, the members of the Central Committee in Paris moved to empower Danon to take a firmer stand on the issue of tuition than the former thought possible.

Although not discussed in the letters, this inflexible stance on tuition may have come about because the Central Committee's members realized they were in a position of power relative to the local Jewish community in that they were funding Baghdad's first school for Jewish girls. Indeed, the organization had been willing to run large deficits in other cities that already had girls' schools prior to the establishment of similar AIU institutions. One such example was Tripoli in Ottoman Libya, where an Italian school for girls, which attracted many middle- and upper-class Jewish girls, began operating in 1877. This was nearly two decades prior to the opening of the city's AIU Girls' School in 1896. Rachel Simon's research on Jewish girls' education in Ottoman Tripoli has highlighted the fact that until the end of Ottoman rule in the city, the AIU Girls' School tended to attract poorer, non–tuition-paying students, whereas the Italian school, which was free, attracted more upper-class girls.[113] However, Simon notes that the Girls' School gradually attracted more upper-class girls during this period.[114] Unlike in Tripoli, where the AIU was apparently willing to subsidize most students' educations in the hope of establishing itself as an alternative to the Italian school in order to recruit more paying students in the future, the AIU's leaders appear to have concluded that they could be more discerning with regard to the Baghdad school.

In addition to not taking Somekh's advice regarding the admission of mostly non–tuition-paying students, the Central Committee decided to include Arabic in the school's curriculum. Danon was able to recruit two young women as teachers in the school: a Hebrew teacher and an Arabic teacher. The former, who also was hired to teach sewing, was totally inexperienced, while the latter had prior experience teaching in Mosul, though Danon claimed that she did not know how to teach groups of students.[115] Danon herself was to teach French and also supervise the other teachers. Indeed, she asserted that her teachers required supervision and training in AIU pedagogy.[116] It is worth noting that the AIU Girls' School in Baghdad was somewhat unique in that it had hired a local female teacher instead of a rabbi to teach Hebrew. Most AIU schools employed rabbis both because of a lack of secular, and especially AIU-trained, teachers capable of teaching the language and to establish cordial relations with the local community.[117]

Perhaps the most pressing organizational challenge facing Danon at this time was the heterogonous mixture of students enrolled in the school. She stated that although she had not yet formed definitive tracks, she had divided the girls into three tracks, which included subdivisions.[118] The First and Second Classes consisted of girls who, like Dola Levy, had spent time studying in the Boys' School, which shows that by the mid 1890s it had become more common for young girls to study alongside young boys. Meanwhile, the Third Class consisted of girls who had either studied some Hebrew in the local communal-run boys' schools or who had never had any kind of formal education.[119] While there were problems, including inexperienced teachers, students with vastly different educational backgrounds, and lower than expected enrollment, the school had opened successfully and, according to the time frame spelled out in Danon's letter from December 1894, on schedule.

Over the course of the year following the school's opening, Danon struggled to alter Jewish community members' views of the importance of primary education for girls while simultaneously taking comfort in the progress her students were making both inside and outside of the classroom. She also continued to monitor her subordinates and engaged in what she believed was a life-or-death fight for the school's continued existence when, in the middle of the year, a dispute broke out over the building that housed the school.

Enrollment and Payment Issues

Although the number of students nearly doubled from twenty-five to forty-eight over the course of 1895, Danon's correspondence leaves little doubt that had she allowed nonpaying students to enroll, the increase in enrollment would have been much more substantial. The figures in Table 1.1 highlight the emphasis that the Baghdad Girls' School placed on accepting mostly tuition-paying students relative to other AIU girls' schools in the Ottoman Empire's Arab provinces in 1895. As shown in Table 1.1, no other AIU girls' school in the Ottoman Arab provinces even approached parity with the Baghdad School with regard to the latter's high ratio of paying to nonpaying students.

Schools in the non-Arab provinces faced similar issues. For example, the Girls' School in the Galata section of Istanbul, founded in 1877, had more non-paying than paying students during its first twenty years of operation.[120] Even in the Girls' School in Salonica, founded in 1874, which scholar Rena Molho argues was successful relative to other schools in attracting paying students in the late nineteenth and early twentieth centuries, only slightly more than half the students were paying tuition in the 1890s, though the situation improved over the next decade.[121] Finally, it is worth noting that evidence clearly indicates that different directors pursued different strategies in the various cities where the AIU operated. According to Erol Haker, Sara Ungar, the director of the Girls' School in Edirne from 1890 to 1911, aimed to admit more nonpaying than paying students to this school in an attempt to attract a higher number of poorer students.[122]

Table 1.1 Total numbers of paying and non-paying students in select AIU girls' schools in the Arab world in December 1895

City	Total number of students	Number of paying students	Number of non-paying students
Aleppo Founded: 1889	70	24	46
Baghdad Founded: 1895	48	34	14
Beirut Founded: 1880	95	13	82
Damascus Founded: 1888	200	77	123
Haifa Founded: 1895	81	26	55
Jaffa Founded: 1894	107	30	77

Source: BAIU

Danon's letters from 1895 and early 1896 repeatedly discussed the haphazard progress made in trying to increase student enrollment. Indeed, this appears to have been the issue that concerned Danon most in the school's first year. In a letter from February, 1895 she mentioned that the school's enrollment had grown from twenty-five to twenty-nine in the weeks following its opening but also noted that the number had recently reached thirty-six before she had expelled seven students.[123] Danon had done this because the girls' fathers would agree to pay only part of their tuition even though they had the means to pay in full.[124] In this same letter she also declared that it was necessary to take a firm stand against wealthy Baghdadi families, as they were not accustomed to others being as obstinate as them.[125] Danon expressed optimism that once these families consented to paying full tuition, others would soon follow suit.[126]

Not everyone was pleased with the director's strategy. Morris Cohen, the aforementioned English teacher in the city's AIU Boys' School, penned a letter to the AJA several months after the Girls' School's opening, requesting funds so that it could admit more nonpaying students to ensure its "permanent existence."[127] The AJA's Executive Committee refused this request, noting that the institution had only just recently opened and that it was too soon to seek changes.[128] Cohen had previously requested unspecified modifications to the school's curriculum, which the Executive Committee had also rejected, so it is likely that he was not pleased with what he perceived to be the school's slow progress in recruiting and educating girls.[129] Cohen's attempts to interfere in the running of the Girls' School are interesting, as he had no formal role whatsoever with regard to the new institution. He did, however, send reports, written in English, back to the AJA to update the Executive Committee on the school's progress.

By May the school's population had increased yet again—to thirty-nine students, thirty of whom were paying. Yet in a letter written in the middle of that month, Danon informed Bigart that the school would have seventy or eighty students, based on the number of parents who tried to enroll their daughters, if not for the school's strict policy of payment enforcement.[130] In the midst of battling parents over the payment of tuition, Danon also engaged in at least one argument with a mother over her three daughters' repeated tardiness. Rather than allow this mother to consistently drop her daughters off after the school day had begun, Danon expelled the three girls.[131] Clearly she was aiming to instill more than just merely financial discipline in the parents. Indeed, Danon's actions in this case indicate that she was trying to make parents understand the importance of adhering to school regulations to drive home the point that their daughters' enrollment in the school was a privilege that should not be wasted. Whether her lack of experience played a role in the severe manner in which she sometimes reacted to students and parents who did not meet her standards remains an open question.

Even with Danon's efforts to accept mostly tuition-paying students, the school still ran at a deficit during its first year of operation. In fact, the majority of the school's funding came not from tuition but rather from AIU and AJA subventions of 1,600 and 800 francs, respectively.[132] Tuition accounted for only 795 francs of the school's income, while 11.50 francs came from unspecified sources.[133] The school spent 2,417.83 francs on salaries, 839.15 francs on rent and classroom furniture and material, and 66.40 francs on unspecified items.[134] This left a deficit of over 116 francs.[135] Thus it is fair to say that since tuition accounted for less than a quarter of the school's income, Danon's goals in forcing parents to pay for tuition likely had more to do with her desire to instill the belief in both Baghdadi Jewish fathers and mothers that a daughter's education was worth paying for, than with her concern over the school's finances. However, it is also evident that Danon aimed to make her school as financially sound as possible, so this factor should not be totally ignored.

The Girls' School's initial financial problems were comparable to, and likely less threatening than, other first and second institutions in the late Ottoman period. For example, the community-run modern Jewish Boys' School that opened in Basra in 1890 repeatedly faced financial shortfalls during its first year of operation.[136] Two generations earlier, in its first two years of operation, the Girls' School opened by the Rothschilds in Jerusalem in 1854, which was later renamed the Evalina de Rothschild School, failed to attract many paying students and often had to pay parents to convince them to send their daughters to the school.[137]

Organizing the Students

Alongside her struggles with parents, Danon labored to place her students in workable tracks and groups, a problem compounded by the facts that the school occasionally both gained and lost students and had low initial enrollment. Over the course of the year, Danon's goal seems to have been to consolidate her students into three workable classes, though at one point, in the middle of the school year, she had to create a Fourth Class. This group consisted of seven veteran students of the Third Class. These students were too advanced to work with the recently admitted students to their class, but were also too weak to join the Second Class.[138] As there were only three teachers in the school, and only two in the afternoon, Danon was forced to place these students in the same class as the three students in the First Class.[139] Although she never explained how, it appears that this situation was resolved sometime in May or June, as her letter from early July mentioned that the school now had three classes.[140] However, Danon may have merely omitted a mention of the auxiliary group in this letter.

While she obviously aimed to provide every student at the school with a stellar education, Danon paid special attention to the girls in the First Class. These three girls had all studied at the organization's Boys' School in Baghdad prior to enrolling in the Girls' School and were extremely advanced. This was the case even when these girls were compared to their classmates in the Second Class, some of whom had also studied at the former institution. In an undated letter that appears to be from late March, Danon relayed her concern for these girls and linked their continued enrollment to the school's future progress.[141] She contended that had these girls been placed with other students they would have left the school, thereby damaging its reputation.[142] Danon, implying that these girls come from well-known families, proceeded to compare Baghdadi Jewish parents to sheep and to claim that these families would not initially send their daughters to the school to gain a solid education. Rather, they would do so only once some of the leading families did so.[143] Thus, she implied that the school's fortunes potentially hinged on its future symbolic status in a community whose members would come to view it as a place they could send their daughters in order to gain, both for themselves and their daughters, a sort of cultural capital. The girls in question, then, were important both because of their academic abilities and their potential roles as passive recruiters for the school.

Supervising the Teachers and Establishing a Curriculum

As previously mentioned, Danon hired two teachers, a totally inexperienced Hebrew and sewing teacher and a slightly experienced Arabic teacher. Although Danon lamented the Hebrew and sewing teacher's inexperience, she believed it also presented an opportunity. In her initial discussion of this teacher, she asserted that one benefit of having hired a younger teacher was that she would be easier to train, as she was not yet set in her ways.[144] Thus, Danon expressed her hope that the teacher's youth and inexperience would make it easier for her to adapt to teaching in an AIU institution.

Furthermore, because the teacher was inexperienced, Danon was able to start her at a much lower salary than the Arabic teacher, who was also a woman.

The Hebrew and sewing teacher was hired at an initial salary of 11.10 francs per month, while the Arabic teacher was paid 33.35 francs per month, even though the latter worked only part time.[145] Additionally, a female staff member was hired to oversee the upkeep of the classrooms at a rate of 8.35 francs per month, and a male doorman and porter was hired at a rate of 16.65 francs per month.[146] Danon noted that the Hebrew and sewing teacher was paid so little because women's work in Baghdad was poorly compensated. She also stated that starting inexperienced teachers at a low salary was a good motivational technique.[147] Indeed, she noted her desire to link future raises to the teacher's ability to adopt Danon's own teaching methodology.[148] Finally, although tangential to the discussion of teachers' salaries, it is worth mentioning that Danon believed the doorman's salary was high, which she viewed as justifiable because he was loyal.[149] She also informed Bigart that the man in question was an Afghani non-Jew, which was important since a Jewish man would lack both the authority and ability to defend the school.[150]

Throughout 1895 Danon struggled to both train and improve the morale of the Hebrew and sewing teacher. She consistently complained about her subordinate's inability to exercise authority over her students and her lack of progress in comprehending AIU teaching methodology.[151] At one point Danon vented her frustration by asserting the school would likely not be able to retain the teacher because she was requesting a raise she had not earned.[152] Additionally, it appears that by the end of the year this teacher had become so angry over her low salary that she had quit her position, though she returned just over two weeks later to ask for her job back.[153] Danon noted that she allowed her subordinate to return, but with the understanding that her raises would be linked to performance.[154]

Fortunately, Danon's only major issue with the Arabic teacher seems to have been linked to the latter's schedule. The teacher could work for only two hours on Sunday mornings and, further, worked only full mornings the remainder of the week.[155] Therefore, Danon and the Hebrew and sewing teacher were left shorthanded for an hour on Sunday mornings and all afternoon each day. At one point she also complained that the Arabic teacher was struggling to adapt to the AIU's teaching methodology, but she likely considered this a minor problem, as she did not repeatedly mention this teacher's shortcomings in her letters, as she did in the case of the Hebrew and sewing teacher.[156] Still, though Danon considered the Arabic teacher to be relatively competent in the classroom, she made consistent attempts to supervise her, while also closely monitoring the Hebrew and sewing teacher.[157] Danon even informed Bigart, that while she herself was constantly busy teaching her own classes, she managed to escape her classroom every now and then to check on these teachers.[158] It appears, however, from the tone of Danon's letters, that she was not pleased with her own ability to supervise and assist them.

It is worth mentioning that Danon, like many other AIU-trained female teachers, had received a Supérior degree from the Institut Bischoffsheim, an elite vocational and normal training institution for female instructors in Paris. The AIU often sent its female trainees to this institution, as it did not establish its own women's training school until the early 1920s. While little research has been done into students' experiences at this institution, according to Frances Malino, "Before graduating from the schools, in addition to the exams for their teaching degree, the students were also expected to pass an exam in Hebrew and Jewish history."[159] Thus, although it is unclear what kind of training she had had in pedagogical theory, Danon had received advanced education in both secular and Jewish subjects.

In terms of curriculum, Danon ensured that her students' education revolved mostly around French, as it was the school's language of instruction, and sewing, as it was viewed as a practical skill.[160] Students received at least ten hours of instruction in each of these subjects each week.[161] Arabic and Hebrew were also key parts of the curriculum, although, because the Arabic teacher worked only mornings and the Hebrew teacher also taught sewing, it appears that students devoted only about five hours per week to each subject.[162] Danon mentioned, as well, that students were also exposed to arithmetic.[163] It is likely that the desire to at least acquaint students with arithmetic was, as in other parts of the Middle East, linked to the women's perceived roles as household managers.[164]

The Girls' School's curriculum was similar, though not identical, to curriculums in other foreign girls' schools in the Ottoman Empire and Middle East during this period, as well as to French girls' primary schools. For example, the AIU Girls' School in Galata, Istanbul, taught French, Judeo-Spanish, since many students were Sephardic, and German, since some students were Ashkenazi and came from Yiddish-speaking families.[165] Like the Baghdad Girls' School, the Galata Girls' School placed a major emphasis on sewing instruction but, in contrast to the former institution, it also educated girls in home economics.[166] St. Mary's School, an Anglican missionary educational institution in Jerusalem during this period, naturally instructed girls in religious subjects but also taught Arabic and English alongside vocational subjects such as sewing and embroidery.[167] This was to prepare girls for marriage and potential work inside or outside of the home.

Supervising Vocational Students

In addition to educating girls in the classroom, the AIU funded apprenticeship programs for boys and girls in cities where the organization operated schools. These programs were aimed at attracting lower- and working-class boys and girls who needed to learn trades to support their families as adults. With regard to female vocational education, the AIU preferred to recruit twelve- to fourteen-year-old girls from poor families who had previously attended their local AIU girls' school.[168] Furthermore, while male apprentices were normally sent to work under masters outside of the confines of the school, the AIU usually built workshops that were attached to girls' schools for female apprentices so they would not have to travel alone in public.[169] Interestingly, since the AIU's female apprenticeship program in Baghdad predated the establishment of the city's Girls' School by over four years, the organization's initial female apprentices had to travel, by themselves, to work under masters throughout the city.

Following the initial girls' workshop's closure in 1886, during Louria's time as director of the Boys' School, Somekh restarted a modified version of the program in 1891. Joseph Danon, Somekh's successor, continued this work upon taking over as director of the Boys' School. Danon was actually responsible for ensuring the program's continuation, as the AIU had only initially provided Somekh with a three-year subvention for its reset.[170] Although Rachel Danon began to work alongside her husband, it appears that he continued to take the lead—possibly because his wife was so busy as the director of a first-year school—in supervising young female Jewish apprentices who were working in various workshops throughout the city.

From one of Joseph Danon's letters, we know that of the twenty female apprentices mentioned by the BAIU for 1895, eleven were embroiderers who worked with wool, silver, and gold, five were embroiderers who worked with cotton, silver, and gold, three were tapestry makers, and one was a dressmaker.[171] These girls all worked under the guidance of local female masters. Both Joseph Danon and a local rabbi, who clearly supported the program, occasionally visited the workshops where the girls were training.[172]

While Rachel Danon was not as active in checking on apprentices as she would be in the future, her husband's views on these apprentices shed light on the organization's goals with regard to less well-off girls and women in the Baghdadi Jewish community. Much of Joseph Danon's focus in his main letter reviewing the work of female apprentices for 1895 was on the link between poorer girls learning marketable skills as craftswomen and their future abilities to find husbands and help support their families. For example, Danon mentioned that these girls received a small salary for their work, which allowed them to, "build a little nest-egg that will aid them in marrying."[173] Furthermore, he noted that by working these girls would be able to help keep their future families out of poverty.[174] Finally, he claimed that the impact of this specific program was so large, and so positive, that it could not be adequately measured.[175]

Joseph Danon's letter indicates that he, like Somekh, Cohen, and his own wife, linked the acquisition of skills by poorer Jewish girls to these girls' roles as future providers or co-providers as wives and mothers. Thus, the acquisition of skills for these girls was important insofar as it kept their husbands and children out of poverty. This is not to say that Danon, or his colleagues, did not want women to gain skills and education for their own personal improvement, but rather to highlight that he seems to have been unable to move beyond his gendered understanding of women's familial roles, even while reporting on a program geared toward preparing them for private-sector work that entailed working in the public sphere.

Modeling Feminine Modernity

Rachel Danon did not view herself only as a director and teacher but, like other AIU female directors, also as a role model for her students.[176] From her correspondence it is clear that she considered the encouragement of students to adopt what she considered to be proper, European methods of hygiene, dress, and manners as a key part of her job. Thus, she was concerned not only with exposing girls to academic studies, but also with changing the way they looked and acted in public. Danon's perception of her own role in this process was similar to the one that scholar Ellen Fleischmann ascribed to American Protestant missionary women in and around Greater Syria in the nineteenth and twentieth centuries. According to Fleischmann, "Through their work with Arab women, the missionary women attempted to shape, construct, and reinforce young women's gendered notions of identity casting themselves in the role of exemplary womanhood."[177] Thus, like the missionaries Fleischmann describes, Danon presented herself as a model of feminine modernity for her students.

Female modernity for Danon seems to have signified cleanliness, hygiene, discipline, manners, and proper dress. In order to become proper wives and mothers, girls needed to acquire these traits. Therefore, Danon viewed the classroom, and really the entire schoolhouse, as a European site where she could model European modernity through the ways she dressed, talked, and interacted with students, teachers, and visitors. Her students would then internalize these ideas and carry them into the outside world.

Danon's letters repeatedly stressed the importance she placed on cleanliness and dress. In her letter discussing the school's progress during its first month and a half of existence, she stated that, "First of all, I have directed all of my efforts towards propriety and have shown myself quite severe in this regard."[178] While lamenting the general state of female cleanliness and style (she mentioned, for example, that girls only did their hair once per week, on the eve of the Sabbath), Danon noted that she initially inspected each student's attire and shoes herself and during the first two weeks had sent away multiple students for failing to meet her standards.[179] In fact, she related that students would often come to school relaying concerns from parents about her strict policy. For example, one girl asked Danon, on behalf of her father, if it was truly necessary to polish her shoes each day.[180] Danon asserted with satisfaction that her policy had worked and that her students were now all passing her inspections.[181] Furthermore, she claimed that since the girls liked her European hairstyle, she had promised to give each girl who achieved a certain goal a similar haircut.[182] She noted that her students were already hard at work in hopes of receiving this reward.[183]

While this earlier letter highlighted some of Danon's goals inside the classroom, a story she told in a later letter casts light on her goal of having students internalize school policies and carry them beyond the confines of the school. In this later letter, Danon related the plea of three students for her to intervene with one of their classmates:

> Madame, they told me, this young girl is going to dishonor the school. She is proper only in class. Yesterday we met her on the street in sandals and without stockings, wearing a stained and torn dress. Is it not a shame for you and for us that she goes out like this when she attends the school?[184]

Although she could not have been happy to hear that one of her students was dressed so poorly in public, the fact that three of her students brought it to her attention must have pleased Danon. On the one hand, the students in question had, after only several months at the school, come to both adopt Danon's views on cleanliness and proper attire and to view themselves as public representatives of the school. On the other hand, the girls were also engaged in a form of self-policing to protect their own reputations, as they were asking Danon to intervene with their classmate so that the latter would not bring shame to the school. In any case, it appears from her letters that Danon's students were adopting aspects of her worldview and also coming to view proper dress, cleanliness, and hygiene as markers of the school's corporate identity.[185]

One additional way that Danon modeled modernity was by presenting herself to the Jewish community as an educated, cultivated, European woman who worked outside the home and, in addition to her formal academic education, was proficient in the practical skill of sewing. Indeed, according to a report from the AJA, which is amply corroborated by Danon's correspondence, much of the opposition to girls' education in general, and learning how to sew in particular, came not from men in the community but from women.[186] In fact, Danon mentioned that mothers had often approached her to ask if their daughters really needed to learn how to sew, since it was a useless skill.[187] The mothers' implication was clearly that middle- and upper-middle-class girls need not acquire any skills that could be used to earn a living, even if such skills would later aid them in managing their own households. Danon lamented the mothers' opposition, as many of the girls were excited to adopt European-style attire and had already accepted her views on modern fashion.[188] Importantly, she continued both to teach sewing and to make the case for the importance of learning to sew when speaking to parents.

Local opposition to women learning crafts and taking part in labor reflected the urban, middle-class outlook of a significant segment of Baghdad's Jewish community, which viewed women having to work as markers of shame for their families. However, in poorer, rural, and even urban Middle Eastern communities, whether Muslim, Jewish, or Christian, families often had no choice but to depend on their female members to work for a living, be it in public or private. In some cases, as Donald Quataert's research has shown, a woman's ability to earn a wage actually increased her appeal as a wife.[189] Among many Baghdadi Jews in the late nineteenth century, the opposite seems to have been true, as families worried that allowing girls to work would both injure the families' reputations and hurt parents' chances of finding a suitable groom for their daughters.

Problems with Materials and Housing

Shifting away from challenges related to instruction or cultural transmission, Danon and her school faced problems posed by both influential community members and the school's building itself during the first half of 1895. Prior to the school's opening, the AIU had been promised material support for school furniture by Abdullah Elias, a prominent Baghdad Jew. Elias, however, soon ran afoul of both Rachel and Joseph Danon. According to Rachel, immediately upon the school's opening, Elias had reduced his support to almost nothing and attempted to link what little help he was still offering to her willingness to admit nonpaying girls, chosen by Elias, to the school.[190] In a letter attacking Elias, Danon stated that these girls came not from the local population but rather from foreign Jewish families living in Baghdad. Rather than accepting these conditions, she rejected Elias's help, fearing that if she acceded to his demands he would gain permanent influence over the school.[191] Based on Danon's desire to accept only paying students it is understandable that she would not have been willing to accept nonpaying students from wealthy foreign families, even if accepting such girls may have boosted the school's reputation. One aspect of this story that stands out is that it appears that Elias was attempting to help the school on the cheap and use his philanthropy to increase his own reputation in certain circles in Baghdad. So while this story highlights a key problem that Danon faced in early 1895, it also indicates that the school was, from its inception, somewhat prestigious, as Elias apparently considered a possible connection with it to be a means of bolstering his own reputation in the city.

Upon opening, the AIU Girls' School in Baghdad was located in a house leased to the organization by Menahem Saleh. It appears that Menahem Saleh was actually Menahem Saleh Daniel, the former Jewish representative to the Ottoman Parliament in the late 1870s and uncle of Sassoon Heskel. Thus, he was not just one of the most prominent Jewish notables in Baghdad but in the entire eastern Arab world. Saleh's decision to rent one of his properties to the school was apparently publicized, as the AJA's Executive Committee sent him a letter expressing gratitude for his work in support of the school's establishment.[192] By June of 1895, two major issues had arisen regarding the house Saleh rented to the AIU. The first was that, although spacious, it was hot and apparently had so many windows that it was constantly flooded with sunlight during the day.[193] This was the opposite problem that the Boys' School had when it first opened in 1864–65, but it was so severe that Danon, copying a practice used by the staff at the aforementioned institution, combined classes in the morning so that students did not have to remain in school during the hot afternoons.[194] It is important to note that school vacations were based on Jewish holidays, so students studied throughout the summer months, suffering through high temperatures, as the major Jewish holidays were in the late summer, autumn, and spring.

The second, and most threatening, problem regarding the school's building was that, during the Passover holiday of 1895, an ownership dispute erupted between Menahem Saleh and several of his family members, most notably his sister Simha Daniel.[195] According to Danon, the latter was the widow of a well-known and influential Baghdadi Jew and had just returned from a stay in the nearby town of Hillah to find a school occupying what she considered to be her own house.[196] Immediately claiming the property as her own, Daniel informed Danon that she would not allow the students to return to school at the end of the Jewish holiday break.[197] Danon claimed that this dispute initially threatened to permanently close the school, as rumors began spreading that it would not be able to re-open.[198]

Danon resolved the situation by spending an evening both explaining the potential negative ramifications for the AIU if the school were closed and appealing to Daniel's ego by paying her numerous compliments.[199] Finally, on the advice of Daniel's brother, Danon signed a contract with the former, recognizing her as the sole owner of the property in exchange for the right of the school to remain in the house.[200] Fortunately, Danon was able to end this dispute prior to the re-entry of students into the school, but it clearly caused her great apprehension.[201] It is worth mentioning that Daniel and another one of her sisters remained in the house and often entertained guests while the students were in class.[202]

Conclusion

Over the course of the Girls' School's first year, its director, Rachel Danon, dealt with numerous issues, ranging from parental opposition to paying for their daughters' education to a dispute over ownership of the school's domicile. By the end of the year, however, Danon, her subordinates, and the school's students had not only persevered, but the institution itself had experienced a near doubling of its student body, the vast majority of whom paid tuition. The school's prestige was also apparently increasing, as Danon, in her final bimonthly review for 1895, covering the months of November and December, proudly informed Bigart that four Muslim girls from prominent Baghdad families had recently enrolled as students. Two were daughters of the Brigadier General, one was the daughter of a Major General, and one was the daughter of the director of the Military School.[203]

Beyond ensuring the school's survival, Danon seems to have succeeded in communicating her, and the AIU's, gendered understanding of the importance of female education to many of the school's students and, likely, their families. Opposition to some of the school's activities would not fade away over the next decade, a period that would see Danon and her successor, Oro Sémach, continue to increase the school's enrollment and expand its activities. However, Danon, through her actions and from the support she received from her staff, her students, the AIU, and the AJA, had set the school on a financially and, perhaps more important, socially sustainable path.

2

FROM DANON TO SUTTON

The Baghdad Girls' School, 1896–1899

Following the AIU Girls' School's successful first year in existence, Danon spent the remainder of her tenure as director working to establish a solid curriculum, improve her teachers' performance, and continue building the school's reputation in the community. During this period the school faced key obstacles, including several housing crises, and at one point Danon even found herself embroiled in a familial dispute involving one of her students. Yet this period also witnessed great social change among the school's student population as a result of Danon and her staff's work and the students' successful adaptation to AIU schoolgirl culture. Moreover, at least according to Danon, this period also saw increasing acceptance of the Girls' School's activities among members of the Baghdadi Jewish community. Although it had to overcome various obstacles during these years, by the end of 1899, the school had clearly solidified its reputation as one of the city's pre-eminent educational institutions.

Enrollment Growth

Interestingly, one of the school's key problems during this period was the rapid annual increase in enrollment, which stemmed at least partly from Danon's success in convincing families both to send their daughters to the school and to pay for their educations. The enrollment increase put significant pressure on the teaching staff as well as the buildings that housed the school. The Evalina de Rothschild School in Jerusalem, which was the pre-eminent modern Jewish school for girls in that city, faced similar challenges during this time, highlighting that demand for modern female education among Jews far outstripped supply in late Ottoman Arab cities.[1] Table 2.1 highlights the annual tuition growth from the school's opening in January 1895 through December 1899.

As can be seen in Table 2.1, the school's population grew by nearly 100 percent over the course of 1895 and then increased at annual rates ranging from nearly 18 percent to 42 percent. From January 1895 through December 1899, the school's population grew by 428 percent. Table 2.1 also highlights how nonpaying students came to constitute a larger overall percentage of the school's population over this period, rising from just over 29 percent in December 1895 to just over 46 percent by December 1898, where it remained through December 1899.

Someone looking only at these numbers might conclude that Danon had relaxed her standards in order to attract a higher number of students, but her letters from this period tell a more complex story. In the spring of 1896 the student population had just topped fifty, though Danon was still refusing to admit many students whose parents refused to pay tuition.[2] By late April 1896, the school's population exceeded sixty, and Danon informed the Central Committee that she believed that she had finally convinced many of the most stubborn families in the community that their daughters' educations were worth paying for.[3] She attributed this change to the girls themselves, who often pleaded with their parents to consent to send them to the school.[4] Danon also noted that a girl from a poor family came to the school by herself to ask to be admitted for free. Danon immediately approved this request.[5] Finally, Danon claimed that the other reason more families were interested in sending their

Table 2.1 Enrollment growth at the AIU Girls' School in Baghdad, 1895–1899

Month/Year	Number of paying students	Number of non-paying students	Total number of students
January 1895	Unknown	Unknown	25
December 1895	34	14	48
December 1896	42	22	64
December 1897	52	39	91
December 1898	61	51	112
December 1899	71	61	132

Source: BAIU and letters found in AAIU Irak V.E.35

daughters to the school was to study handicrafts, which she noted was a part of the school's curriculum that had initially met with great disapproval.[6]

Perhaps the most prestigious occurrence in this period was the Ottoman governor of Baghdad's decision to send his two daughters to the school in June 1896.[7] Danon viewed this as especially impressive considering that, in her view, Turks rarely allowed their daughters to leave their homes.[8] The girls remained in the school for only three weeks because their father was transferred to Damascus. However, they apparently were so enamored with their time there that their father informed Danon that he planned to enroll them in the AIU Girl's School in Damascus.[9]

The school's student population barely grew over the remainder of 1896, apparently partly because of illnesses circulating both within the community and the school. In a letter from December 1896, Danon mentioned that the school had recently lost five students, including two as a result of sickness.[10] Two of the other girls had been removed because their parents disliked the way the school taught Hebrew—though, in this instance, Danon did not blame the Hebrew teacher—while the fifth girl had been expelled for poor behavior.[11]

Although she had earlier expressed optimism that community members had finally accepted the need to pay for girls' educations, in early 1897 Danon criticized Baghdadi Jews for their avarice. She stated that she often had to argue with parents to receive a small amount of tuition, while the same parents would not hesitate to buy expensive jewelry for their daughters.[12] Still, the school's population continued to increase, reaching eighty by the end of May 1897.[13]

By the beginning of 1898, the school's population had surpassed ninety students, and it reached 105 in May of that year.[14] As evidenced by the enrollment statistics in Table 2.1, 1897 and 1898 were the years that witnessed a significant increase in nonpaying students as a percentage of the school's overall student population. While Danon did not discuss this in detail, one of her letters from mid-1898 mentioned that she had recently begun to admit more nonpaying students because of a recent commercial crisis and the high cost of living in the city.[15] Danon had previously shown herself willing to allow poorer students to attend the school for free, and it appears by 1898 she had softened her stance on tuition a bit based on the community's changing short-term economic fortunes.

In late 1898, Danon submitted a request, which was subsequently approved, to leave Baghdad to return to France for a short period of time before assuming a new position.[16] By the time of her last report on school enrollment in March 1899, the school counted 112 students, which Danon noted was approximately the same number that the Boys' School had when she and her husband had

Table 2.2 Comparison of paying and non-paying students at the AIU girls' schools in Baghdad and Jaffa, 1894–1899

Month/Year	Baghdad	Jaffa
December 1894	0	107 (30 paying)
December 1895	48 (34 paying)	107 (30 paying)
December 1896	64 (42 paying)	167 (32 paying)
December 1897	91 (52 paying)	254 (29 paying)
December 1898	112 (61 paying)	280 (29 paying)
December 1899	132 (71 paying)	247 (43 paying)

Source: BAIU

arrived in the city in 1893.[17] While the school's growth was certainly impressive, it was not unusual for newly founded AIU Girls' schools (see Table 2.2 for a comparison with the Jaffa school, which was founded in 1894). However, this fast growth contributed to the school's housing problems.

Housing and Logistical Problems

In April 1896, the school's growing population had already led Danon to request authorization to have more furniture made for her students.[18] By late August, however, the school faced a bigger problem. Menahem Saleh's sister, Simha, who had been living in the house since the middle of 1895, had become too great a distraction to ignore. Danon asserted that Simha had come to believe that the organization had wronged her in some way, and she had been doing whatever she could to annoy the school's students and staff.[19] Referring to Simha as an "uneducated woman whose reputation is not intact," Danon accused her of showering insults upon her domestic staff in front of students and of showing several Muslim women, who were smoking cigarettes, around the house during school hours.[20] Additionally, Simha had become angry with Danon when Danon refused to admit a daughter of one of Simha's friends. Danon claimed this friend was not a reputable person.[21] Even worse, Simha had not only refused entry to Danon and the local Ottoman Director of Education when the latter's envoys had attempted to enter the school, but had also peppered them with insults.[22]

Unfortunately for the school, when Rachel and Joseph Danon approached Menahem Saleh about this matter, he refused to intervene, stating that he had little influence over his sister.[23] This forced Rachel Danon's hand, and she decided to abandon the house in favor of another domicile. After spending the

September and early October holiday break searching for and negotiating over a new house, she signed an expensive lease that allowed the school to reopen on time.[24] Although Danon lamented the small size of the new building, she implied it was the best she could do given the time constraints under which she was operating.[25] She also complained that the rent for the new building was stretching the school's budget.[26]

By May of 1897 Danon had concluded that because of the school's enrollment growth her students required both more furniture and more space.[27] During his visit to the school a couple of months later, even the French Vice Consul in Baghdad told Danon that the students required a new building.[28] Thus, for the second time in less than a year, she set about searching for a new building to rent. In late October it appeared that Danon had located a suitable building and had reached a verbal agreement with its owner.[29] Unfortunately, she soon reported that the owner, whom she identified as a Muslim, had backed out after the papers had been drawn up because he did not want his house turned into a "Midrash."[30] Danon underlined the word "Midrash" in her letter, likely pointing out the absurdity of someone confusing her school with an educational establishment devoted to the study of religion and Hebrew.

After failing to change the owner's mind by offering more money, Danon succeeded in finding a larger but still unsuitable location for the school.[31] While she had no choice but to rent the new building because of the lack of viable alternatives, Danon requested that the Central Committee look into either purchasing or constructing a permanent home for her school.[32] Unfortunately for her, such a project was not undertaken for several years.

Supervising Teachers and Adapting the Curriculum

Danon began her second year as director with the intention of mentoring the school's Hebrew and sewing teacher and the goal of devising a stable curriculum. Unfortunately, the school's rapidly increasing student body and the birth of her second child, which forced her to suspend her duties at the school for several months in early 1896, worked to slow her progress in accomplishing these tasks.[33] With regard to the latter development, Danon's husband Joseph spent two hours per day at the Girls' School in order to supervise and assist its staff during her absence.[34] As Frances Malino has shown in her research on female AIU directors, one benefit of having husband and wife teams run boys' and girls' schools in the same city was that one could aid the other if he or she was unable to carry out his or her professional duties for an extended period of time.[35]

Upon her return to the school after her maternity leave, Danon joyfully informed the Central Committee that her policy of focusing on sewing instruction had helped disabuse local Jews of the idea that it was dishonorable for girls and women to learn a craft.[36] At the same time, however, she stated that the curriculum's heavy emphasis on sewing, which required two hours per day from students, and her need to supervise the sewing teacher, had prevented her from giving students more than an hour per day of French instruction.[37] Furthermore, because of the school's increasing population and her need to supervise other teachers, Danon requested that the Central Committee send her an AIU-trained assistant to alleviate some of her burden in mentoring both students and faculty.[38] It is worth pointing out that in early 1896 Danon received criticism form the Central Committee for not teaching Jewish history to her students. In response she informed her superiors that even her best students lacked the French skills to study such a complex subject.[39]

One person Danon did not want to be considered for this position was Dola Levy, the young woman her husband's predecessor, Saul Somekh, had successfully helped enroll in the AIU's Teachers' Training School in Paris several years earlier. Danon seems to have had no reservations regarding Levy's character or abilities but opposed her candidacy solely because she was a native of Baghdad.[40] The Central Committee concurred with her opinion.[41] This corresponds with Frances Malino's contention that after some trial and error the AIU had decided to disallow graduates of its Paris teaching program to return to their cities of origin in fear they would not be able to establish themselves as authority figures in their native communities.[42] Furthermore, according to Malino, "For the parents, especially the mothers, whose longings for their young daughters permeate the Alliance correspondence, this separation entailed almost unbearable sacrifices."[43] This appears to have been the case with Levy's mother, who, unlike her husband, could not be convinced to accept the fact that her daughter was not a candidate for the school's position. She asked both Danon and local community members to intervene on her daughter's behalf with the Central Committee in Paris, but her requests were ignored.[44] Instead the Central Committee sided with Danon and decided to send Faride Sutton, a twenty-year-old woman originally from Beirut, to assist her.[45]

Danon spent much of the remainder of 1896 anxiously awaiting Sutton's arrival. While she appreciated her current teachers' desires to perform well in the classroom, she believed that despite their hard work they were still not making sufficient progress.[46] By the start of 1897, however, Danon had started to grow critical of the school's Arabic teacher. She contended that this teacher lacked the required knowledge to teach her subject but could not be let go because of the lack of other suitable candidates for the position.[47] Danon's criticisms of this teacher would continue throughout the remainder of her time in Baghdad.

Sutton's arrival in early March 1897 energized Danon and allowed her to implement some curricular changes. Most significantly, she immediately commenced having students in the First and Second Classes study French two hours per day instead of one. She also implemented changes in both the Hebrew and Arabic classes.[48] In the former she ordered the teacher to cease working with students on varied readings from the Torah and to instead focus on ensuring students would first learn the Ten Commandments and daily prayers by heart before moving on to more advanced topics.[49] She stated that because of the local rabbis' focus on weekly Torah readings as opposed to the Ten Commandments and basic prayers, many members of the community had studied Hebrew and Judaism for eight to ten years but still lacked knowledge of the religion's basic tenets.[50] Danon additionally took it upon herself to teach religious stories to these students, as she believed the Hebrew teacher lacked the aptitude to impart moral lessons to them.[51]

Danon's intervention in the Arabic class was perhaps even more radical. Claiming that the Arabic teacher's practice of trying to make students memorize grammatical rules by heart had failed and that her dictation exercises lacked adequate explanation, Danon used her limited knowledge of Arabic and her advanced knowledge of French grammar to both write and suggest questions for the Arabic teacher to ask the students in class.[52] She noted that it must have been humorous to see a French woman explaining Arabic grammatical rules to native speakers of the language.[53]

Sutton made a good first impression on Danon, who thought Sutton had a charming personality and lacked only experience.[54] Indeed, Sutton's first year at the school appears to have gone very well, with Danon even praising her for her hard work during her own extended absence in late 1897 after the birth of her third child.[55] However, Sutton soon fell ill for a period of time, prompting her superior to cover some of her classes and allowing her to observe the former's results.[56] After spending parts of two weeks in Sutton's classes, Danon concluded that although Sutton was hardworking, her pedagogical methods needed significant improvement, especially with regard to penmanship.[57] She especially faulted Sutton for being unable to help the students in the Third Class make simultaneous progress, stating that this class had three or four subdivisions.[58] Still, Danon claimed she did not want to spend too much time discussing her assistant's faults, asserting that with time and training Sutton would become an excellent teacher.[59]

It is clear from Danon's correspondence that she believed that Sutton made progress over the course of 1898 and early 1899. Danon's chief concern about her assistant during this period was that she could not endure Baghdad's harsh summer climate.[60] By March 1899, Danon had come to appreciate Sutton's work and also to praise the school's Hebrew teacher for her improvement.[61] The same could not be said for the school's Arabic teacher, whose presence in the school Danon had come to regret by early 1899, though she claimed she could not replace her.[62]

One area where Danon seems to have failed to meet her own goals was with regard to the school's Third Class. Over the course of her four-plus years at the school she had aimed to have the students in this class learn and progress as one group, but neither she nor her assistant were able to accomplish this. While Danon expressed disappointment that Sutton had failed to remedy this situation, she herself had also been unable to do so either before or after Sutton's arrival. The main obstacle appears to be the school's growth. Every time the class seemed to be making progress, new students would enter the school and naturally be placed among the least advanced students.[63] Thus, Danon's goals for this class appear, in hindsight, to have been unrealistic.

Her motivations, however, are understandable since the Third Class was the largest in the school. Although Danon did not consistently update the Central Committee on the makeup of each class, one of her letters from mid-1897 provided an overview of class enrollment and how many students in each class paid tuition. As of August 1897, the school had eighty-two students, fifty-three of whom paid tuition.[64] The First Class was by far the smallest, with twelve students, nine of whom paid tuition; the Second and Third Classes had, respectively, twenty-six and forty-four students with twenty and twenty-four tuition-paying students, respectively.[65] So, at least as of August 1897, more than half of the school's students were in the Third Class.

Both Danon and Sutton, who in her capacity as an AIU teacher also wrote letters to the Central Committee, often discussed their pedagogical goals, linking their implementation to the goal of liberating their Baghdadi co-religionists from their perceived backward ways. Upon arriving in Baghdad, Sutton reported her first impressions of the community to her superiors in Paris. Based on her report, which is similar in tone and content to earlier reports written by male AIU representatives, she viewed Jewish women in Baghdad as being confined to the home, forced to think only of housework, and devoid of any opportunity to take part in intellectual pursuits.[66] Unlike her male colleagues, however, Sutton's report merely provided the context to elaborate on her pedagogical goals and opinions on students' needs and abilities. She contended that since girls often married young, even those who attended the Girls' School could hope only for a brief stay.[67] Therefore, the school's teachers had only a few years to both educate their students and alter their worldviews.

As a result of her impressions and previous training, Sutton argued that instructors should have two main goals, both of which were linked more to social than educational change. First, she contended that teachers, in order to avoid alienating students, should not move too quickly to challenge local customs.[68] Second, instructors should work slowly but firmly to civilize their students.[69] Additionally, because of what they perceived as the backward society in which their students had been socialized, both Sutton and Danon viewed their students as being, at least at first, incapable of higher-order abstract reasoning and in need of clear explanations and concrete examples to facilitate learning.

One example of Danon's perceptions of her own students' abilities comes from a story she related to the Central Committee shortly after Sutton's arrival in March 1897. While teaching French, Danon held a picture of an apple in her hand and asked her students, ranging in age from six to eleven, to identify the object.[70] Her students were stumped, not because they lacked the requisite knowledge of French vocabulary to answer the question, but because they lacked the ability to associate abstract words with actual items.[71] After two students failed to identify the object, with the first guessing that it was a cat and the second that it was a lantern, Danon asked her three-year-old daughter, who had accompanied her to school that day, if she knew what the object was.[72] Her daughter correctly identified it as an apple, driving home the message to her mother that the school's students needed to focus on simple concepts if they were to progress in their learning.[73]

Finally, it is worth noting that after spending almost a full year in Baghdad, Sutton identified arithmetic as the subject with the most immediate real-world benefit for students.[74] She viewed arithmetic as important because she observed that, whether Jewish, Muslim, or Christian, Baghdadi women were responsible for doing much of their families' shopping yet were often unable to perform simple calculations in the marketplace.[75] Thus, similar to Danon's prior focus on sewing, Sutton hoped to enhance the school's reputation by improving instruction in a subject with real-world implications for nearly every one of her students in their future roles as wives and mothers.

Student Progress Inside and Outside of the Classroom

Danon's supervisory work vis-à-vis the school's teachers and, in 1898–1899, her AIU-trained assistant was not an end in itself but rather was obviously geared toward improving student learning. The students' progress in the classroom, both in academic and vocational subjects, slowed a bit in early 1896 while she was on maternal leave but, at least according to Danon, slowly regained its prior momentum following her return.[76] By July 1896, she proudly claimed that students in all three classes were making great progress in all subjects, especially French and sewing.[77] Unfortunately, summer heat took its annual toll on the school's students, leading to numerous student absences and uneven learning outcomes.

Following Sutton's arrival, the school's students appear to have begun progressing rapidly in their studies. In August 1897, Danon expressed her happiness in the students' performance in all subjects, including arithmetic.[78] Later in 1897, Danon gave birth to a third child, a son, and had to take a couple of months away from her academic duties. However, in contrast to what occurred during her absence in 1896, she was pleased to find her students doing excellent work upon her return to the school in early 1898.[79] Danon continued to laud her students throughout the remainder of her tenure in Baghdad, although she occasionally pointed out areas in which they needed to improve. One such area was memorization, which Danon asserted was a skill all Baghdadis needed to work on.[80]

Even prior to Sutton's arrival, Danon remarked that one aspect of school culture that had changed was student appearance. By late 1896, Danon informed the Central Committee that most students had adopted European dress and hairstyles, which she associated with both moral and physical improvement.[81] Furthermore, she was pleased with their discipline and desire to learn.[82] It appears, then, that by the end of the school's second year in existence Danon had succeeded in creating a modern schoolgirl culture in the Girls' School.[83] By schoolgirl culture, I mean that students had come to accept, adapt to, and internalize a set of disciplinary, aesthetic, and intellectual norms promulgated by Danon and, to a lesser extent, her staff.[84] The establishment of such a culture, as in other modern girls' schools in the region, whether run by Jewish or non-Jewish organizations, was essential to ensure that Danon's students would be at the forefront of a cultural revolution, or regeneration, in Baghdadi Jewish society.[85]

As previously mentioned, Danon was pleased to find that her students had continued to make great progress in the classroom during her 1898 maternity leave. She was even more impressed to find that her students had not at all abandoned their European dress and hairstyles during her absence.[86] The change in student appearance effected by the Girls' School is even more remarkable if one believes Sutton's contention that it was the students themselves who introduced these new styles, via the classroom, into their own households.[87]

Just prior to her departure from Baghdad, Danon penned a reflective letter on her time at the Baghdad Girls' School. In this letter she praised her students both for their academic work and their social change. She contended that an AIU academic and moral education had made her students superior to their fellow citizens, and noted proudly that, "one is astonished at the French air that breathes through their bodies."[88] Indeed, Danon's letter repeatedly mentioned how her students had become more European in culture and outlook, highlighting that she viewed her role as a cultural missionary whose tasks included the spread of European cultural values to her students. Furthermore, after stating that her own students had adopted modern European dress, she expressed her hope that in the future an entire generation of Baghdadi Jewish women would follow their example, thus showing that she hoped her own students would model modernity for their co-religionists, just as she was doing for them.[89]

The AIU and Child Marriage

One of the main problems that female directors and teachers throughout the AIU's network focused on solving was child marriage. From Baghdad to Fez, AIU teachers complained that child marriage robbed girls of their education and innocence and gravely harmed Jewish societies.[90] The AIU was obviously not the only institution to rail against child marriages in the Arab world, as Christian missionaries, the AJA, colonial governments, and indigenous reformers also derided and worked to end the practice.[91]

In her discussion of child marriage among Jews in the Middle East and North Africa, Rachel Simon notes, "Most brides were in their early teens and grooms somewhat older; in many places single girls in their mid-teens were considered old spinsters, almost unmarriageable . . . Marriage of minors below the age of 10, took place relatively rarely . . ."[92] Reasons for child marriage varied depending on geography, class, and whether families lived in urban or rural areas, but family economics and the desire to arrange solid matches for children certainly played a role.

While in the mid–nineteenth century it had been common for Jewish girls to marry at the age of ten or eleven, by this century's close it was far more common to find girls entering into marriage at thirteen or fourteen.[93] In 1894, the community's leaders stipulated that girls should not marry before the age of sixteen, though based on letters in the AIU archive it appears that this was not, or could not be, enforced.[94] Thus, it makes sense that the AIU Girls' School's first director, who had arrived in Baghdad in 1893, would place the goal of weakening the institution of child marriage among the city's Jewish community among her top priorities.

The Story of Mouzli Haim

Perhaps the incident that best highlighted both the school's impact on its students and Danon's multiple roles as director, educator, diplomat, and cultural emissary was one involving a student, Mouzli Haim, and her family:

> Last Monday the sister of Mouzli Haim, who is a thirteen year old student in our Superior class, came to me: "Is Mouzli here?" she asked me anxiously. Upon my negative reply she told me that her sister was to become engaged that evening and that when she learned about the engagement she fled the house. She then told me that her sister must have come to me and that I should exhort her to be docile and use my influence to convince her to get married. I answered that that was beyond my role and that I could not mettle in family affairs that did not concern me.
>
> I will not hide from you that a profound send of pity came over me; I had in one minute envisaged the situation: the parents tempted by the fortune of a man, 15,000 (Turkish) liras, wanted to force their unfortunate thirteen year old daughter, free of worries and happy to be in school, to marry a young man she had never seen and who could only promise her happiness through his riches.
>
> The sister therefore left me and came back a few moments later with her two brothers and Mouzli, who had been found with our Arabic teacher. Upon arriving my student burst into tears. I let the first tears pass and asked her the cause of her emotion. Indignantly she held back her tears, and told me that they wanted, in spite of her own wishes, to unite her, a thirteen year old girl, with a 32 year old man with no education, having not attended the Boys' School, and who, in addition, had physical defects. She did not fear to declare to me in front of her sister that the only motive that pushed her mother to arrange this marriage was the suitor's immense fortune, that she would never consider it, and moreover that she would refer the matter to her father in San Francisco, who had been away from Baghdad for twelve years, whose authorization was absolutely

necessary in such a circumstance. I was amazed at this vehemence, at this energy, and especially the good sense and calmness of this girl. The sister, furious, responded that in Baghdad a young girl must never be permitted an opinion on matters of matrimony and must only yield and bow her head before the decision of the parents, regardless of what they decide. And the sister [Mouzli] replied, "Then why have you sent me to school to be instructed there? Why have you had me open my intellect?" The two brothers looked to their sister to answer in the same manner.

At this moment the mother and aunt of this young girl arrived saying that everything was ready, the papers, the witnesses and that they did not know how to explain the delay. You can imagine how embarrassing the situation was in which I found myself, wanting neither to contradict the plans of these people nor to push a thirteen year old into such a union. I started to talk to the mother and quite gently I showed her that she could do great harm to her daughter, in the state in which she found herself (she had burst into tears again), if she forced her to get engaged on that same day; that it was better to postpone, which would thus give her the time to learn new information and to persuade Mouzli, etc. Thus I succeeded in reconciling these issues; the family going away but the girl remaining with me until nightfall fearing a trap. Even today at school she told me that they pester her each day, that they come to her and say despicable things because of her resistance.

I leave it to you to judge, Sir, the conduct of the family and the young girl. For me I would be enchanted if this villainous custom of marrying off young girls of ten, eleven, or twelve years of age were to disappear. Is it not necessary for the girl to first be prepared for the duties of marriage and motherhood before assuming such roles? How is she capable of even understanding them at eleven or even at twelve or thirteen? It is perhaps why we find so many broken homes in Baghdad, so many families whose father has left without even saying where he had gone. I hope that the passion showed by Mouzli spreads to her companions, as it will be one of the fortunate results of the Girls' School.[95]

Mouzli's story is interesting in that it provides us with insight not only into Danon's thoughts on the matter at hand but also those of the student and her family, though these are obviously mediated by Danon. Furthermore it places Danon at the center of both an intra-familial dispute and a cultural clash between her own "modern" European values and those of the Jewish community in Baghdad.

Besides highlighting the evils of child marriage, the story of Mouzli was also worth relating because of the girl's response. She had, at least in Danon's telling, internalized AIU norms and adopted the organization's culture, providing her with the strength to both conquer her emotions and stand up for herself to her own mother, even in front of a nonrelative. By linking her own social change to the education she had received, Mouzli demonstrated that the two were intertwined. The self-advocacy and rational arguments employed by Mouzli were precisely the types of moral and intellectual change Danon wanted the school to effect in the community. Additionally, by fleeing her home for the safe confines of the schoolhouse Mouzli highlighted both where she felt most secure and most accepted. The school literally acted as both a safe and foreign space while simultaneously being located in Baghdad.

Yet the story also illustrates the challenges a first-generation student faced at the time. While Mouzli had changed as a result of her education, her uneducated sister continued to adhere to local custom by arguing that girls had no choice but to accept decisions made by other people. Interestingly, it appears that Mouzli herself was attempting to use long-accepted gender norms to her advantage by claiming that only her father, who as a man was the head of the family, could sanction her marriage. Ultimately Mouzli triumphed, but as Danon related, she continued to face harassment at home, illustrating once again that her only safe space was the schoolhouse. In a sense, this story highlights how the schoolhouse acted as both a second home for students and a contested space where different cultural values came into conflict.[96]

Danon's dilemma in this situation stemmed from the AIU's policy of having its agents stay out of familial disputes.[97] Yet, since the family had effectively surprised her in her own place of work, she had no choice but to involve herself in some way. Her solution was not perfect, for it left Mouzli open to constant harassment at home, but it did give her student time to continue her education and, perhaps, to try to convince her family to change their minds with regard to her impending engagement and marriage.

The story also sheds light on Danon's views of social deficiencies among Baghdadi Jews. By connecting the practice of child marriage to the breakdown of the Jewish family, Danon was challenging not just the morality of a local practice but its efficacy. Furthermore, she blamed Mouzli's situation on her mother's greed, for the only reason the marriage was to take place was because of the intended groom's wealth and, presumably, social position in the community. Mouzli's mother was not considering what was best for her daughter, but rather what was best for her family's reputation.

Finally, Danon's words and actions indicate that she was not necessarily arguing that women needed to have unlimited agency in their own lives. After all, she still identified wife and mother as the two main roles a young girl would assume as an adult. Rather, she was asserting that by forcing a young girl into a marriage before she had the proper moral and educational training to assume her future roles as wife and mother, Baghdadi Jews were hurting both girls and society. The issue was not that Mouzli would never assume such roles—it was that she needed more time in school to prepare for them.

Thus, the school's activities were both the catalyst for this familial dispute and its ultimate solution. By imparting moral and intellectual education to local girls, the school had influenced one of its students to challenge local customs. Unfortunately, Mouzli lacked the tools to succeed on her own, as she remained the only member of her family with an education. Only by educating more girls, and for longer periods of their lives, could the AIU ignite a communal revolution that would overturn the practice of child marriage. This would lead to better-educated girls who would be well-prepared mothers and wives, which in turn would lead to stronger and happier families.

Unfinished Business: Vocational Education

While Danon was generally pleased with the educational and social progress her students made during her time in Baghdad, in her final year at the school she concluded that the AIU needed to improve and expand its vocational program for girls. In a letter from June 1898, Danon attempted to convince the Central Committee to build a workshop dedicated to training girls to become seamstresses and designers.[98] She contended that because of her school's existence many Baghdadi Jewish women had come to adopt European fashion but, since only Catholic Nuns worked as seamstresses, there was a lack of supply in the city.[99] Predicting that in three or four years nearly all Baghdadi Jews would abandon their own styles for European ones, Danon contended that the construction of a workshop would not only lead to increased revenue, since the workers would sell their products, but would also help meet the community's demands.[100] The seamstresses in this workshop would take orders for both European and local styles and for both leisure and professional outfits.[101] Danon hoped that AIU vocational students would come to dominate the fashion industry in Baghdad.

While Danon may not have been aware of its existence, it is worth noting that the Evelina de Rothschild School for Girls in Jerusalem, which at this point was linked to the AJA's educational network, had such a workshop that employed over a dozen of the school's graduates.[102] She was, however, certainly aware that AIU girls' schools in other cities, especially in Anatolia, had such workshops, which besides providing girls with suitable and profitable technical educations also ensured that young girls did not have to travel about town by themselves on a daily basis.[103]

Interestingly, Danon believed the future director of such a workshop should be an AIU-trained girl from Baghdad, since she would have knowledge of both European and Baghdadi fashions.[104] This obviously went against the AIU policy of refusing to send Paris-trained teachers back to their cities of origin. Further, Danon stated that a local girl would be well suited to train other local teachers in both foreign and local design and production.[105] Therefore, she requested and immediately received permission to begin considering possible candidates among her veteran students.[106]

Danon soon identified three suitable candidates, but she ran into cultural obstacles. She claimed that families were not only reticent to allow their daughters to leave the country but that many still believed that it was dishonorable for their daughters to work for a living, even if the families could benefit from daughters who earned money.[107] As a result of these concerns, two of the students sadly informed Danon that their parents refused to consent to allow them to study in Paris.[108] Fortunately, the third student's parents granted her permission, which Danon attributed to the fact that she had been enrolled at the school since its establishment in 1895.[109] Therefore, Danon requested permission to begin training her thirteen-year-old student, Farha Yehouda Lévy, for her new role and to take her to Paris upon Danon's departure from the city.[110]

It appears that the Central Committee ordered Danon to subject Lévy to a series of exams to ascertain whether she was ready to undertake advanced study in Paris. While Lévy scored well in arithmetic and grammar, she fared poorly in her knowledge of French.[111] Danon claimed that this was a result of her own inability to spend more than one hour per day teaching French until after Sutton's arrival and expressed her confidence that Lévy had the ability and work ethic to rapidly improve her proficiency in this subject.[112] Apparently fearing that her superiors would reject her student's candidacy, Danon reminded them that it was nearly impossible to gain parental consent to take daughters out of the country.[113] Furthermore, she stressed that while at present Lévy was unprepared, the Committee needed to consider the future.[114] In the future, she contended, Lévy would be able to return to Baghdad as a woman who could raise up other women, thus leading to a new era for all Baghdadi Jews, which Danon claimed was the AIU's main goal vis-à-vis women's education.[115]

In late 1898, the Central Committee consented to Lévy's candidacy, and Danon promised to work independently with her to expedite the learning process.[116] However, since Danon was in the process of preparing to permanently leave Baghdad, it is unclear to what extent she followed through on her promise. Indeed, in her letter tracing the history of the school penned just prior to her departure, she once again lamented the poor state of vocational education. She stated that the students were dispersed among individual mistresses throughout the city, making it difficult to supervise them, and argued that the organization needed both a workshop attached to the school and a capable teacher.[117] Moreover, it does not appear that Danon brought Lévy with her to France upon her departure from Baghdad, perhaps because Danon was ill and traveling with her entire family. Thus, while she began an important conversation regarding the construction of a vocational workshop and the reorganization of the school's vocational program, and even identified a future candidate to direct the school, her hasty departure from the city appears to have ensured that she failed to achieve the goals she set for this project.

The Personal and Professional Struggles of a Female Director

Thus far this study has focused on the workings of the school and the role of its director, both inside and outside the classroom. Danon's letters from these years, however, also provide important insight into her personal and professional struggles as a female educator working for the AIU in Baghdad. The study of the personal lives of female educators working for the AIU is an emerging subject of interest and highlights both the opportunities and limitations these women encountered while working for the organization.[118] Moreover, by examining the private as well as the professional lives of AIU female educators, scholars can better understand how these women perceived and constructed their own identities in both the domestic and public spheres in their multiple roles as directors, teachers, wives, and mothers.

During her first two years in Baghdad, Danon did not discuss many details of her personal life in her letters, though she occasionally mentioned important developments, including the birth of her second child and the health of members of her family. However, upon the arrival of Faride Sutton in early 1897, Danon penned a long letter to the Central Committee in which she discussed how her professional life required her to make great sacrifices in her personal life. The main impetus for Danon's letter was not Sutton's arrival but rather her salary. Danon declared that she was humiliated to learn that her new assistant was to earn a higher salary, 1,800 francs per year, than she received,

1,600 francs per year, even though the latter lacked experience and was to be her subordinate.[119]

In making her complaint to the Central Committee, Danon made sure to note that she did not work at the school to make a lucrative living but rather to work toward the, "rapid uplifting of our Baghdadi coreligionists."[120] Still, she stated that as a result of her work in the school she had left her children in the hands of untrained caretakers and had been forced to neglect her duties as a household manager.[121] Danon implored the Committee to at least raise her own salary to make it equal to Sutton's before Sutton read future budget reports and realized that she earned more money than her own superior.[122]

Jacques Bigart, the AIU's Secretary-General, sent Danon what she considered to be a warm letter, though its exact contents are unknown, to which she replied that she was satisfied and would not raise the issue again.[123] Although it took nearly a year, the Central Committee ultimately voted to raise Danon's salary to 1,800 francs per year, as she had requested.[124] Yet Danon complained once again, though this time less overtly; while thanking the Committee for their decision, she expressed her hope that her superiors would, in the near future, increase her salary again so that she earned more than Sutton.[125] She claimed that her request was not the result of avarice or jealousy but rather because as director she needed to be in a firm position of authority over her subordinates and a higher salary, even if only slightly, would convey such a message.[126]

In her letters discussing her disappointment with her salary Danon had to balance a need to be assertive, in that she was requesting a raise, with the expectation that as a female educator she show both restraint and deference. Thus, it makes sense that she would discuss how the sacrifices she had made as a director in her professional life had negatively affected her performance in her roles as mother and wife in her personal life. In doing so she was, in a sense, feminizing herself, in her superiors' eyes. By portraying herself as a mother and a wife, and not merely as a professional seeking an increase in salary, she was likely trying to make her demands seem less assertive and, perhaps, more palatable for men accustomed to imagining women, even educated ones, more in domestic than professional roles.

Requests for salary increases were actually very common among both male and female AIU teachers throughout the organization's network. Aron Rodrigue, in his analytical sourcebook on the AIU's work, *Jews and Muslims*, includes letters by two male teachers in early twentieth-century Iran and Morocco expressing discontent over their pay.[127] Research by Frances Malino and Joy Land on AIU female directors in Morocco and Tunisia, respectively, has also highlighted that female teachers in the Maghreb often complained about their low salaries, although such complaints did not lead these women to abandon their posts.[128]

Danon's request for permission to leave Baghdad in late 1898 also sheds light on challenges facing female AIU educators. She made this request because doctors had informed her that her oldest child, then five years old, could not tolerate Baghdad's climate and might even die if the family remained in the city.[129] While Danon and her children were to leave the city, Joseph was to stay behind for a period of time both to continue running the Boys' School and to help in supervising the Girls' School until a permanent replacement could be found for his wife.[130] It is important to note that the Danons do not seem to have considered leaving either of the younger children in Baghdad with Joseph. Rather, it appears to have been expected that Rachel, as the mother and wife, would take time out of work to tend to all of her children, even the two who were not ill, while her husband continued his work at the schools. This incident provides evidence that female AIU educators were expected to be the first to sacrifice for their families, even when both they and their husbands were in charge of AIU institutions.

It warrants mention that requests to relocate to other cities also appear to have been common throughout the AIU's educational network. This makes sense, especially for those stationed in the Arab world and in Iran, as teachers in these areas often chronicled the tragic impacts that outbreaks of disease had on local communities and the teachers' own families.[131] Teachers in these areas also frequently reported that they felt isolated and yearned to be closer to family or to reside in or near more cosmopolitan cities.[132] Although it cannot be stated definitively, it is likely that female teachers requested transfers in order to properly care for family members, whether children, siblings, or parents, more frequently than did their male counterparts. Indeed, in her research on female teachers in Morocco, Frances Malino has shown that women's family networks remained central to their lives throughout their careers.[133]

Finally, Danon once again invoked her maternal role in her final letter from Baghdad, which reviewed the school's brief history. In this letter she mentioned that her regrets regarding her departure were linked to a feeling of maternal attachment to the school's students.[134] Indeed, her letters throughout her tenure indicate that she viewed herself as a maternal role model for the girls. In a sense she was raising a generation of modern Jewish girls who would then go on to raise their own modern daughters, thus revolutionizing Baghdadi Jewish society. Therefore, it makes sense that just after Danon expressed regret for her impending departure, she mentioned that the school was positioned to elevate Jewish women in the community.[135] In her maternal role Danon had prepared her students and subordinates for a future without her.

An Interim Director

Following Danon's departure from Baghdad in April 1899, Sutton assumed the position of interim director of the school.[136] In her new role, Sutton had to act, as Danon had done prior to her arrival, as both teacher and director and was also responsible for inspecting the students' dress and cleanliness.[137] Fortunately, Joseph Danon had remained in Baghdad and provided significant aid to Sutton and her staff. Upon assuming her new position, Sutton began to repeat one of her predecessor's complaints. In a letter from May 1899—which could have been written by Danon in 1895—Sutton mentioned that eight new students had enrolled in the school, with six of the new students paying tuition, but stated that more students would have enrolled if not for the question of tuition.[138] Among the new students was a Turkish Muslim student.[139] Sutton's initial report was slightly kinder to the school's Arabic teacher than Danon's reports had been. However, considering that she stated that this teacher lacked both methodological training and experience, it is unclear whether Danon had finally replaced the teacher in question prior to leaving the city or if Sutton was merely commenting on the abilities, or lack thereof, of the original woman.[140] I believe, however, that she was discussing the original Arabic teacher since Sutton's replacement, Oro Sémach, later fired the teacher after voicing similar complaints to Danon.[141] Sutton was also a bit more critical of the school's students than was her predecessor, noting that while generally hardworking they could also be indolent.[142]

Shortly after Danon's departure, the Central Committee offered Sutton a teaching position at its new school in Tehran.[143] Although flattered, Sutton informed the AIU that because of her own inability to tolerate Baghdad's climate she needed to depart from the city following the new year to allow her mother to help her recover from her maladies.[144] Rather than immediately accepting the position, she insisted that she could only make a decision once she had healed, though she did state that in any case she would not be able to continue working in Baghdad in 1900.[145] Ultimately, Sutton ended up going to Aleppo, not Tehran, after leaving Baghdad shortly after her replacement's arrival.

In the midst of the Central Committee's offer to relocate Sutton to Tehran and her request to return home so that her mother could care for her for a period of time, the Girls' School faced a legal challenge from the Ottoman government stemming from its founding five years earlier. As discussed in the previous chapter, upon the school's establishment, Joseph Danon had employed legal trickery to ensure the school would open. In fact, because he had feared a lengthy wait if he had tried to register the school as a new institution with the authorities in Istanbul, he had claimed that the school was merely an offshoot of the Boys' School.[146] Thus the school could claim to have pre-existed the new Ottoman law enacted in 1893 requiring the central government to approve the opening of any new schools throughout the empire.[147]

In May 1899 Danon had received a request from the Ottoman Director of Education for official proof that the school had in fact pre-existed the recently passed law.[148] He thus asked local rabbis to sign a document certifying that the school had indeed broken off from the Boys' School, but the rabbis refused to take part in his ruse. Instead he succeeded in convincing local notables to sign a document that the rabbis would then notarize.[149] Although he expressed fear that the interim Director of Education would not accept such documentation, by late 1899 the Ottoman authorities had granted the school official recognition.[150] The AIU's desire to circumvent Ottoman law, however, may explain why the BAIU sometimes listed the Girls' School's establishment as having been in 1893, which is the year the new law came into force, when in fact the school did not open until 1895 and had not even been approved until late 1894.

Sutton handled the challenging hot summer months by limiting schooling to five hours in the morning, as Danon had always done.[151] Her correspondence provides important information about the subjects that students studied. During summer, students studied one hour of Hebrew, French, and Arabic per day and normally studied sewing for two hours per day.[152] However, it appears that Sutton took time away from Arabic, Hebrew, or sewing for the First Class, as she mentioned that she taught these students Jewish history and arithmetic. She also spent an hour per week teaching them either general history or geography and one hour per week teaching them both natural science and a Great Writers course.[153] During Sutton's tenure we also know that the First Class was divided into two divisions; the Second Class consisted of one division, and the Third Class, as always, consisted of several divisions.[154]

As a result of persistently inadequate housing, which was consistently exacerbated by the summer heat, Joseph Danon appointed a committee of five local Jewish notables who were supportive of the AIU's activities to study the costs and logistics of purchasing land and constructing a permanent home for the Girls' School.[155] Unfortunately, the committee failed to make progress, and

Danon was unable to find a more suitable building to rent, leaving the school in its inadequate locale.[156]

Even with the housing problems, the school continued to flourish. Sutton also seems to have grown more comfortable with her interim role over the course of the summer and, as Danon had often done, started to share her opinions on aspects of the school that required work. For example, she expressed fear that the three girls who constituted the top division of the First Class would leave the school if they could not be given more advanced instruction.[157] These were presumably the same three girls Danon had focused on retaining in 1895. Sutton also advocated for the creation of a permanent Fourth Class, which would entail additional staff.[158] The school actually would have suffered an even more pronounced staffing shortage had Sutton allowed more nonpaying students to enroll, but she continued to refuse to do so.[159] She did, however, mention that many fathers in the city were withholding their daughters from the school rather than consenting to pay tuition in the hope that Sutton's replacement would be more flexible on this issue.[160] Still, the school's population did increase by twenty over the course of 1899, and by the time Sutton's replacement arrived in December the school had 132 students, 71 of whom paid tuition.[161]

Conclusion

The four-year period from 1896 to 1899 saw a significant expansion of all aspects of the AIU Girls' School, from enrollment to staff to subjects taught. In addition to its growth, the school also weathered adversity in this period, including a dispute with a local notable, multiple problems with the buildings in which it was housed, and the premature departure of the its first director, who had done so much to both establish and nurture the school's development. At the turn of the century, following the completion of the school's fifth calendar year of existence, not only had the Girls' School proved that it could survive, it had become part of the cultural fabric of the city's Jewish community.

3

MAKING ADJUSTMENTS

Oro Sémach's Tenure in Baghdad, 1899–1904

In late 1899 Oro Sémach replaced interim director Faride Sutton as the Baghdad Girls' School's second permanent director. During her four and a half years in Baghdad, Sémach labored to build upon Danon's foundation by expanding key aspects of the school's mission and curriculum. This work included establishing new classes, introducing new subjects, recruiting current and former students to work as group monitors, setting up a library, and organizing meetings and activities for former students. In addition to Sémach's work inside the classroom, she and, especially, her husband Yomtob, who replaced Joseph Danon as the director of the Albert Sassoon School, took active roles in trying to convince the Central Committee to either build or purchase a permanent building for the Girls' School.

Oro Sémach's tenure as director also saw increasing acceptance of the school's activities by members of the community and key social changes, including a later marriage age, for current and former Girls' School students. However, during this period the school had to deal with significant challenges, including outbreaks of Bubonic plague and cholera, constant staff shortages, and an inadequate building. Finally, Sémach herself experienced great personal joy in the births of two children but also personal tragedies that included the death of one of her children and the loss of her sister to cholera. Still, throughout these ups and downs, the school continued to flourish in large part because of its director's able leadership and the beneficial policies that she implemented.

A New Director

Oro Sémach arrived in Baghdad in December 1899. Originally from Bulgaria, the twenty-five-year-old Oro Sémach had, over the previous seven years, served the AIU as an assistant in Tangiers, Morocco, and as director in both Tatar-Bazardjik in Bulgaria and Damascus in Ottoman Syria.[1] Upon her arrival in Baghdad, she found the Girls' School to be in fine working order, for which she credited both Rachel Danon and Faride Sutton.[2] She was especially pleased with how well the school was functioning considering its relatively recent establishment.[3] In fact, within weeks of taking over as director Sémach happily reported that her students had greatly impressed a group of visitors, which included the French Consul in Baghdad. The visitors were pleased to find that some of the students spoke French without an accent and had become proficient in sewing.[4] What stood out most to the group, according to Sémach, was the students' simple, proper attire, which stood in contrast to the ornate and disgraceful dress of most Baghdadis.[5] Indeed, she reported that the students did not appear to be Baghdadi.[6]

Unfortunately, Sémach was faced immediately with Sutton's desire to depart Baghdad. While she initially did not want the Central Committee to consent to Sutton's request, Sutton's poor health soon convinced Sémach to acquiesce to her desire to leave.[7] Still, fearful of being left to run the school on her own, Sémach begged the Committee to ensure that a replacement was en route to Baghdad prior to Sutton's departure.[8]

Interestingly, Sémach's first complaint mirrored one that Danon had made in early 1897. Upon seeing the school's budget for the first time Sémach was shocked to find that Sutton earned 1,800 French francs per year, whereas she earned only 1,700.[9] Rather than demanding a raise, she merely informed the Committee that she was, "sure that this situation has not escaped the attention of the Central Committee and no doubt you have now adjusted my salary so as it reflects the moral distance which exists between a director and an assistant."[10] Although the matter is not discussed in these letters, Sutton's salary likely was higher, at least initially, than either Danon's or Sémach's because she was a single woman living alone in a city far from her family. It is unclear, however, whether her salary was higher than that of her superiors in order to lessen the burden of living alone in an area so far from the Mediterranean or because the Central Committee's members believed that they could pay married women a lower salary since their husbands were also employed.

This issue lingered over the course of at least the first part of 1900. Sémach was still disappointed after receiving a 100 franc raise, as it appears that the Central Committee also raised her assistant's salary by 200 francs, thus increasing the salary gap between the two women.[11] Sémach stated that the salary discrepancy was abnormal and humiliating for her and also wrote that the four raises she had received over her eight-year career had been so low as to more accurately reflect reprimands rather than rewards.[12] When the Central Committee, after apparently increasing her salary to equal Sutton's, informed her that both her predecessor and Sutton had earned 1,800 francs per year, Sémach responded by accurately surmising that this must have been a great embarrassment for Danon, who probably let it pass only because it is so difficult to discuss money.[13] She also noted that her husband's salary, which was 4,000 francs per year, should not affect hers.[14] Unfortunately, Sémach's correspondence file for the second half of 1900 is blank, and her husband's letters do not discuss her salary dispute. Therefore, it is unclear whether this issue was resolved to Sémach's satisfaction.

What is clear, however, is that, like her predecessor, Sémach did not hold Sutton's salary against her. In fact, she was highly complimentary of her assistant, and on learning of Sutton's final request for a change of post, praised her work to her superiors in Paris and lamented the void Sutton's departure would leave at the school.[15] Besides lauding Sutton's work in Baghdad, Sémach recommended her for a directorship position should an AIU girls' school have a vacancy in the near future.[16] However, likely alluding to Sutton's health problems, she requested that the Central Committee send a healthy replacement to Baghdad who could tolerate the region's harsh climate.[17] Interestingly, Sémach's adjustment to teaching in the Girls' School seems to have been relatively smooth, which highlights how successful Danon had been in leading the school during her tenure. Sémach's only issues resulted from the impending departure of her capable assistant and her frustration over earning less than a subordinate.

Enrollment Growth and Its Discontents, 1900–1904

Upon Sémach's arrival in Baghdad in December 1899, the Girls' School had 133 students, one of whom appears to have left by that month's end, based on the BAIU's year-end count.[18] Over the next five years, including the second half of 1904, during which time Sémach had been replaced by an interim director following her own permanent departure from Baghdad, the Girls' School continued to grow at a steady rate, though slower than previous years. The only exception, as shown in Table 3.1, occurred in 1904,

Table 3.1 Enrollment growth and breakdown of paying and non-paying students at the AIU Girls' School in Baghdad, 1900–1904

Month/Year	Number of paying students	Number of non-paying students	Total number of students
December 1900	99	67	166
December 1901	112	78	190
December 1902	118	83	201
December 1903	126	87	213
December 1904	110	60	170

Source: BAIU

which marked the first year the school suffered a net decline in enrolled students.

By 1900, the school's growth had become limited not by middle-class families refusing to pay the required tuition, though that remained an occasional problem, but rather by the small size of the school's building and the relatively small staff the school employed.[19] In fact, it appears that for the first time in the school's history its director had to turn students away because of lack of space. Indeed, following the break for the Jewish holidays in spring 1900, forty-eight students applied to enroll in the school, but Sémach could accept just sixteen applicants.[20]

Although the Central Committee sent Jamilé Douec as a replacement for Sutton in late 1900, increasing student enrollment and growing demand for the school's services led Sémach to request a second assistant in early 1901.[21] By May of that year Sémach had started expelling small numbers of students she believed were not working hard enough in order to make room for more deserving ones.[22] She did not regret these expulsions, however, as she compared lazy students to parasites feeding off the school.[23] Near the end of 1901, Sémach once again informed the Central Committee that an inadequate building and a staff shortage were hindering the school's enrollment growth.[24] In fact, the building was so overcrowded by this point that in December 1901 Sémach had left an entire class outside for part of the day due to lack of space.[25] She rationalized this decision by stating that since the cold season in Baghdad was so short she thought it better to keep students on school grounds where they could at least spend part of the day learning rather than being turned away and left in ignorance.[26]

Perhaps the only positive resulting from the school's inability to admit each applicant was that the quality of the student body improved. In early 1902, Sémach reported that she had been able to admit only twenty-two of seventy-five applicants but praised her new students' intelligence and hard work.[27] Sémach also increased the school's staff by hiring one of the First Class's students, Farha Chalom, as a monitor, which meant she would instruct small groups of students when the school's teachers were working with other groups.[28] While Chalom's hiring helped, it was much too little to make a significant difference in the school's functioning.

In fact, Sémach again voiced her desire for a second assistant and claimed that in order to improve the lives of women in Baghdad the school should be trying to enroll as many students as possible.[29] By making such a case, Sémach was separating herself a bit from her predecessor, who had advocated a slow and steady approach to attracting students. The difference in these approaches to the issue of enrollment increases was likely a result of the two directors' different circumstances. Danon had led the school during its formative years and was most concerned with ensuring that she placed the school on sound financial footing while simultaneously building its reputation. Sémach, in contrast, had the good fortune of succeeding Danon after the latter had accomplished her initial goals and so was able to shift part of her focus to expanding access to the school's services.

Sémach continued making her case in favor of expanding the school's staff and the construction of a new building in the summer of 1902. In fact, she adopted a more aggressive tone with the Central Committee by claiming that the AIU had refused to make great sacrifices for the residents of Baghdad, though it had done so for less important communities.[30] She argued that the AIU was far more generous in Damascus, where she had served prior to coming to Baghdad, and expressed her disappointment that she had still not received permission to hire a new assistant.[31] According to Sémach, the Girls' School in Baghdad was not only running a budget surplus but was doing so even while the Central Committee had withheld the annual 800 franc subvention the Girls' School received from the AJA.[32] Furthermore, she noted that the school was in such demand that parents had begun offering her nearly three times the requested maximum monthly tuition to accept their daughters, but she had to reject these offers.[33]

Unfortunately, the Central Committee was either unwilling or unable to provide immediate support, as evidenced by a letter from Sémach from late 1902 in which she repeated the same complaints.[34] She had, however, succeeded in getting the Committee to agree to send a second assistant in the future, though she had demanded that one be sent immediately.[35] In fact, Sémach had become so desperate that even after asking why the annual AJA subvention was still being withheld from the school, she offered to pay for a second assistant out of the school's budget surplus.[36]

Sémach grew even more frustrated over the next several months. While revisiting the issue of a second assistant during the summer of 1903, she once again reiterated her willingness to pay such a person's salary out of the school's local revenue.[37] Furthermore, she criticized the Central Committee for decreasing the organization's annual subvention to her school.[38] Ironically, her reports about the school's progress were consistently positive during this period, indicating how effective she and Douec were as educators and administrators.

It is unclear why the Central Committee refused to provide either adequate financial or staff support, at least from Sémach's perspective, but there are several possible explanations. First, the organization was in the midst of expanding its presence in Baghdad by adding a Talmud Torah to the Boys' School to attract more male students. Second, the AIU had, over the past seven years, been expanding into new areas, including Ottoman Libya, Egypt, Rhodes, and Iran, and was soon to convert the Jewish community's Boys' School in Basra into an AIU institution. Thus, the organization may have been stretched economically. Third, building on the previous point, the fact the Girls' School in Baghdad was requiring less financial help each year in order to maintain the status quo may have convinced the Central Committee to focus its attention on improving other schools as opposed to helping an already self-sufficient institution. In a sense, then, the Girls' School may have been a victim of its own success. There is also a fourth possible explanation. As will be discussed in the next section, the Central Committee and Yomtob Sémach were in touch with expatriate Baghdadi philanthropists who were considering donating money to build a new Girls' School. This may have led the AIU's Paris leadership to wait to see how much aid non-AIU sources would provide the school before committing precious AIU funds to the cause.

In any case, Sémach continued to express her disappointment with the Central Committee and to advocate for a second assistant.[39] Following this most recent complaint, in the summer of 1903, her superiors informed her that they had failed to send her a second assistant because of their own candidate shortage in Paris.[40] By late 1903, Sémach, after hesitating to do so for some time, decided to ask the Central Committee to send her sister, Louna Gueron, who had been employed as an assistant in Philippopolis for the previous seven years, to Baghdad to teach sewing.[41] She seems to have believed that her superiors would hesitate to agree to her request, so she made sure to note the school's desperate need of a teacher, her failed efforts to recruit teachers from the AIU Beirut School, and her knowledge of her sister's capabilities.[42]

The Central Committee approved this request, and Gueron arrived in Baghdad in mid-December 1903.[43] However, the Committee did not approve Gueron's appointment as an assistant, forcing Sémach to list her as a teacher.[44] Unfortunately, shortly after Gueron's arrival, Sémach's assistant, Jamilé Douec, requested permission to leave Baghdad in the near future.[45] Although disappointed, Sémach supported Douec's request, noting that Douec was extremely fatigued.[46] Douec's request, however, appears to have been initially rejected, likely because the Sémachs soon left Baghdad, for what was supposed to be a brief period of time, making Douec's presence in Baghdad a necessity.

In mid-1904, Sémach and her husband left Baghdad, partly so their children could recuperate and have time away from the region's severe climate. In fact, one of their sons had died during their time in Baghdad, though it is unclear when.[47] Just prior to the couple leaving Baghdad, Sémach's sister Louna had married Solomon Halfon, an assistant at the Boys' School.[48] While the Sémachs were away, a cholera outbreak devastated Baghdad, hitting the Jewish community particularly hard. In September 1904, Louna contracted cholera and passed away.[49] As a result of her sister Louna's death, Oro Sémach informed the Central Committee that she could not return to Baghdad, as she had lost both a sister and a son there.[50] Thus, Sémach never returned to Baghdad, and her school was left without a permanent director for a short time. During this time, the school's population appears to have decreased as a result of parents keeping their children out of school.[51] It is also likely that some students either died or moved away during the outbreak, as Nissim Albala—Yomtob Sémach's permanent replacement, who arrived in late 1904—mentioned that the Jewish population in the city had markedly declined during this period.[52] Thus, the cholera outbreak clearly caused the decline in the school's population in late 1904, though the numbers rebounded almost immediately in 1905.[53]

Housing Issues and Opportunities

Unlike her predecessor, Sémach did not take the lead in searching for new homes for the school, although she certainly voiced her opinions for the need of new buildings when necessary. Instead, her husband Yomtob took on this responsibility. Yomtob actually inherited this role from Joseph Danon, who had spent part of his final year in Baghdad, following his wife's departure from the city, trying to lay the groundwork for the construction of a permanent home for the Girls' School. Prior to his departure, he had created a local committee responsible for devising plans to purchase land in the Jewish quarter for this undertaking.[54]

Upon taking over the responsibility for meeting with the committee his predecessor had organized, Yomtob noted that the estimate he received for construction of a school, including the purchase of land, was approximately 120,000 francs.[55] This was apparently too expensive for the AIU, but he soon came up with his own idea. Realizing that the Girls' School would soon have to relocate, since its current building would be put up for sale in the near future, Yomtob advised the Central Committee to not even consider purchasing the building and instead to consider purchasing the homes of three poor families in the Jewish quarter next to the Boys' School.[56] These homes could be bought and demolished for 10,000 to 12,000 francs each.[57] In a follow-up letter, he noted that including the construction of a new school, the entire cost of this plan would amount to only 40,000 francs.[58] Furthermore, he proposed to use the new building for the Boys' School and to convert his school's current building into the Girls' School.[59] After conducting additional research, Yomtob noted that a total of five buildings could be purchased and advised his superiors to purchase these homes.[60] He also asked for permission to write to the AJA in London to request financial support for this scheme.[61]

While the AIU did not give Yomtob approval for this undertaking, the Central Committee had apparently granted him permission to write to the AJA about the issue. The latter organization forwarded him a letter from a Jewish philanthropist in Hong Kong named Eskell, which had originally been sent to Sassoon Heskell. Eskell was a former AIU student from Baghdad, who wanted to provide funds for a Jewish hospital in Baghdad and who mentioned that his brother was planning to give the AIU money for the construction of a building for the Baghdad Girls' School.[62] Eskell's brother was Elly Kadoorie, a well-known industrialist and philanthropist whose wife, Laura, was from the Sephardic British Mocatta family, which was prominently involved in AJA operations. Since Eskell's letter to London was dated June 14, 1900, it is clear that Yomtob's letter to the AJA, which must have been written in late July 1900, was not the catalyst for such a plan.[63] This letter led to an extended correspondence between Yomtob and the AIU regarding the Kadoorie family. This family, which was also offering to provide funds for a Girls' School building, were descendants of Baghdadi Jews born in Bombay and had moved to East Asia for business reasons in the late nineteenth century.[64]

The Kadoorie family's negotiations with the AIU and AJA regarding the school appear to have been relatively bumpy. In May 1901, Yomtob reported that the family had realized the undertaking was more expensive than previously thought and had tabled the plan indefinitely.[65] Yet by July 1901 he claimed the issue had been resolved and that the construction of a building would be relatively simple.[66] In October 1901, Laura Kadoorie, in whose name the building was to be constructed, wrote to Oro Sémach to discuss the Girls' School and to inform Sémach that she was donating money to establish an annual prize fund for the school's students.[67] By November 1901, the AJA's Executive Committee received word that the Kadoorie family was offering 10,000 pounds for the school's construction.[68]

Only several months later, in February 1902, Yomtob informed the Central Committee that the Kadoorie family had decided to once again postpone construction of a Girls' School building until an unspecified future date.[69] This decision caught Oro Sémach by surprise and inspired her to float her own plan. Contending that the Girls' School needed immediate help, she advocated creating a smaller Girls' School for working-class students devoted only to sewing and Arabic.[70] While she did not go further into detail about her plan, it appears that since it might be years before a larger general building was constructed, she believed one short-term solution was to have two girls' schools with different missions. The original school would focus on general and moral education, and the other devoted solely to teaching practical skills.

Sémach returned to the need for a new building several months later, though she had apparently dropped her proposal of creating a second school. At this point she stated that she was not looking for a luxurious mansion but rather a modest building that would allow the school to double its population, tuition collection, and influence.[71] Meanwhile, Yomtob and Oro Sémach received mixed messages over the summer regarding the possibility of the Kadoorie family providing money for the school. Yomtob initially believed that the AJA, for unspecified reasons, was holding up progress, but by late June 1902 he had concluded that the Kadoorie family was indeed serious about paying for the construction of a new building.[72] In August, however, Oro Sémach noted that the project seemed to be close to being abandoned.[73] Her husband concurred, and in December he informed the Central Committee that the plans appeared to have been aborted.[74]

At this point, Yomtob made an impassioned plea to the Central Committee to provide the Girls' School with the funds to purchase or build a new school. He argued that the AIU had established the Girls' School to both uplift women and families and noted that the school was now reaching its limit, as it was nearing 200 students.[75] He rhetorically asked if the Central Committee considered its job accomplished by having a successful school with only 190 students.[76] Furthermore, noting that the community had no other school for girls but, counting the AIU Boys' School, had 5,500 male students currently enrolled in some sort of educational program, he contended that the organization needed to expand its educational program to include more girls.[77]

While the Central Committee urged Yomtob and Oro to remain patient, as its members hoped that the Kadoorie family would opt to provide funding for the construction of the school, Yomtob continued to search for possible buildings the organization could purchase. He soon identified the house of Saleh Juda, which belonged to four brothers, two of whom lived in Baghdad and two of whom lived in India.[78] Yomtob informed the Central Committee that the house could be purchased for between 20,000 and 23,000 francs and asked for a quick decision, as the Girls' School's lease was to expire in seven months and the house in question needed significant renovations.[79]

The Central Committee relayed this news to the Kadoorie family, who immediately agreed to provide the funds to purchase the home.[80] Yomtob now planned to purchase a house to construct a school for 600 students, which would include fifteen classrooms and two rooms designed specifically for sewing instruction.[81] Unfortunately, not only could the brothers not agree with one another on a price, but after learning that the Kadoorie family had provided the AIU with the funds to purchase the home, they took a firmer stand in the negotiations.[82]

Yomtob soon feared that not only would the brothers be unwilling to sell their property but that the Ottoman government would hold up such a purchase, at least for a period of time, because the property would have to be registered to Narcisse Leven, the President of the AIU.[83] Because of his problems with the Juda family, he also informed the Central Committee that the prospect of creating a school for 600 students in the short term was likely unrealistic and that the organization would have to consider scaling back its plans.[84] While Yomtob was certainly attached to the idea of the construction of a Girls' School, the events of the summer 1903, especially his discussion of the need to request permission from Istanbul to construct such a building, indicate that he had not done the proper background research on this issue over the previous four years, even as he had constantly advocated for such an undertaking.

Yomtob soon wrote to the Central Committee claiming that it would be nearly impossible to gain Ottoman permission to build a French school in Baghdad registered to a foreign national.[85] In order to get around this issue, he proposed four plans. The first was for the organization to purchase a house in Leven's name, construct a school building, and then have Leven lease the school to the AIU.[86] However, Yomtob doubted that the authorities would approve of such a duplicitous move.[87] A second plan would be to use the AIU's contacts with local foreign consulates to secure permission, but he feared that this would create permanent tension between Ottoman educational authorities and the Baghdad Girls' School.[88] The third plan would be for Leven to purchase the land and then gift it to the Girls' School, at which point the director, Oro, could request the construction of a school.[89] From a later letter it appears that this idea would have been acceptable since the Girls' School already enjoyed official Ottoman governmental recognition.[90] A fourth plan would be to purchase the school in the name of an Ottoman citizen.[91] In a later letter, Yomtob advocated listing Elly Kadoorie, the businessman who was promising money on behalf of his family, as the building's owner since he was an Ottoman citizen.[92] Yomtob's plans, which varied in their levels of deception, highlight the bureaucratic obstacles the AIU faced when considering even purchasing land to construct a Girls' School.

The failed negotiations with the Juda family ensured that Yomtob and Oro Sémach would have to either sign a new lease to keep the Girls' School in its current building or search for a new temporary home for the school. In fact, Yomtob entered into negotiations with the current building's owners for a two-year lease prior to the Jewish holiday break in October 1903.[93] The owners, however, were reluctant to sign, and did so only after a long period of deliberation, forcing the school to extend the holiday break by five days.[94]

Over the course of 1902 and 1903, Oro Sémach had maintained a regular correspondence with Laura Kadoorie. In some cases, Sémach would write her letters in English, and Kadoorie would answer in French.[95] Thus, while Elly Kadoorie was negotiating with male members of the AIU's Central Committee and Yomtob Sémach, Oro Sémach was engaging in her own form of diplomacy by befriending Laura. In October 1903, Laura sent Oro a generous donation to be used to throw a party on the day the future school, which was to be named for her, was opened.[96] Sémach appreciated the gift but noted in her letter to the Central Committee that the AIU had yet to even purchase the land the school would one day stand on.[97]

Interestingly, in October 1903, Yomtob expressed the concern that Elly Kadoorie's promised contribution would not be enough to pay for a building that would house 600 students.[98] However, several months later, Kadoorie and the Central Committee informed him that the goal should be to purchase suitable space for the construction of a school that could house one thousand students.[99] Yomtob agreed that this plan was the most rational, at least in theory, because it would ensure that the organization would never need to make additions to such a school.[100] Yet, in practice, he argued such a task was impossible at present since the building would have to be in the Jewish quarter and the properties there were too small to accommodate such a project.[101] He also noted that the cost would be over 100,000 francs just for the land.[102] Rather than waiting for the perfect situation, he lobbied the Central Committee to send him the funds necessary to purchase a medium-sized plot of land. The organization could use this land to build a smaller school at first and then to slowly purchase the surrounding properties and convert them into school buildings as the opportunity arose.[103]

The Central Committee granted Yomtob permission to search for properties that would suit his plan and to discuss sales prices with the owners, though it did not authorize him to actually make any purchases.[104] He identified houses belonging to the Chemtob and Soffer families that he believed would serve the organization's purposes.[105] Yomtob succeeded in convincing the Central Committee to allow him to purchase these homes, and by late March he claimed that the purchases were complete and had been registered under the name of Narcisse Leven.[106] Unfortunately, Saleh Soffer decided to abrogate the agreement, a move that caught Yomtob totally by surprise.[107] Yomtob was distraught because he had already agreed to purchase Chemtob's home; since the homes were next to one another, he wanted either to purchase both homes or neither.[108] He informed the Central Committee that it would have to provide some compensation for the Chemtob family, and that it was not worthwhile to pursue legal action or to try to engage the French consulate on Leven's behalf.[109]

As the Sémachs left Baghdad shortly after this incident, and ultimately did not return to the city, Soffer's actions ensured that the project of purchasing land would be tabled for at least another year. Thus, the Girls' School remained in its inadequate building. Still, although he ultimately failed to achieve his goals during his tenure, Yomtob's advocacy had helped attract strong support for the construction of a permanent home for the Girls' School from the Central Committee and the Kadoorie family. While Yomtob and Oro would be long gone from Baghdad, their immediate successors would eventually get to enjoy the fruits of Yomtob's labor.

Schooling in the Time of Cholera

Inadequate housing and staff were not the only obstacles the school encountered during Sémach's tenure as director. In mid 1901, a disease began spreading throughout the city, and even survived the hot summer months.[110] By early 1902, the disease, now identified as Bubonic plague, was still spreading, and many families in the city's Jewish quarter had become infected.[111] In March 1902, a thirteen-year-old girl from the school's First Class died of the illness.[112] Her death had a demoralizing impact on her classmates and the school.[113]

During March and the first half of April approximately half of the Girls' School's student body was absent each day.[114] Oro Sémach noted that some families had left the city, while others had requested that their children be granted a semi-permanent break from the school until the disease disappeared.[115] Sémach granted such permission, as she did not want to assume responsibility for forcing children to spend time in school where they could potentially become infected during an epidemic.[116] However, she also believed that city authorities and families could have prevented the epidemic. Unfortunately, a combination of uncleanliness, poor housing, unhealthy air, individual fears of governmental scrutiny for contacting medical officials, social customs, and an incompetent government had ensured the plague's continued spread.[117] In fact, ten days before her student had died, Sémach had noticed that the girl was sick and recommended that she take the afternoon off from school to take a walk in the fresh air.[118] The student refused because as a thirteen-year-old girl she was soon to be married and thus could not take walks by herself in public.[119] Instead she remained confined to the school and her home, ensuring that she would not breathe fresh air.

Fortunately, the hot summer months of 1902 succeeded in killing the Bubonic plague, and the school's students returned to class and resumed making great progress.[120] No other major epidemic appears to have broken out during 1902 or 1903, but a cholera outbreak in early 1904 forced the school to close for a short time.[121] Sémach blamed part of this outbreak on local Shiites whose unsanitary practices allowed the disease to fester.[122] It is worth noting that Sémach's attempts to respond to the plague and cholera outbreaks by reinforcing student and familial cleanliness, and attempting to change certain local practices, mirrored similar undertakings by Annie Landau at the Evalina de Rothschild School in Jerusalem. Landau devoted a significant amount of time in 1902 to teaching students and their parents about cleanliness and germ theory so as to maintain calm and mitigate the effects of a recent cholera outbreak.[123]

Shortly after the cholera outbreak in 1904, Sémach and her husband left Baghdad, but the disease continued to ravage the community throughout the summer months. During this period, the school's temporary director was Jamilé Douec, Sémach's assistant. In August, Douec informed the Central Committee that the school had to close for a period of time because of excessive summer heat; she also told the Committee that many parents were refusing to send their children to school because of fear of cholera.[124] It was during this time that Sémach's sister Louna contracted a fever that subsequently turned into cholera and soon killed her. In the midst of the cholera outbreak, local authorities placed much of the city under quarantine, and the school closed down for another period of time.[125] Although the outbreak had not been completely contained, Douec tried to reopen the school after the Jewish holiday break in late October, but of the 200 students who were enrolled, only sixty showed up for class, so she delayed the re-opening.[126] Many families had once again pulled their students out of school, and many of the middle- to high-income families abandoned Baghdad for the countryside, where they spent several months waiting for the epidemic to ease.[127] As previously mentioned, the cholera outbreak was the first problem to cause a significant short-term decline in the school's population, and also ensured that Yomtob and Oro Sémach would not return to the city.

Organizational and Curricular Challenges

During her time as director of the Baghdad Girls' School, Oro Sémach made several key changes to both the school's curriculum and organization. Some of these changes resulted from her need to adapt to staff shortages; others occurred because of the progress that the school's students had made and because of the school's increasing prestige in both local and expatriate Baghdadi Jewish circles. Although Sémach departed Baghdad prematurely, in May 1904, and never returned, her reforms certainly left their mark on the school.

The first major change initiated in the school during Sémach's tenure was actually not her idea but resulted from an AIU order. In early 1900, in order to improve student morale, the AIU issued a circular ordering its institutions to cease any type of corporal punishment.[128] Sémach's correspondence says nothing about this matter, but her initial assistant, Faride Sutton, wrote a long letter to the Central Committee in response to this decree. Although she saw benefits to both engaging in and refraining from corporal punishment, Sutton ultimately stated her approval of the new policy. She liked that it both freed the teacher from constantly policing student infractions and aimed to change students' behavior not by scaring them but by appealing to their hearts and minds.[129] Sutton's comments indicate that the AIU was aiming to promote what modern scholars of education refer to as intrinsic motivation for learning, or self-motivated learning, as opposed to extrinsic motivation, or reward-based learning.[130]

Sémach's first key organizational challenge was Sutton's departure in early 1900, as the latter's replacement did not arrive for over eight months. During this time, Sémach was unable to focus solely on her own teaching, as she believed she needed to consistently supervise the school's other teachers, in whom she placed little confidence.[131] As a result of her increased workload, she was unable to admit many new students to the school in January 1901, as doing so would have necessitated the creation of a fifth class, which was impossible because of the staffing shortage.[132]

Even with her workload, Sémach succeeded in both expanding instruction in several subjects and introducing others. Danon had previously expanded the curriculum, but Sémach's goal upon arriving at the school was to shift a bit of the school's emphasis away from language instruction toward the study of other subjects. In arguing for this shift, Sémach praised her predecessor by contending that Danon's focus on languages had laid the foundation for students to study more advanced topics.[133] Thus, she introduced a science course into the school's curriculum and expanded the study of history, geography, and religious history to the lower classes.[134] Further, since she had finished teaching contemporary history to the First and Second Classes at an earlier date than anticipated, she introduced an Ottoman history course to these students.[135]

Although Sémach had students devote less time to the study of languages, especially Arabic and Hebrew, she continued to stress the importance of sewing, and students continued to spend two hours per day on this subject.[136] This is not to say, however, that language study was ignored or denigrated. In fact, in late 1902, the Girls' School received a generous donation from Silas Sassoon, a Baghdadi Jew living in India. Sémach proposed to use the funds to establish a library for the school.[137] Sassoon was the same man who had offered to fund the short-lived vocational workshop in 1886 in order to keep it open. Sémach had two main goals in establishing the library. First, the Girls' School was relatively far from the Boys' School, from which the girl students borrowed books. A library would make it easier for the Girl School's students to access books.[138] Second, she hoped a library would attract former students of the school and allow them to continue educating themselves and conversing with other educated girls and women long after having graduated and married.[139] The new library, which was subsequently approved, was to include works by eminent European and American authors, including Miguel de Cervantes, Harriet Beecher Stowe, Charles Dickens, and Molière.[140]

During her time at the Girls' School, Sémach made significant changes to the school's teaching staff. Shortly after her arrival in Baghdad, she had floated the idea of hiring some of her more advanced students as monitors, meaning they would be responsible for instructing less advanced students in subjects they had mastered.[141] She noted, however, that it would not be possible, at least initially, to pay wealthier students to take these positions because their families viewed it as shameful to have their daughters work for money.[142] Instead, Sémach hoped to "make them work for the glory of contributing to a work of progress and civilization."[143] She had another goal as well—to ensure that instead of leaving the school, older girls would remain as part-time monitors so the AIU would continue to influence their moral development.[144] In any case, Sémach began engaging advanced students from less well-off families as monitors in 1901.

In early 1902, however, she succeeded in convincing Farha Chalom, a student in the First Class from a wealthy family, to take a paid position as a monitor.[145] Sémach lauded Chalom's work but also mentioned that after accepting the position she was so embarrassed to accept money that she cried the first time she was paid.[146] Still, hiring Chalom was important both because the school faced a perennial staff shortage and because it set a precedent for other intelligent, educated girls from wealthy families to accept paid teaching positions at the school.

Chalom performed so well as a monitor that Sémach was able to make a change that she viewed as long overdue. Having been consistently disappointed with the school's Arabic teacher, Sémach finally fired this teacher in January 1903.[147] Unfortunately, she could not replace the teacher since she could not hire a male teacher, and she claimed no capable women were available in Baghdad.[148] Instead she asked Chalom to improve her Arabic skills so she could take over this position. Chalom thus began taking private lessons with a tutor, presumably male.[149] At the same time, Sémach hired a fifteen-year-old girl from the First Class, Regina Masri, to help instruct lower-level French courses.[150] Sémach never regretted her decision to fire the Arabic teacher, although doing so must have slowed student progress, as the subject could not have been taught in the immediate aftermath.[151] It appears, however, that Sémach tasked Chalom with teaching Arabic by some point in the spring and certainly by the summer.[152]

Sémach's innovations were important to the school's development, as she not only expanded the school's monitorial system but proved that the school could prepare its own students for, albeit low-paying, teaching positions in the school.[153] In doing this, she was able to meet the demands of a growing student body in the midst of a severe staff shortage. Introducing the monitorial system also allowed Sémach to continue accepting new students, though the building's flaws certainly ensured that admissions would be limited. In fact, by 1903, when the school counted 190 students, she had established a fifth class, and by late

1903, when the school counted more than 200 students, she had established a sixth.[154]

Finally, it is worth noting that even following Sémach's departure in mid-1904 and her sister's death several months later, the school continued to function well. This was largely a result of the monitorial system Sémach had implemented. In late 1904, Douec informed the Central Committee that the school's staff had been reduced to three—Douec and two monitors— as the Hebrew teacher had fallen ill.[155] Although the school's population had declined sharply as a result of the cholera outbreak and the school's permanent teaching staff had been reduced to one, thanks in part to Sémach's innovations and Douec's hard work, the school survived this trying time.

Establishing a Womens' Society

The aforementioned establishment of the library allowed Sémach to focus part of her efforts on maintaining links with the school's former students. By early 1903 she had begun planning regular meetings for the school's former students in this new space in order to allow these girls to continue to benefit from the AIU's civilizing mission.[156] Over the course of 1903 Sémach founded the Society for Reading for the school's former students, which by January 1904 had grown into a charitable society.[157] She noted that this was the first-ever women's society in Baghdadi history.[158]

In addition to academic pursuits this organization solicited donations and purchased cloth to make into linen, which the school's Third and Fourth Classes then turned into finished products to be donated to a pharmacy devoted to poorer Baghdadis, presumably Jews.[159] Besides establishing links with former students, Sémach's new society allowed her to involve the school's current students in helping less-fortunate Jews, which was in keeping with the AIU's goal of creating international and local Jewish solidarity. This was thus a way for native Jewish women with AIU educations to contribute to their community's regeneration, which was part of the organization's central mission.

Semach's work in this last regard was similar not only to that of other AIU schools, but to AJA schools as well. Returning to Laura Schor's research, it is worth noting that Annie Landau, the headmistress of the Evelina de Rothschild School in Jerusalem during this period, worked to instill the importance of volunteer work and charity in her students.[160] For example, Landau's students would bake cookies for an annual bazaar and then donate all proceeds back to the school.[161] Volunteer work and charity were clearly part of not only the AIU's mission but also the European-Jewish concept of international Jewish solidarity.

The importance of Sémach's creation of a women's society should not be overlooked, especially when placed in a Middle Eastern context. Throughout the late nineteenth and early twentieth centuries, women's societies proliferated across the region. According to Ellen Fleischmann, "The first women's associations generally focused on improving the status of women through working in such areas as health; the care of poor women, infants, and orphans; vocational training; and literacy."[162] Such organizations also allowed upper-class women to become acquainted with the challenges faced by lower-class women, and by members of society in general.[163] In doing so, these organizations helped lay the foundation for women's solidarity in Middle Eastern societies.[164]

Furthermore, the creation of women's organizations often represented women's first forays into politics. Fleischmann contends, "Women's very recognition of the need for the social welfare services their organizations provided constituted a kind of tacit political act and implicit criticism of the deficiencies of prevailing political and social institutions."[165] Although Sémach did not reference politics when discussing this society's establishment, Fleischmann's comment is clearly applicable with regard to the society's relationship to the Jewish community, as it was clearly fulfilling a need that the Jewish community's leadership was either unwilling or unable to address. In doing so, the group's members showed that educated Jewish women could put their skills to good use on behalf of the entire Jewish community. While the letters housed in the AIU's archive do not specify the kind of impact the women's society had on the school's reputation, it would have been unlikely to harm it.

Finally, it must be noted that the creation of the women's society was meant to improve its members' access to the public sphere. One of Sémach's chief goals in creating the society was clearly to ensure that her former students would have an excuse to continue visiting the Girls' School even after they graduated and married. Although we lack evidence to fully corroborate this claim, it is likely that these graduates' continued affiliation with the school and work on behalf of the community increased the community's acceptance of the idea of girls and women spending significant time outside of their homes.

Vocational Training, Sewing Instruction, and Housework

While her predecessor had lobbied for the construction of a workshop to serve vocational students, preferably one that could be attached to the school, Sémach was not in favor of such a project. Just after her arrival in Baghdad, she informed the Central Committee that the school did not need a standalone workshop for the thirty apprentices under her partial supervision, as many of these institutions had closed in other cities after training enough pupils to satisfy local demand for goods and instruction. Instead the school required a dedicated and knowledgeable instructor who could teach both vocational and academic students.[166] It appears that the student Danon had started grooming to travel to Paris had changed her mind, or perhaps her parents had changed their minds, as Sémach recommended trying to recruit a future permanent sewing instructor from among the school's poorer students.[167] This was because poor students would presumably be allowed to work for a living. Further, Sémach linked the recruitment and training of a sewing instructor to the school's development, as training girls who could not only make their own European styles clothes but also serve clients in the Baghdad would greatly expand the school's influence.[168] It is worth mentioning that Sémach noted that some of the apprentices were actually learning how to iron, though she did not discuss whether these students would continue to work under local masters outside of the school.[169]

The Central Committee, which had previously supported, at least verbally, Danon's plan to construct a workshop, lent its support to Sémach's plan and asked her to send a detailed plan for the creation of such a venue for students at the Girls' School.[170] However, Sémach responded to this request by stating that it would be impossible to submit such a plan since the city lacked a capable instructor.[171] Indeed, in a subsequent letter she stated that there were girls who wanted to travel to Paris to train to become teachers, but their parents refused to allow them to do so.[172] Instead she asked if she could send letters to colleagues in other schools offering a competitive salary, which would entail an additional subvention of 1,000 to 1,200 francs for a well-trained instructor who would consent to move to Baghdad.[173] Sémach did not envision the workshop as being a permanent institution but rather a five-year project.[174]

In early 1901, Sémach once again took up this issue and reported that her attempts to recruit a teacher from Beirut had proved futile since teachers there earned good money and thus refused to travel to Baghdad.[175] She also noted that it was essential to hire a foreign teacher since even if one of her own students were granted parental permission to train to become a sewing teacher, it would be several years before the student would be able to return to the school to teach.[176] The Central Committee did not accept Sémach's assertion that there were no capable local sewing instructors and informed her that since the apprenticeship program had been in existence for ten years there certainly were capable teachers in the city.[177] Sémach responded by claiming that all of the apprentices had mastered only different kinds of embroidery and were not suited to teach sewing.[178] She claimed that the city lacked even one Jewish master of sewing, noting that the first Jewish girls who were learning how to sew properly were not apprentices but rather students at the Girls' School.[179] Since she had failed to convince any of her students' parents to let their daughters travel to Paris for training, Sémach advised her superiors to find and send a capable master who could, over the course of several years, train about twenty apprentices plus the school's regular students.[180] Thus, she was hoping to improve the apprenticeship program at least partly in order to develop a candidate pool of future sewing instructors.

Unfortunately, the Central Committee would not consent to recruiting a suitable candidate, leading Sémach to return to the subject in early 1902. By this point she had grown frustrated and stated that the current apprenticeship program could not continue as currently constituted.[181] She contended that only an experienced and European-trained instructor in charge of a dedicated workshop could even partly resolve the situation.[182] Sémach clearly believed the Central Committee could recruit a qualified candidate and tried to convince its members to do so by linking the program's potential improvement to the school's future progress.[183]

The Central Committee's continued refusal to send a sewing instructor to Baghdad and Sémach's continued failure to recruit one from Beirut, even though she had—certainly with AIU approval—offered to pay such an instructor 1,600 to 1,800 francs, led her to finally request that her sister be sent to the city.[184] This was not a perfect solution, but it would allow Sémach, her sister Louna Gueron, and Douec to share the burdens of teaching this subject. Unfortunately, Sémach's premature departure and Gueron's untimely death shortly thereafter ensured that the organization's local apprenticeship program and the school's sewing curriculum would not be overhauled.

Still, during her time in Baghdad, Sémach was able to introduce at least one key change. Shortly after arriving in the city she had purchased the school's first sewing machine, allowing her students to both learn how to sew by hand and to operate a modern machine.[185] Additionally, she mandated that the four apprentices studying ironing had to come to the school once per week to practice their craft, and also to instruct her own students in this subject.[186] Toward the end of her time in Baghdad, she advised the Central Committee that the new school building, whenever it was constructed in the future, should have a separate room for culinary instruction since knowledge of cooking was essential to both wealthy and poor women.[187] Thus, although, like her predecessor, Sémach would not see her plans realized vis-à-vis vocational training and sewing instruction, she both left her mark on these programs and provided her superiors in Paris with ideas on how these programs could be improved.

Social Change and Persistent Challenges

During Sémach's four and a half years in Baghdad she occasionally discussed key social changes among the city's Jewish community. In the middle of her tenure she was surprised but thrilled that a local rabbi, who she claimed had great authority and implied had previously been critical of the school, asked her to admit his daughter.[188] She informed the Central Committee that this was part of a broader trend of formerly critical community members making amends with the Girls' School.[189]

Less than a year later she penned a letter to her superiors in which she contended that the school was held in such high regard that, "even the most intransigent mother-in-law does not fear sending her daughter-in-law there."[190] This statement is telling, as Sémach was not referring to current students but rather to former students who had left school, married, and moved to their husbands' homes, where they often lived under the protective rule of their husbands' mothers.[191] Thus, many former students who just five years earlier would have lacked the ability to travel outside the house at all as teenagers, whether married or unmarried, now had access to a nonfamilial community.[192] It is important to note that Sémach relayed this information in the context of her discussion of the importance of the library for the school's current and former students and the need to devote a larger space for it whenever the organization constructed a new building for the school.[193]

Unfortunately, when the school closed during holiday breaks and heat waves, which amounted to approximately two months per year, the girls were unable to leave their homes.[194] This held especially true for students in the school's First Class, who tended to be between the ages of twelve and fifteen.[195] During one such break, Sémach invited the wife of the Russian consul in Baghdad, who had told Sémach of her desire to review the students, along with over a dozen other European women in the city, to a party she organized near the school so that these women could meet the members of the First Class.[196] Not only were these women pleased to find what Sémach referred to as a "corner of true civilization in the Jewish quarter," but they also showered the girls with compliments for their knowledge of French, propriety, modern sensibilities, and sewing ability.[197] While male officials, whether from the Jewish community, Ottoman government, or foreign governments, often visited the Girls' School, it is telling that Sémach did not invite any men to the party she organized outside of the school. Although students' parents viewed the school as a safe space, school-related events conducted in public spaces were still clearly viewed skeptically.

In addition to providing a safe space for current and former students, Sémach also noted that the school had helped effect a change in the marriage age for its students. While in the past these girls would have likely been married off between the ages of ten and twelve, she noted in 1902, that many girls who had attended the school now married at the ages of seventeen or eighteen.[198] This clearly was not the case among most Baghdadi Jews, who continued to force their daughters to marry at younger ages.[199] Still, that many graduates of the Girls' School were marrying at later ages clearly signified a change in these girls' identities, at least from the AIU's point of view. As Sara Regeur argues, a rising marriage age signaled modernization in Middle Eastern Jewish communities.[200] While this study does not attempt to engage in debates over what constitutes modernization, Sémach clearly viewed later marriage ages as a sign of progress.

Convincing parents to delay their daughters' wedding age had been one of Danon's goals as well, as she had argued that girls required proper education before they could be capable wives and mothers. The wedding of a former student provided Sémach's assistant Jamilé Douec with the opportunity to discuss both how an AIU education had prepared this girl for marriage and motherhood, and also how such education had created a bit of distance between the girl and her new in-laws:

> The whole city was talking about Regina's wedding. I should tell you first that Regina is one of our former students. People were saying, "Yes, Regina is *à la franca*. She is making her own trousseau with the help of a seamstress who comes from the West. She is sending for clothes from Europe, she won't accept jewelry from here, and her hair is all curled like a sheep."
>
> The day of the ceremony people came from every part of town to see the young bride *à la franca*. As she was one of our students, I thought it important to go see her that day. The crowd was thick; with difficulty I was led through it to a room on the second floor. The young bride had just finished dressing. She looked beautiful but exhausted. "Why do you look so tired?" I asked her.
>
> "It's because I've worked very hard, night and day, with only one person to help me." And tears began to well in her eyes.

There was a lady who was a friend of mine in the room; she came over to me and said, "Do you see how the poor thing has grown thin? Well! It's because she's had to fight; she has fought for every item in her trousseau. And it's not because her parents refused her anything, but because the things that were brought her were not to her taste. Her parents want her to buy a fabric which is too gaudy. She won't accept it. Or else it's an ankle bracelet they want her to wear. She refuses. Or else they want her to wear rouge and henna on her hands and to paint her nails black; she protests. Again today," my friend continued, "she sent for me to come to her aid. She wanted to wear her hair the way she's used to wearing it in school; they wouldn't let her do it. They were trying to force her to hang heavy gold rings on the end of her braids. The poor girl isn't used to them; they would make her ill."

She started coming to school when she was still very young, so she has never worn them. "The poor little thing," I thought to myself. Finally the groom arrived. A rabbi gave the blessing. What a contrast there was between those two young people. In her white satin dress with a long flowing train, carrying orange blossoms, a net veil covering her face, she was altogether the European bride but for the few excessive adornments that it had been impossible not to wear.

He wore a *ziboun* woven in gold thread, with a great cloak over his shoulders. He must not have attended the school and so had not had time to become a little civilized. But what difference does that make? Now his wife is seeing to that task. She has him wear European dress, she dines at the table with him and not in the kitchen, in contrast to all the other women in Baghdad, and against the wishes of everyone in the family, she dresses according to what she sees in the newspapers she receives.

She does not hide herself from visitors, even when they are gentlemen coming to see her husband. She has not forgotten the school and, with the permission of her husband, she stops by from time to time to visit her former classmates. She takes as much care of her home as she does her person. A short time after her wedding I visited her at home, and the house was clean and in good order. Even now she must often struggle to maintain what she has accomplished.

Sometimes her husband refuses all change; she is often mocked by her in-laws. From a distance, her husband's mother and sisters look upon her actions with apparent malevolence. They tell each other, "We'll see if she will be able to do this, if she really knows how to sew." They are biased

> against the girls from the school because the latter know how to read books, and in this place a *savante* (that is what people call the girls who have finished school) could never be a good housekeeper. But our former students are proving these people wrong. They have been successful in whatever changes they have undertaken in their homes, and now people are finding them sensible and capable.
>
> Regina has a baby and she takes care of him well enough. The first few times she gave him his bath her mother-in-law ran out of the house saying that Regina was going to kill her child. But she does not run away anymore, for she sees that the baby looks healthy. She even takes pleasure in seeing him clean and nicely dressed.
>
> This is a student who truly has succeeded, but how much she had to go through to do it! At the same time there are others who fail in spite of their great energy. The proverb says, "The goat cannot graze beyond the length of its tether." No doubt it tries to reach farther but resigns itself when it cannot.
>
> In the end, these first students are victims, for it is hard to live in a house where everyone looks at you with an air of defiance. The struggle against so many people joining forces against them, against their ideas, against their actions, is very difficult for these young women to endure. Nevertheless, their efforts are not lost. What they have not been able to attain for themselves, they will leave for their children to do. A new generation will begin with them. It will be more enlightened, more aware, more capable of understanding the morality taught them in the schools. Here, as in all noncivilized countries, women are very ignorant. They do not accept innovations. They are like servants in the home but they always manage to get their husbands to do what they want. This power of influence is truly extraordinary. Because it is so, once this influence starts being exercised by the young women who have studied in our schools, it will serve to improve the conditions of family life.[201]

In terms of both what it explicitly and implicitly states, Douec's letter is probably the most insightful individual letter regarding the goals of AIU female education in Baghdad and its positive and negative impacts. As Rodrigue notes, this letter highlights the symbolic importance of Western dress as a signifier for social change and identity in late Ottoman Baghdad.[202] From Douec's perspective, Regina's Western dress signified her identity as a modern, Westernized

Jewish woman, whereas her husband's attire clearly marked him as an uneducated—or at least not AIU educated—Baghdadi Jewish man who was in need of regeneration. Furthermore, Regina had clearly internalized AIU teachings, as she had abandoned ornate local jewelry and fashion for simpler European styles.

Douec also linked Regina's European style to the public's fascination with her wedding. It appears from her writing that even non-Jews were interested in discussing this spectacle. Clearly there was also a class component to the wedding and Regina's tastes, as her less well-off classmates would certainly not have been able to afford to hire a foreign seamstress or to order specially made clothes from Europe. Regina's tastes were consistent with those advocated by the AIU. For example, Paméla Dorn Sezgin states that as a result of the AIU's work, by 1900 the traditional European white dress had replaced local fashion for brides in Istanbul.[203] Regina thus represented a modern Jewish woman who in many ways had more in common with Jewish women in Western Europe, and other cosmopolitan cities in the Ottoman Empire and North Africa, than she did with most Jewish women in Baghdad.

Yet beyond the aesthetics, the wedding symbolized the metaphorical marriage of West, as represented by Regina, and East, as represented by her husband. Douec clearly felt badly that Regina had to marry a man who lacked her level of education and did not share her cultural tastes, but she also was confident that Regina would be able to slowly change her husband into a modern man. In other words, she would be able to "civilize" him. This sentiment clearly reflected perhaps the most important goal the AIU had in extending education to girls, which was to use educated women as conduits of cultural change within the household.[204] In her purportedly natural role as homemaker and wife, Regina would set about remaking her husband in the AIU's image and ensuring that her child would be raised with her mores, and not those of her husband's family.

Unfortunately, as represented by Regina, this letter also made the point that the Girls' School's first cadre of students faced significant challenges. For Regina, these challenges came both from her own family, who pressured her to adhere to traditional Baghdadi fashion, and her female in-laws, who believed that her education rendered her unsuitable for traditionally feminine tasks in the private sphere.[205] While perhaps comical to read for an educated audience, Regina's mother-in-law's reaction to the way she bathed her son symbolized localized culture shock, as this action appeared both foreign and unsafe to the older woman.

Although Douec noted that Regina's mother-in-law eventually accepted and even lauded the former's parenting style, she also mentioned that other girls had not been so fortunate. In fact, she went as far as to state that the first girls were the unlucky ones. Indeed, as Danon's earlier letter detailing the struggles of Mouzli Haim showed, the school's first students struggled to adapt their modern educations and identities to communal norms that had little space for them.[206] When discussing the impact of modern education, including the AIU, on Jewish girls in the Arab world in the late nineteenth and early twentieth centuries, Rachel Simon states, "Although it provided graduates with some qualifications that were needed in society, it also created high expectations that could not always be met: the society at large changed at a slower pace culturally, socially, economically, and technically."[207] Thus, the struggles of the first students who studied at the Girls' School may have been unique in Baghdad, but they were not unique in the broader context of Ottoman Jewish history in this period.

Finally, Douec's letter illustrates the continued influence of the school on its graduates. Regina had already learned to sew, as she demonstrated to her mother-in-law and sister-in-law, and had clearly learned how to run a household. Douec, however, noted that she continued to visit the school. As has been discussed in the past two chapters, Danon had worked to make the school a European space for her students, while her successor labored to ensure that it would remain a safe space for the school's graduates. Girls like Regina thus had the opportunity to continue their moral and intellectual educations even after graduation and also could have the identities they developed as schoolgirls reinforced as older teenagers or adults. It is worth noting, however, that although the AIU's education had led Regina to refuse to follow traditional customs such as eating meals in a separate room from her husband and excusing herself when unrelated male visitors came to her house, she still needed to ask her husband's permission to travel outside of the home. Therefore, it is clear that the AIU had succeeded in breaking certain cultural barriers but, when out of the classroom, its early graduates still had to navigate through a world that was very different from the one for which the school had prepared them.

Life in the Desert: Oro Sémach's Personal Struggles in Baghdad

Like Danon before her, Sémach faced obstacles in both her personal and professional life in Baghdad. As previously discussed, she initially sparred with the

Central Committee over her salary, and though she gave birth to two children during her time in Baghdad, she lost both a child and her sister during this same period. In reading her letters, one gets the sense of a diligent teacher trying to balance her work and home life while feeling overburdened in both spheres, at least in part because of her residence in a relatively remote, though heavily populated, Ottoman province. This theme of the remoteness of Baghdad was articulated clearly in her final letter in which she discussed the various challenges she and her family had faced in Baghdad, including the ravages of exotic diseases and the loss of her son "in the desert."[208]

Excluding the deaths of her son and sister, the issue that seemed to most trouble Sémach during her time in Baghdad was her sister's treatment by the AIU. As has been discussed, she had spent several years lobbying her superiors to send her a second assistant, or at least a competent sewing instructor. Finally, in late 1903, the Central Committee consented to send her sister, Louna Gueron, who was working in the organization's school in Philippopolis, to assist her. Unfortunately, a major misunderstanding arose between Sémach and the Central Committee with regard to Gueron's new position.

Sémach had expected that her sister, who had earned 950 francs per year as an instructor in Philippopolis, would receive a significant raise. She assumed her sister's salary would be between 1,350 and 1,400 francs per year, since she had previously offered to pay a competent sewing instructor or assistant between 1,600 and 1,800 francs per year.[209] The Committee, however, merely raised Gueron's salary by 10 francs per year.[210] Although Sémach had not promised her sister a significant raise, it is clear that she had expected her to receive one, and the fact that this did not happen only increased her anger toward her superiors.[211] Sémach's disappointment with the Central Committee on this issue appears to have been exacerbated by her previous struggles with its members.

This is not to say that Sémach appears to have regretted her decision to work for the organization but rather to show that she suffered a bit of burnout. As a director, Sémach had been tasked with lobbying both the community and the AIU on the behalves of her students, subordinates, and school. As a mother, she labored to raise healthy, well-educated children in a remote corner of the Ottoman Empire. Additionally, in her role as a sister, she worked to ensure that her sibling would be respected professionally and be able to support herself financially. By 1904, Sémach had achieved great success in her role as director, but even before her sister's untimely death later that year, the years in Baghdad had clearly, and understandably, taken a significant toll on her.

Conclusion

Sémach's tenure in Baghdad was a trying time for the school but also a period that witnessed the school gain increasing local and foreign support and recognition for its activities. Building on her predecessor's successful work, between late 1899 and mid-1904, she succeeded in both modifying the school's curriculum and expanding its influence over current and former students. During this period, she and her staff began to see positive results in the form of confident, educated, European-oriented graduates and former students who, as Danon had hoped, attempted to use their AIU educations to change their own families' norms and tastes. Like Danon, Sémach ultimately found that life in Baghdad was too difficult to endure, but her work helped to ensure that by the end of its first decade in existence the Girls' School had succeeded both as an intellectual and cultural institution.

4

FROM THE BAGHDAD GIRLS' SCHOOL TO THE LAURA KADOORIE SCHOOL FOR GIRLS, 1905–1915

During its first decade the AIU Baghdad Girls' School had succeeded in establishing and sustaining a strong academic reputation and had experienced significant growth. As this chapter will show, the school's second decade, the vast majority of which coincided with the administration of Marie Albala, witnessed continued, if inconsistent, enrollment growth and a further strengthening of the school's reputation among both Baghdad's Jewish and non-Jewish communities. This period also saw the long-awaited expansion of the school's vocational program and the construction of a spacious permanent school building. Indeed, as will be shown, the construction of a permanent home significantly increased the school's population, even leading to the establishment of a preschool attached to the building. Meanwhile, Albala's focus on vocational training highlighted her commitment to what she believed to be the regeneration of the local Jewish community's poorer members. Unfortunately, the onset of World War I slowed the school's progress, and wartime events led to the school's nearly eighteen-month closure starting in October 1915.

A Time of Change: Baghdadi Jews and the Revolution of 1908–1909

Before discussing developments in the Girls' School in the final decade before the outbreak of World War I it is important to provide some context on Ottoman developments in this period. Most important, this period witnessed the Committee of Union and Progress' (CUP) Revolution of 1908, which saw the re-instatement of the Ottoman constitution and parliament, and the CUP's successful resistance of the counter-revolution in 1909, which resulted in Sultan Abdulhami II's permanent exile.[1] The CUP Revolution has often been portrayed as an attempt by secular, modernizing reformers to pursue constitutionalism and integration in order to strengthen the bonds of Ottomanism among all, or at least most, citizens regardless of religion or ethnicity. This interpretation has recently been forcefully challenged by Bedross Der Matossian, who asserts: "The reality is that constitutionalism failed to create a new understanding of Ottoman citizenship, grant equal rights to all citizens, bring them under one roof in a legislative assembly, and finally resuscitate Ottomanism from the ashes of the Hamidian regime."[2] Still, it is clear that many communities throughout the empire welcomed the revolution and hoped it would signal a period of greater imperial unity and strength.

Baghdadi Jews belonged to one such community. In the revolution's immediate aftermath many Jews took to the streets to celebrate and even welcomed the arrival of compulsory military service for all Ottoman young men.[3] Sassoon Heskel was soon elected as one of Baghdad's representatives in the Ottoman parliament. Although many Baghdadi Jews had prospered under the autocratic rule of Abdulhamid II and had even come to place great trust in the central government's ability to serve and protect their community, many of these same people viewed the revolution as an opportunity for further integration.[4] Part of this can certainly be attributed to the AIU's educational work, which imbued male students with notions of civic equality and participation while preparing them to engage productively in a globalizing world.

The revolution's aftermath, however, was not all positive for Baghdadi Jews. In fact, in 1908 and early 1909 there was sporadic violence directed against members of the community by Sunni Muslims who were sympathetic to the old order.[5] The situation calmed down after the suppressing of counter-revolutionary forces in Istanbul in 1909 but did not stabilize completely until the arrival of Nazim Pasha as governor of Baghdad in 1910. During Pasha's brief time in Baghdad, which ended in early 1911, he received strong support from the city's Jews, many of whom actually took part in public demonstrations on his behalf.[6] Such displays of overt political sentiment arguably marked the arrival of large-scale public Jewish political activity in Ottoman Baghdad.

While Baghdadi Jews shared the excitement of their coreligionists throughout the empire with regard to the revolution, their experience of its aftermath differed in at least one significant way: no segment of the community seems to have been influenced by Zionism or to have viewed its cultural and political variants as alternatives to Ottomanism. This certainly differentiated the Baghdadi Jewish community from those in cities such as Jerusalem, Salonica, Istanbul, and even Damascus.[7] Indeed, in an interview with a European Jewish paper Sassoon Heskel came across as ignorant of basic political Zionist ideology.[8] Following the revolution, Baghdadi Jews clearly viewed further integration into the empire as the only viable path. Unfortunately, the community's high hopes would be dashed with the outbreak of war and the accompaniment of strict military governance.

Recovering from Cholera: The Enrollment Explosion in the Girls' School in 1905

Marie Albala, formerly Khiat, was born in Tunis in 1877. In 1895 she received her teaching degree in Paris and then spent nearly two years, from 1896 to 1898, working as an assistant at the Girls' School in Tunis. It appears that while in Tunis she met Nissim Albala, an assistant teacher at the city's Boys' School who was eight years her senior, and married him in 1897. After leaving Tunis, the Albalas worked as directors of the Boys' and Girls' Schools in the Anatolian city of Bursa until 1904, at which point they were transferred to Baghdad.

The Albalas arrived in Baghdad in February 1905, though Marie spent much of the couple's first week in the city recuperating from fatigue from her journey.[9] Based on Nissim's initial letter, it appears the couple found the city, the Jewish community, and the AIU's schools in disarray as a result of the cholera epidemic.[10] In her first letter to the AIU, Marie praised Jamilé Douec for single-handedly directing the school for most of the previous year, though she noted that the latter's inexperience as a leader had hindered the school's progress.[11] However, she also mentioned that she was impressed by the students' appearance, intelligence, attention to detail, polite manner of speaking, and skills in handicrafts.[12] Albala also spoke approvingly of her initial meeting with the Society of Former Students, which Sémach had referred to as a charitable society, who continued to use the school as a meeting place. She noted that these girls were fortunate to have such a space considering that most teenage girls and young, unmarried Baghdadi girls lived in relative seclusion.[13] It is unclear if this society had changed its title or if different directors merely referred to it by different names.

Albala had little time to settle into her new position before enrollment and lodging issues once again appeared. As shown in Table 3.1 in the previous chapter, the cholera epidemic of 1904 had reduced the school's population to 170 by the start of 1905. Yet by March the population had risen to 199, and the school was once again running out of space for classes.[14] By June the situation had become even more pressing, as Albala claimed that over the previous three months over 100 girls had applied for admission but none had been accepted because of the school's lack of space.[15] Although she admitted it was difficult to find a building that could comfortably house between 400 and 500 students, Albala argued that the current building was both too small and too hot during the summer to serve as a suitable schoolhouse.[16]

Fortunately, Nissim was able to find a more suitable home for the school toward the end of the summer. The new building consisted of two separate houses connected to one another, though initially one of the houses was under construction and unusable.[17] Marie informed the Central Committee that once the construction was completed the new building would be able to hold approximately 450 students.[18] The main problem she now foresaw was that the school would soon face a shortage of teachers and, because the rent for the new school building was much higher than that at the previous location, the Girls' School's budget lacked the money to pay for new teachers.[19]

It appears that her letters failed to move the Central Committee, though strong demand for girls' education helped mitigate part of the problem. While Albala did not receive a new AIU-trained teacher, she was able to hire three former students to work as monitors in the school.[20] This was made possible by the admission of nearly 200 new students, nearly all of whom paid tuition.[21] Albala attributed this to parents' desires to educate their daughters and willingness to meet all of the school's tuition demands.[22] By the end of 1905, the school had 430 students, of which 285, just over 66 percent, paid tuition.[23] Rachel Danon's insistence, a decade earlier, that the school force able families to pay tuition for their daughters had not paid immediate dividends for Danon, but by 1905 it had clearly proved to be a successful policy.

Student Enrollment and School Construction, 1906–1910

Enrollment remained over 400 during much of 1906, which continued to put a strain on the school's teachers. To add insult to injury, in early 1906 the Central Committee authorized one of Albala's assistants, Rosa Farhi, to transfer to the Girls' School in Hamadan, Iran.[24] As Douec had been transferred to Aleppo the previous year, this left Albala with one assistant, Esther Valadji, in whom she claimed to have little confidence.[25] Valadji resigned shortly thereafter, leaving Albala without a Paris-trained assistant and with a student body numbering over 420.[26] Albala requested more assistants, but the Central Committee initially agreed to send her only one.[27] As a result she mentioned that she was able to admit only a tiny fraction of the 200 students who hoped to enter the school at the beginning of the 1906–1907 academic school year in October 1906.[28]

Although she did not discuss it in detail, it appears that Albala admitted a significant number of nonpaying students throughout 1906, perhaps because she assumed that the number of paying students would remain constant. If this was her thought process, she was mistaken. By the end of 1906 the school's population had declined slightly to 398, but the number of nonpaying students had increased to 170 from 135 the year before.[29] The number of paying students had thus declined from 285 to 228. In her first letter in 1907, Albala noted that many paying students had dropped out of the school because their parents, reverting back to tradition, refused to continue paying tuition.[30]

Over the course of 1907 both the number of paying and nonpaying students declined so that by December of that year the school's overall population had declined to 332, which included 226 paying students.[31] Both the school's total population and its number of nonpaying students rose over the course of 1908. By December of that year the school's population had risen to 395 while the number of nonpaying students had risen to 192.[32] In a letter written in July 1907, Albala mentioned that at the time of her arrival in Baghdad the school had very few impoverished students, but that she had admitted many more, bringing the number to 70 out of 400 total students.[33] Although she did not explicitly state that her goal had been to attract nonpaying students, it does seem that she was far more willing than her predecessors to do so.

While the school's population declined slightly throughout 1907 and 1908, it was during this time that the Kadoorie family in Hong Kong formally agreed to build a new, permanent home for the Girls' School. By December 1907, the Kadoorie family had purchased land in order to begin construction of the new building, which was to last nearly four years.[34] As a result of this momentous development, Marie Albala began to make plans to enroll more students, as on completion the new school would hold over 1,000 students.

A cursory glance at the BAIU's statistics for 1909 would lead one to conclude that the school's population continued to stagnate, as at year-end the school counted 399 students, with 207 paying students and 192 nonpaying students.[35] Albala's letters, however, tell a more complicated story. The school was forced to move again, in mid-1909, and ended up in a much smaller building.[36] As a result, Albala had to send a large contingent of nonpaying students away for several months.[37] Further, she enrolled 160 students who would not be able to enter the school until the new building was finished.[38] Thus, Albala stated that the official statistics understated the school's official population by nearly 200, though in reality the official count ignored only the contingent of nonpaying students she had sent away in the short term.[39] It also appears that if many nonpaying students had remained in the school, the school would have, for the first time in its history, had more nonpaying than paying students enrolled.

In early 1910 Albala notified the Central Committee that, although the new building was not yet complete, the school had been renamed the Laura Kadoorie School for Girls.[40] The school remained in a small building over the course of the year, though the student population grew to 429, with 229 tuition-paying students and 200 nonpaying.[41] The Girls' School was so cramped that Albala even requested that it be transferred to the section of the new building that was completed.[42] She stated that she hoped the new building would be totally complete by Passover, in spring 2011, though considering she had recently lamented the lack of progress at the construction site, this wish appears to have been overly optimistic.[43]

The Opening of the New Building of the Laura Kadoorie School for Girls

Although she had hoped to move her students into the new building by May 1, construction delays forced Albala to accept the need to remain in the current building during much of 1911, and also resulted in the school's population growth remaining flat.[44] In anticipation of the new school's opening, the AIU had also sanctioned the building of a communal apartment for single female teachers.[45] The apartment was to include six fully furnished bedrooms and a common dining room and was scheduled to be ready in October 1911.[46] It is likely that part of the rationale for building such an apartment was to help the school retain single teachers by making their private lives more comfortable and increasing their ability to socialize with colleagues outside of the schoolhouse.

In the fall of 1911, as the new school building was nearing completion, the Albalas began planning a major party to accompany the school's opening. The school's inaugural celebration took place on November 14, 1911. The guest list included foreign notables, members of the local Jewish community, the Kadoories, and the Ottoman governor of Baghdad.[47] Unfortunately, both Nissim and Marie Albala's letters recapping the inauguration are mostly illegible, but the former's correspondence includes a long speech that he presumably gave at the event.

Nissim's speech provided a brief history of the AIU in Baghdad from the 1860s through 1911, and eloquently connected the AIU's goals with the historical and contemporary needs of the Baghdadi Jewish community and the

Ottoman Empire. Indeed, he began his speech by linking female education with the communal and national well-being:

> The celebration today will mark a memorable date in our scholarly annals. It will open a new era of moral regeneration for our Baghdadi co-religionists. Sirs, it is a well-known truth to say that instruction is the most powerful tool of progress and that the schools are the foundation of national and individual prosperity. But in a province such as Iraq where education remains held back, it is useful to constantly proclaim this truth especially with regard to female education, which is generally neglected. However, the teaching of women is a chief necessity. The woman, guardian and mistress of the family, holds between her hands the education of children and, consequently, the future of the family and the nation. It is therefore important to prepare her for this difficult task by strengthening her heart and enlightening her mind.[48]

He once again returned to the theme of patriotism at the end of his speech, directing his concluding remarks toward the Ottoman governor of Baghdad:

> The Alliance, which has, in Turkey, pursued a noble task in a disinterested manner, will be happy to hear a restatement of support from the authorities. The government has always considered the schools of the Alliance, from where numerous generations of educated citizens have been imbued with gratitude towards and learned to be conscious of their duty to the Ottoman homeland, and who at the time of the Revolution voluntarily rushed to take their places among their Muslim and Christian brothers to defend endangered freedoms, to be a helpful tool and has always treated it with the utmost kindness. It is in keeping with these patriotic sentiments that we will continue to prepare our students to contribute to the greatness and prosperity of the Ottoman Empire.[49]

Clearly Nissim was aiming to earn the continued support of the government by highlighting the AIU's contributions to the Ottoman Empire and its graduates' contributions to the CUP revolution of 1908–1909.

Beyond his desire to ingratiate himself and his organization with Ottoman authorities, the most striking aspect of Nissim's speech was his direct linkage between female education and the future well-being of the Ottoman Empire. Previous male and female instructors in Baghdad had, like him, noted the link between female education and the regeneration of the Baghdadi Jewish community. However, by linking the AIU's work to the future success of the now CUP-ruled empire, he was arguing that the Laura Kadoorie School was not only an important Baghdadi institution but an important Ottoman one as well. While male AIU teachers in Baghdad had long linked male education to the strengthening of Ottomanism, it is unclear when either male or female AIU teachers came to view female education in this light. It is possible, likely probable, that it was the 1908–1909 revolution's impact on the local Jewish community that influenced AIU teachers to begin to portray the Laura Kadoorie School's work as contributing to imperial, and not just communal, interests.

While the beginning and end of the speech dealt with the link between education and patriotism, Nissim also made sure to speak directly to local Jews in attendance. First, he argued that Jewish tradition had historically valued female education by drawing from the Bible and the work of Maimonides.[50] However, he claimed that the goal of the Laura Kadoorie School was not to create a cadre of intellectual women, but rather to help develop educated but skilled women who would be able to provide intellectual and emotional support for their husbands and children.[51] Thus, he reiterated the long-held AIU goal of viewing girls' education as complementary, not equal, to boys' education. Finally, as an intelligent and experienced director, he made sure to pay numerous compliments to the Kadoorie family for their financial support.[52]

Although certain aspects of his speech seem to have been innovative in a Baghdadi Jewish context, the overall content was fairly typical for an advocate of women's education in the late nineteenth- and early twentieth-century Arab world. It was common for such activists to legitimate their ideas through references to religious tradition and, as Ellen Fleischmann has pointed out, to view women's status as a "barometer of a society's modernity."[53] By the early 1910s it had also become common for advocates of women's education to link women's education to national or imperial prosperity.

It does, however, appear that Baghdadi society lagged behind other parts of the Ottoman Empire and much of the eastern Mediterranean Arab world with regard to debates centered on women's education and the link between women's progress and national prosperity. For example, in 1910, Jamil Sidqi al-Zahawi, a Baghdadi Muslim writer and legal scholar, published an article in an Egyptian newspaper that blamed Muslim backwardness on women's oppression.[54] The article caused a major uproar in Baghdadi Muslim circles, and al-Zahawi was subsequently dismissed from his position at the Baghdad Law School.[55] As a well-respected scholar and a Baghdadi Muslim man, al-Zahawi should have been well placed to make such an argument without fearing retribution.

In contrast, just several weeks before Albala had given his speech in Baghdad, Esther Azhari Moyal, a Jewish woman from Beirut who had traveled widely throughout the Ottoman Empire, Egypt, and Europe, delivered a graduation speech at the American College for Girls in Beirut that was very similar to his.[56] Moyal focused much of her speech on the link between education and national prosperity. In one section she noted:

> You see those who hold you back, whose hearts are obliterated by God, saying that there is no point in education and that every dirham spent on it is a waste since our Eastern traditions dictate that a woman's place is in the home, where no activity enlightens her mind and no art raises her mental capacities, nor expands the boundaries of her imagination. No, my dear ladies, you will prove these demagogues utterly wrong and show that life's good things and created by us, women; that we bequeath morals to the nation's sons, who are our fathers, brothers, husbands, and sons.[57]

Indeed, Moyal's speech actually went beyond Albala's by calling for greater equality between men and women, rather than only painting women as intellectual and moral companions and supporters of men.[58] Perhaps Moyal's speech would not have been too radical for an AIU audience in Baghdad, but it likely would have been so for a general Baghdadi Muslim or Jewish audience.

The Impact of the New Building

Immediately following the new building's inauguration, the Laura Kadoorie School experienced rapid growth. By January 1912 its population had increased to 706, and Marie Albala noted that twenty-three of these students were members of prominent non-Jewish families.[59] Twenty of these students were either Armenian or Greek, while three were Turkish, and two of these three were daughters of high-ranking Ottoman military officers.[60] Albala claimed that the school's work in the years immediately preceding the opening of the new building had strengthened its reputation among various non-Jewish communities in the city and that the inaugural ceremony had further enhanced its prestige.[61]

While the building was now adequate, the school still faced a staff shortage and increasing demand for education from the Jewish community. At this time the school's 706 students were divided into fourteen classes, which must have put great pressure on individual teachers.[62] Meanwhile, Albala claimed that the school included only about 300 poor students, as the majority of the students were from middle-class to wealthier families.[63] She asserted that if the AIU hoped to reach the thousands of poor Baghdadi Jewish girls, it would need to establish additional schools.[64]

Unfortunately for the AIU, not every segment of the Jewish community was pleased with the school's elevated profile. Albala asserted that a group of local rabbis had long opposed the school's work but had recently cast baseless accusations against one of her assistants, Léa Policar. According to Albala, the rabbis had sent a letter of complaint to the local scholarly committee accusing Policar of committing six transgressions against Jewish tradition in her teaching.[65] Most notably they claimed that she had taught students that God does not exist and that a woman's monthly menstruation period does not render her impure.[66] Albala, who, as will be discussed, was very critical of assistants at times, forcefully defended Policar in her letter to Paris and noted that not only had she not made the statements the rabbis attributed to her, but she also lived a moral private life.[67] In fact, Policar was unaware of some of these accusations, and Albala did not want to inform her of the accusation regarding impurity that was leveled against her.[68] Albala viewed these accusations as a way for the rabbis to create a public outcry against the school, which would lead to the community calling for its closure.[69] While this incident rattled Albala, it likely blew over quickly, as Policar did not mention it in any of her letters. In fact, in her letter from late 1912 requesting a transfer, Policar, a native of Bursa, cited the impact of Baghdad's inhospitable climate on her health as the sole reason for her desire to leave the city.[70]

While Albala was writing to defend Policar, the school was undergoing further construction. The Kadoorie family had donated additional money to the school to build a preschool for younger children. This new annex was finished in late December 1912 and was named the Eliezer Kadoorie Institute.[71] Albala mentioned that the new preschool was open to boys and girls aged four to seven.[72] She also noted that this preschool was not aiming to compete with the Menahem Daniel Institute, which had opened nearly a decade earlier, as each school catered to a specific segment of the community.[73] Although she did not say so explicitly, Albala clearly viewed the Eliezer Kadoorie Institute as an elite institution for children of educated members of the community and, especially, children of former AIU students.[74] Indeed, she noted that her goal was to ensure that the majority of students would pay tuition and had set strict financial criteria for admission to the school.[75]

Although the increase in student enrollment did have a positive impact on the Laura Kadoorie School's prestige, it also placed the institution under new financial stress. This was because the major growth in student enrollment in late 1912 and early 1913 came from the admission of poor students. By mid-1913, not counting preschool or vocational students, the school had 800 students, 400 of whom were from poor families.[76] In addition to not collecting tuition from these students, the school provided many of these students with free meals and free clothing.[77]

As Albala labored to convince the Central Committee to send financial support for her less-fortunate students, she also struggled to find local sources of support. During her early years she had often been able to count on the support of the charitable society that her predecessor had helped establish, but by 1912 this group had apparently stagnated and was not able to offer as much material support as it once had.[78] Albala attributed the group's struggles to the stifling social environment in which women in Baghdad lived.[79] In response to the group's struggles, she renamed it the Society of Married and Unmarried Former Students and made direct appeals to former students in the community to join.[80] Apparently, these appeals met with some success, as Albala claimed, in September 1913, that the reformed society counted about fifty members and was looking for recognition and a small subvention from the Central Committee to supplement the funds it had already raised.[81] The reformed society's goals were mainly aimed toward feeding and clothing the school's poor students, goals Albala clearly believed would significantly aid the institution's future progress.[82]

Overall, the new building made a significant and positive impact on the school's functioning and prestige. While the school experienced some opposition from conservative rabbis and struggled to adequately respond to the influx of nonpaying students in 1912 and 1913 (see Table 4.1), it continued to enjoy strong support from important segments of the local Jewish population as well as important non-Jewish families. Perhaps most notably, following the new building's opening in late 1911, Albala no longer complained about a lack of space, which had been a recurring theme in directors' correspondence since the school's founding in 1895.

Albala and Her Assistants

In many ways Albala benefitted from the strong foundation she inherited from her predecessors. However, as a result of the school's success she came to struggle with an issue that Danon and Sémach could have only hoped to deal with: how to supervise a large teaching staff and a large student body. Indeed,

Table 4.1 Enrollment growth and breakdown of paying and non-paying students at the AIU Girls' School/Laura Kadoorie School for Girls in Baghdad, 1905–1913

Month/Year	Number of paying students	Number of non-paying students	Total number of students
December 1905	285	145	430
December 1906	228	170	398
December 1907	206	126	332
December 1908	203	192	395
December 1909	207	192	399
December 1910	229	200	429
December 1911	337	369	706
December 1912	349	433	782
December 1913	384	404	788

Sources: BAIU (1905–1906, 1908–1911, 1913) and AJAR (1907 and 1912)

under Albala, the school's culture underwent significant change as a result of the school's quadrupling in student population between 1905 and 1913. Whereas Danon and Sémach were able to both actively supervise their assistants and teachers while also giving personal attention to students, Albala had no choice but to focus most of her efforts on the former at the expense of the latter. Thus, much of her effort, especially in her later years at the school, was focused on advising, monitoring, and evaluating her AIU-trained assistants.

Her first major challenge with regard to her assistants involved Esther Valadji, a woman in her mid-twenties who came to Baghdad in 1906, clearly as a demotion, after having directed the AIU Girls' School in Fez, Morocco, for the previous three years. Albala expressed her disbelief that Valadjii had been able to direct a school for three years, as she often contradicted herself in class and employed creative but ultimately flawed teaching methods.[83] Indeed, Albala noted that this assistant was "the first victim of her inventions." Still, she informed Bigart that Valadji was receptive to her advice and hardworking.[84] In any case, Valadji left the school a few months later and apparently discontinued working for the AIU.[85]

During her first three years at the school, Albala relied heavily on monitors to both supervise students and teach classes. Her most valuable monitor in this period was her sister, whom she referred to as mademoiselle Khiat.[86]

Unfortunately, Khiat left the school for health-related reasons in mid-1907, putting even more strain on her sister's staff.[87] In July and October 1907, Albala pleaded with the Central Committee to send her additional assistants to relieve her, and her assistant Rosa Braun's, burden.[88] The Central Committee was apparently unable to honor this request, though an undated letter from Bigart, most likely from March 1908, assured her that the Central Committee was doing everything possible to find her assistants for the following year.[89]

In August 1908 Albala believed she would soon suffer another setback, as it appeared that Braun would be leaving the school in the near future. However, Braun ended up staying another two years.[90] Finally, in December 1908, a second assistant, Joya Simhon, a native of Haifa, arrived in Baghdad.[91] Albala's initial comments about Simhon illustrate why it was likely so difficult to recruit female assistants for the school. When Simhon arrived, she had little money and no place to stay, and ended up sleeping, by herself, in one of Albala's children's beds.[92] Several months later, Albala learned the Central Committee was sending her two additional assistants, Rebecca Confino and Alice Picciotto, though their arrival date was not yet known.[93]

During her first several months at the school Simhon proved herself to be a capable teacher. Albala praised her work and predicted that with time and experience she would become an even stronger teacher.[94] At the same time, Albala also spoke highly of Braun's work. In fact, even though the school required Braun's services, Albala attempted to convince Bigart to let her leave Baghdad in order to improve her health.[95] Bigart had previously ordered Braun to remain in the city, leading Albala to intercede on her behalf.[96] Albala asserted that the AIU owed Braun because of her fine work over a period of three years in a remote location.[97] Bigart and the Central Committee were apparently unmoved.

One of the new assistants, Confino, finally arrived in September 1909, but after several days of work she fell ill and needed to take a two-week leave of absence.[98] Still, the arrival of Confino and Picciotto allowed Albala to revamp her own schedule and to keep parts of her mornings free instead of constantly monitoring classes.[99] It is also worth noting that Albala spent two to three hours per day monitoring teachers at the Menahem Daniel Institute, even though it was not associated with or even near the Girls' School.[100]

The new assistant Picciotto clearly made a positive first impression on Albala, as the latter put the former in charge of the school during a leave of absence she took in mid 1910.[101] Albala lauded Picciotto's work in a letter from late 1910 and informed the Central Committee that she, more than any other assistant, merited an increase in salary.[102] In fact, a week later, Albala penned a follow-up letter detailing this assistant's excellent work and once again asserting she deserved an increase in pay.[103] The Central Committee agreed, and in early February granted Picciotto a modest raise.[104] Picciotto, however, did not remain at the school much longer, as she became engaged to Moïse Abrevaya, a former assistant at the Albert Sassoon School and current director at the Boys' School in Basra; later that year, she moved to Basra, where she continued to work for the AIU.[105] At about the same time, Simhon became engaged to Maurice Sidi, the headmaster at the Boys' School in Mosul and soon left Baghdad as well.[106] By mid-1911, Confino had also departed, leaving Albala only with Policar, as Braun had departed in late 1910.[107]

In early 1912, the Central Committee sent four additional assistants to the school: Flora Nahon, Leila Chalom, Rebecca Termin, and mademoiselle Abulafia. These four assistants made terrible first impressions on their new director because of their behavior outside of the school. Albala noted that they had offended the local community by publicly mixing with and entertaining Jewish and non-Jewish men in their newly built common apartment.[108] This was problematic for two reasons. First, the Kadoorie family had funded the construction of the apartment, and Albala did not want their local relatives to relay to them scandalous news about what happened there.[109] Second, the apartment was located next to a rabbinical court, and Albala feared that local rabbis would be offended by her assistants' behavior.[110] She ultimately forced her new assistants to sign contracts pledging to never allow unaccompanied male visitors into the apartment, while her husband forbade his male assistants from visiting the apartment.[111]

Albala's problems with Termin and Nahon extended into the schoolhouse as well. Both Albala and Termin wrote to Paris regarding two incidents.[112] The first incident involved Termin and Nahon. According to Albala, Termin was supposed to work with the Second Class for several days while another assistant was absent, but by the third day she had abandoned her post. When confronted, Termin claimed that her director had erroneously accused her of ordering Nahon to take her place. Meanwhile, Albala asserted that this is what Nahon herself had told her. Termin complained that Albala had publicly reprimanded her, as if she were a student. The second incident occurred when the teachers were lining their students up to leave their classrooms. Albala made a public announcement, which Termin must have initially believed pertained only to students, telling students to remain quiet while everyone was lining up, but then she noticed Termin talking to a fellow teacher. Termin contended that she was having a private conversation and that when Albala noticed it she looked specifically at her and said, "My comment was especially for you Madame Termin." It seems that from Termin's perspective she was merely speaking quietly to a colleague, but Albala saw her behavior as undermining the discipline she wanted her staff to instill in the students. Although problems between the two continued, Termin remained at the school until 1914.

Unfortunately for Albala, in early 1913 she lost one of her most valued assistants, Léa Policar. The latter had spent much of the previous year fighting off various illnesses and often had to leave class early. Although she had spent three years in Baghdad, Policar, a native of Bursa, had never adjusted to Baghdad's harsh climate, and so Albala wrote to the Central Committee on her behalf asking that she be reassigned.[113] Several months later, Albala lost two additional assistants, as Rosa Farhi, who had started at the school in 1904, left in 1906, and returned in 1912, transferred to Hilla, while Abulafia married and left the school.[114] In response to the loss of Policar, Farhi, and Abulafia, Albala requested three new assistants for 1914.[115] Albala, however, left the school herself in late 1913.

Albala and Vocational Education

Like her predecessor, Albala took a great interest in the AIU's female vocational projects. During her first year in Baghdad, in 1905, she worked to revamp and expand the program. On taking over, she had counted twenty-eight female apprentices, which included two ironing apprentices who learned their craft at the school and twenty-six apprentices training as embroiderers throughout the city.[116] Albala complained that the apprentices working outside of the school labored for free and often lacked enough money to purchase shoes so they could walk comfortably to their workshops.[117] She noted that even after they began earning money, their salaries were often very low.[118] Contending that weaving was more lucrative, Albala announced her intention to open a weaving workshop at the school.[119]

In April 1905, she purchased a couple of weaving looms and started a carpet-weaving workshop at the school.[120] She claimed that the weaving itself was not technically complicated but required great patience.[121] She also noted that several families from the local Shiite population in Baghdad were renowned for their weaving skills, so she hired a young woman from one of these families to work at the school to train the apprentices.[122] The woman did not last very long, however, as she apparently feared that the apprentices were learning how to weave too well too quickly and would eventually compete with her for clients.[123] It is unclear whom Albala found as a replacement, but the workshop continued to function.

One major problem of the vocational program was that it lacked an adequate alumni network. According to Albala, of the numerous former apprentices, dating back to the early 1890s, only fifteen were employed, and only six worked with apprentices.[124] Two of these women employed one apprentice, one employed two, one employed three, and one, Salha Haim, employed thirty.[125] Further, these masters and their apprentices did not work year-round but for only four to six months per year.[126] Thus, one of Albala's goals was to help create a strong network of graduate masters who would train Jewish girls and help them earn a decent living.

In late summer 1905, Laura Kadoorie sent the Girls' School a new subvention in order to help establish a sewing workshop at the school.[127] The main issue, however, was one that Sémach had also dealt with. Albala alluded to a complete lack of sewing instructors in Baghdad capable of making high-quality, fashionable dresses, and claimed that European women, surely wives of businessmen and government agents, living in the city often made their own dresses.[128] In October she reported that one of her aides had found a foreign seamstress, Madame Alcales, who wished to work at the school. However, Albala believed that Alcales would not accept less than 200 francs per month, a sum that the Central Committee was apparently unwilling to pay.[129] It appears that these negotiations failed, as by January 1906 Bigart had tasked Albala with trying to find a seamstress from Bombay and paying her salary largely out of Kadoorie's subvention along with funds from tuition.[130]

While discussing finances associated with hiring a foreign master seamstress, Albala mentioned that all students who wanted to study under such a master were tuition-paying students from wealthy families, as these families valued a woman's ability to sew.[131] This is interesting, as Sémach and Danon had previously argued that most well-to-do families did not want their daughters to learn a craft. There are several possible explanations for this disparity. First, Albala was clearly referring to daughters from the wealthiest Jewish families in Baghdad, whereas her predecessors may have been referring to middle- to upper-middle-class families. Building on this first point, a second explanation may be that the wealthiest families had had greater exposure to western European norms, whether because they had traveled to India, Europe, or even Istanbul, or because they had had more contact with Europeans in Baghdad. Thus, they may have been more comfortable than many of their co-religionists with the idea of a skilled daughter. A third explanation, presuming that even the wealthiest Baghdadi Jewish families had in the recent past opposed their daughters undertaking this kind of training, is that upper-class Jewish social mores had changed radically, at least with regard to girls learning how to sew. It is, unfortunately, unclear which of these explanations is the most accurate, but based on previous directors' experiences I would lean toward the third. Finally, it should be noted that the tuition-paying girls who wanted to study under a master seamstress do not appear to have been vocational students but rather academic students. Thus, Albala did not view the school's vocational goals as necessarily separate from its academic goals.

Despite the problems Albala had in setting up a sewing workshop, by early 1906 the carpet-weaving workshop was doing quite well. In fact, in January 1906 there were already fifty-seven apprentices[132]—this despite the workshop no longer being located in the Girls' School, which had recently moved to a new building. The workshop had first been transferred to the Albert Sassoon School for a short time and was currently located in a building that the Albert Sassoon School had recently acquired.[133] Albala attributed the popularity of the weaving workshop to the fact that embroidery, the field most Jewish female apprentices had gone into, paid so little money.[134] Interestingly, one group attracted to embroidery was older members of the school's First Class. In mid-1906, Albala had created a small embroidery workshop in the school for thirteen former members of this class who wanted a reason to remain in school, and thus not be secluded in their homes, and so asked their director to allow them to perfect their sewing and embroidering skills.[135]

Even though the carpet-weaving program declined slightly during late 1906 and early 1907, it remained the most important vocational program associated with the school.[136] In April 1907, the vocational program counted eighty-five apprentices, a number that excluded students enrolled in the Girls' School who received vocational training as part of their academic curriculum.[137] Fifty of these apprentices studied carpet weaving. Albala noted that she had bought four Singer sewing machines and eight apprentices were training on them.[138] Fifteen girls were working outside of the school as embroidery apprentices, although Albala mentioned she was phasing this program out because it did not lead to lucrative salaries.[139] Thus, she had not accepted new applicants to this program for some time.[140] An additional ten girls worked as apprentices under lace masters, and two worked as ironing apprentices at the school.[141] These two girls were also tasked with teaching older students at the school how to iron.[142]

Although source material is sparse for 1907, a report from July suggests that the vocational program suffered a major setback in the first part of the year because many apprentices started refusing to work for free. In response, Albala, who had long lobbied the Central Committee to send money for this purpose, began paying these girls a modest daily stipend to cover their basic necessities.[143] She claimed that this new policy worked to re-invigorate the program, though she also noted that it put some strain on the school's finances since she was using tuition revenue to pay these stipends.[144]

The vocational program underwent a major transformation in late 1907 and early 1908. In November 1907, Albala permanently severed the carpet-weaving workshop from the school, stating[145]

> [s]ince its creation which took place in April 1905, we have trained around a dozen capable workers who are now working at home. Each of these workers has three of four apprentices under her surveillance. Given these circumstances it was useless to keep our workshop, the revenue of which covered neither the costs of training the apprentices or paying the instructor. The goal had been to teach carpet weaving to members of the poor classes and this has been accomplished. Several workshops are now functioning in the city in Jewish houses. Moreover, our instructor has continued to operate the workshop at her own expense by increasing its size and will continue to train students.[146]

Thus, the weaving workshop was a victim of its own success. It is important to note that the workshop must have trained between fifty and seventy-five girls during its two and a half years of existence. Since, as Albala noted, only about a dozen of these girls became trusted master weavers, it is likely that many who studied at the workshop struggled to compete with their classmates, not to mention other weavers in the city, and never used their skills to earn a living.

After closing the carpet-weaving workshop, Albala replaced it with a sewing workshop, which she and her predecessor had wanted to open.[147] In fact, Albala cited great communal support for its establishment.[148] Although she had hoped to find a foreigner to run the workshop, she ended up hiring a former student from her school instead because she believed it was impossible to find an ideal foreigner.[149] Albala informed Bigart that her new hire was well placed to serve local Jewish clients, as these women were not too demanding in terms of quality.[150] Further, as her predecessors had predicted, the new workshop succeeded in stealing Jewish clients away from the Catholic Sisters' workshop, and Albala mentioned that many of her school's graduates had begun to buy their clothes exclusively from the new workshop.[151] Finally, the workshop employed twenty-two apprentices, most from poor families, though the seamstress must have also worked with wealthier girls who attended the Girls' School.[152]

The sewing workshop continued to function well throughout 1908, and in 1909 Albala informed Bigart that the workshop run by Catholic Sisters had lowered the prices of their products in an attempt to retain clients.[153] Albala had also opened, in late 1908, a new workshop for making lingerie.[154] Part of her goal in doing this seems to have been to continue to train embroiderers and to steer them toward making more lucrative items. As Albala could not find a local master to run this workshop, she assumed the responsibility and hired an experienced apprentice to assist her.[155]

In April 1909, she wrote that the young woman in charge of the sewing workshop was performing adequately but, as she had never left Baghdad, required careful supervision when trying to teach students how to make more complex items.[156] However, a month later Albala claimed that the workshop was functioning so well that it had continued to steal clients from the Catholic Sisters' workshop.[157] Indeed, she claimed that her workshop's victory was even more impressive, as the master seamstresses at the Catholic workshop came from France. She also proudly mentioned that her sewing workshop had impressed a wife of one of the agents at the local Russian consulate.[158]

As a result of her workshop's success, Albala informed Bigart that she planned to expand it and admit more apprentices.[159] In fact, a month earlier she had stated that her school's workshops were always busy and that she sometimes had to refuse orders from clients.[160] In explaining her plans to expand the workshop, she wrote:

> In Baghdad more than anywhere else there is still a lot to do with regard to vocational work. The younger indigenous generations, Christians and Jews, are beginning to adopt European fashion. They are adopting embroidered lingerie. The rich families are numerous. The European colony is increasing each year. With a strong sewing instructor, a trained embroiderer, we will do excellent business and will help many poor girls find work.[161]

While Albala was certainly pleased with her native master seamstress, she clearly believed that the workshop required a more skilled, and likely older, director. Her letter also attests to the significant cultural and economic changes taking place in Baghdad. It is worth pointing out that Albala's letter from May was written just weeks after the counter-revolution against the CUP Revolution of 1908 had been put down and Sultan Abdulhamid II had been sent into exile. These events obviously did not dampen her optimism; her letter is evidence that the local Jewish community had made it through the events of 1908–1909 and retained confidence.

In early 1910, Albala traveled to Europe and spent part of her trip searching for a more capable sewing instructor to run the sewing workshop.[162] By this time the two workshops together had sixty apprentices.[163] Albala noted it was essential to find a capable instructor, as her own responsibilities were to increase once the school's new building opened.[164] During her trip she met a well-trained Jewish woman willing to move to Baghdad and to sign a three- or four-year contract—but only if the AIU would subsidize her trip to and from Baghdad and pay her 200 francs per month.[165] Albala requested a new 2,400-franc-per-year subvention from the Central Committee in July, but she was apparently turned down, as in December she noted that she would begin looking for a capable sewing instructor who would be paid out of school revenue.[166]

While trying to convince Bigart and the Central Committee to provide further financial support to her workshops, Albala discussed what she believed to be the most important aspects for girls' education in Baghdad. Like her husband, in the speech he was to give at the inauguration of the new building a little over a year later, Albala emphasized that intellectual training for her students was important but that moral training was her chief goal.[167] She further linked vocational training to the development of a young woman's moral character and contended it was essential to help young Baghdadi girls develop practical vocational skills that would allow them to become capable household managers.[168] Indeed, Albala's assistant Alice Piccioto noted that although they had great ability in handicrafts, Baghdadi girls required close supervision, as they came to the workshops lacking motivation and direction.[169] In other words, the workshops helped develop the apprentices' moral character by teaching them to have a strong work ethic.

It is worth noting that Albala's predecessors had viewed vocational education as essential for both rich and poor girls, as the former would learn to become more capable household managers and the latter would be better able to support themselves financially. Albala, however, at least based on her letters, seems to have taken this a step further. She viewed vocational training as not just essential for the training of both rich and poor girls, but also as a way to increase contacts among rich and poor Jewish women as well as among women from the city's various communities. Just as Danon and Sémach had worked to turn the school into a safe and neutral space where Jewish girls would be allowed to congregate, with parental approval, even outside of school hours, Albala aimed with the workshops to create a space where poorer Jewish women would sell quality products to wealthier Jewish and non-Jewish women. The workshops also increased the school's name recognition throughout the community, and helped former graduates stay in contact with students through the placement of orders and visits to the workshops to pick up their items. Finally, the workshops were, in a way, part of the AIU's modernizing and regenerating mission. They were geared toward producing European-style products for indigenous women who already had acquired such tastes, as well as for European women living in Baghdad. However, Albala also appears to have wanted the workshops to create an even larger market for European fashion, thereby effecting further societal change, both for the Jewish community and the larger Baghdadi community, through local adoption of new aesthetic preferences.

At the start of 1911, Albala had once again located an excellent foreign candidate to come run the sewing workshop. Rachel Danon, the former director in Baghdad and current director at the AIU Girls' School in Alexandria, had identified a certain Madame Bignens, a European woman living in Alexandria, as the ideal candidate.[170] In her letter to Bigart, Albala made sure to mention that Danon had extensive knowledge about Baghdadi society, and that Danon agreed with her regarding the need to bring in a foreign master seamstress.[171] The major issue was that Bignens wanted a salary of nearly 240 francs per month and for the AIU to pay 800 francs for her and her husband's voyage to Baghdad.[172] While Albala noted that her workshops had achieved a surplus of nearly 250 francs during the previous calendar year, she still needed both AIU support and approval to hire Bignens.[173]

As Albala's separate negotiations with Bignens and the Central Committee were taking place, her indigenous master seamstress was also requesting an increase in her salary from nearly 84 francs per month to somewhere between 125 and 150 francs per month.[174] Albala reminded Bigart that her current seamstress required constant supervision and mentioned that many of the elite clients had little confidence in her ability to make high-end products.[175] Further, she argued that since her current seamstress' salary had to be greatly increased anyway, the Central Committee should just spend a little more to attract a highly capable master.[176]

The Central Committee appears to have balked at both the high salary and the steep cost of Bignens's family's travel, as she ultimately was not hired.[177] In a letter from February 1912, Albala mentions that the Central Committee authorized her to pay only 200 francs per month for a master seamstress.[178] In January 1912, she once again complained that supervising the workshop's master seamstress and her apprentices was detracting from her other responsibilities, which had increased because the school had recently admitted many new students following the opening of the new building.[179] However, it is worth mentioning that the workshop must have been functioning well, as two new assistants, Leila Chalom and Rosa Farhi, in their initial letters to Paris after having started teaching at the school, specifically noted they had been impressed by the students' ability and work in handicrafts.[180]

Over the course of 1912 and 1913 the workshops continued to flourish, while the number of apprentices surpassed 100.[181] Still, Albala was growing increasingly displeased with having to run the school and manage two workshops while also supervising apprentices.[182] Unfortunately for Albala, and perhaps for her apprentices and students, the AIU never consented to provide the necessary funds for her to hire a high-caliber master seamstress.

Although she had clearly become frustrated with her superiors, Albala oversaw a major expansion of the school's vocational program. When she had arrived at the school there were only twenty-five apprentices, and over 90 percent of them worked under masters not affiliated with or located at the school. By the time she left the school in late 1913, the vocational program counted over 100 apprentices and had established two workshops. Actually, it had established three if one counts the successful carpet-weaving workshop that flourished from 1905 to 1907. Furthermore, her apprentices' products were in great demand and had helped increase her school's prestige. By any measure, Albala's work in the vocational sphere was exceptional.

Albala's Struggles with the Central Committee

Like her predecessors, Albala consistently complained to her superiors in Paris about her low salary. Upon her arrival in Baghdad, she was receiving an annual salary of 1,500 francs.[183] She complained that, like Sémach before her, she was making less than two of her assistants, who earned 1,700 francs and 2,100 francs per year, respectively.[184] Nissim Albala also sent a letter of support on behalf of his wife, informing the Central Committee that if they had known that Marie was not going to receive a raise they would not have agreed to be transferred to Baghdad.[185] Marie Albala did not receive a raise at that time, and later, in 1905, she once again requested an increase, stating that she deserved at least 1,800 francs per year.[186] By early 1906 she had received a raise to 1,700 francs, which she and her husband still considered too low.[187] It is worth noting that Nissim Albala's salary in early 1906 was 2,500 francs per year, which he also believed was far too modest for a director with fifteen years of experience working for the AIU.[188]

In late 1906, Marie Albala once again complained to the Central Committee that since a recent AIU circular had promised bonuses for directors to take up residence at important posts such as Iran and Iraq, she and her husband deserved a bonus.[189] She requested an additional 500 francs per year.[190] Albala's request was to no avail, as in a letter from November 1908 she lamented that she had not received a salary increase since January 1906.[191] By late 1910 she had received an additional 200 francs per year, bringing her total compensation to 1,900 francs per year, but she argued that a director with her experience deserved at least 2,200 francs per year.[192] The Central Committee voted Albala an increase in response to this letter, but exactly how much they increased her salary remains unclear.[193]

Following the opening of the new building, Albala once again requested a salary increase. In this instance she argued that she deserved more money because of her increased workload, even complaining that since the Central Committee refused to provide her with enough money to hire a capable master seamstress she was burdened with supervising both the masters and apprentices in the school's two vocational workshops.[194] The Central Committee refused Albala's new request, stating she had already received a significant raise the previous year.[195]

Albala issued a new request for a raise in late 1912. She noted that the school's population had increased from 200 to 780 during her nearly eight years in Baghdad, while she actually was responsible for over 1,000 students when apprentices and preschool students were included.[196] The Central Committee responded favorably to this request. Albala received an additional 200 francs per year, bringing her salary to either 2,300 or 2,400 francs per year, assuming that her previous increase, which the Central Committee had called "significant," had been for either 200 or 300 francs per year.[197] Even though she supervised more students than her husband, her salary in 1913 was still lower than his initial salary in 1905, which he had considered low.

Toward the end of her stay in Baghdad, Albala had perhaps her greatest disagreement with the Central Committee. In October 1913 the Central Committee appointed Nissim to be the new director at the Moïse Allatini Boys' School in Salonica and appointed her to be the director of the kindergarten attached to the Popular Girls' School.[198] Salonica at this time had two boys' schools, a main girls' school, and a popular girls' school. Nissim informed Bigart that the couple could not accept this post, as Marie deserved to direct the main girls' school, since she had clearly proven herself to be a superior director in Baghdad.[199] Ultimately, the Central Committee retracted the Salonica appointments and instead appointed the Albalas to direct the Boys' and Girls' Schools in the Couscoudjouk section of Istanbul.[200]

The New Director: Rebecca Bassan

Although the Albalas remained in Baghdad until January 1914, they were replaced by Isaac and Rebecca Bassan as directors of the Albert Sassoon School and Laura Kadoorie School in late November 1913.[201] Isaac Bassan was a Bulgarian national and experienced director who had led schools in Hamadan, Iran, Bursa, Gallipoli, and Aleppo. Rebecca Bassan was an Ottoman citizen who had directed schools in Bursa, Gallipoli, and Aleppo.

Interestingly, Rebecca Bassan was extremely disappointed in the state of her new school, for which she blamed her predecessor. She claimed that Albala spent only ten hours per week in the school, preferring instead to focus the vast majority of her time at the workshops.[202] In fact, Bassan referred to Albala as a "director in name only."[203] She also noted that assistants were often unsupervised and taught students merely to memorize, not to understand, academic material.[204]

According to Bassan, Albala had also allowed the school's nourishment program to suffer, which meant that many poor students were not receiving adequate meals during the school day.[205] Additionally, she claimed that the sewing instructor was paid too much for doing too little and had acted merely as Albala's personal seamstress.[206] She consequently fired the sewing teacher and replaced her with a monitor to supervise the apprentices.[207] Bassan was also critical of the state in which the Albalas had left their residence, which she and her husband inherited. She stated that the Albalas had left nothing behind and also requested an additional 1,000 francs, which she claimed is the amount the Albalas had received upon arriving in Istanbul, as an installation bonus in order to furnish her home.[208]

Finally, Bassan accused Albala of using school funds for her own purposes and falsifying budgetary reports. For instance, Bassan claimed that the school's maid never set foot in the school itself but instead spent her days working in the Albalas' home.[209] She accused Albala of charging her own personal transportation costs to the school[210] and contended that Albala profited handsomely off fines she collected from her assistants, sometimes taking home as much as thirty extra francs per week.[211] Thus, Bassan concluded, the school's finances should have been in much better shape than she found them.

The End of the Ottoman Period: 1914–1915

Although Bassan was not pleased with the state of the school she had taken over, she noted that there was great demand for its services.[212] However, she was surprised to find that many wealthy Baghdadis were averse to paying tuition for their daughters' educations and, like her predecessors, refused to budge on this issue.[213] Unfortunately, it is unclear what kind of progress she made with regard to this or any other issue as both her and her husband's correspondence say very little about the school's progress in 1914 or 1915.

However, based on a letter Rebecca Bassan wrote in 1917, just after the British arrived in Baghdad toward the latter part of World War I, it is possible to determine in very general terms what happened to the Girls', and Boys', School in Baghdad in 1914 and 1915. With the Ottoman entry into World War I in late 1914, the Ottoman government began censoring mail to and from the AIU schools in Baghdad.[214] As a result, staff at these institutions appear to have lost effective contact with the Central Committee in Paris.[215]

It is important to note that the AIU schools did not close immediately following the outbreak of the war. While it appears they lost students, Rebecca Bassan noted that the Ottoman government in Baghdad treated Jews well during early and mid-1915.[216] The community started coming under increasing pressure in late 1915 with the arrival of a new governor, though the schools remained open.[217] According to Bassan the closure of the schools was linked to a scandal involving three assistants at the Girls' School: Sultana Levy, Claire Levy, and Regine Gueron. These three unmarried women apparently scandalized the community by publicly mixing with Jewish and non-Jewish men at night.[218] In response, Rebecca Bassan imposed fines on these women.

Although the details are sketchy, it appears that these three women were in secret correspondence with Heskel Nehama, a thirty-three-year-old AIU-educated Baghdadi Jew who had previously directed the Boys' School in Kirkuk and wanted to replace Isaac Bassan as the head of the Albert Sassoon School.[219] Bassan claimed that the three women, in collusion with Nehama, used their close contacts with influential Ottoman, presumably Muslim, officials to have her husband arrested on October 16, 1915.[220] Isaac Bassan was immediately deported to Mosul, and the schools did not reopen until the British arrived in early 1917.[221] Following the schools' closures, they were transformed into hospitals until the British chased Ottoman forces from the city.[222]

Finally, Nehama never succeeded in taking over the Albert Sassoon School, as he was murdered in early 1916 while walking with Claire Levy.[223] According to Nehama's wife, Levy had been fond of singing in public, and her husband had found her walking alone one night and, not wanting to see a young woman alone on the street, offered to walk her home.[224] In contrast, Rebecca Bassan implied that the two were having an affair and that they often took night walks together.[225] Based on the limited evidence, it is impossible to ascertain the truth of their relationship.

Conclusion

As this chapter has shown, the Laura Kadoorie School not only functioned effectively during Albala's tenure from 1905 to 1913 but also continued to expand its activities until the onset of World War I. In addition to receiving a new permanent home during this period, the school established two well-regarded vocational workshops and a preschool, and the school's academic population increased by about 400 percent. Although Albala's tenure was later criticized by her successor, it is clear that her work in Baghdad had been successful. Unfortunately, the combination of war, a loss of contact with Paris, and local machinations combined to force the school to close in late 1915, ending, at least briefly, two decades of successful work and nearly continuous growth. While the school would reopen in early 1917 and continue functioning for another thirty-four years, the school's closure in 1915 marked the end of an era.

5

THE AIU GIRLS' SCHOOLS IN HILLA, MOSUL, AND BASRA, 1911–1915

This chapter shifts the focus from the Laura Kadoorie School in Baghdad to the AIU Girls' Schools in Hilla, Mosul, and Basra. Since these institutions were all founded near the end of the Ottoman period, there is much less source material available than for the Laura Kadoorie School. Furthermore, these schools were all founded relatively shortly after the AIU established boys' schools in these cities, at least when compared with the organization's history in Baghdad. As a result, this chapter aims to tell a brief recuperative history of these schools' origins, curriculums, goals, and challenges, but it cannot go into great detail on these subjects. Still, the chapter discusses how the AIU extended its network of girls' schools beyond Baghdad and should serve as a foundation for future studies on secular Jewish education outside of Baghdad in the late Ottoman and post-Ottoman periods.

The Founding of the Hilla Girls' School

Hilla is a city located south of Baghdad near the ruins of the ancient city of Babylon. In the late nineteenth and early twentieth centuries it housed a small but important Jewish community of just over 1,000.[1] In 1906, at which point the AIU's educational network in Ottoman Iraq consisted of multiple schools in Baghdad and a boys' schools, founded in 1903, in Basra, Moïse Soussa, an agent of Menahem Saleh Daniel, wrote to the Central Committee requesting a school.[2] Soussa mentioned that at this time the city had only one Talmud

Torah, which had about 150 students, 30 of whom paid tuition.[3] Furthermore, he promised that locals would provide some of the funds for the school via synagogue collections and a tax from kosher food sales.[4]

The Central Committee responded favorably to Soussa's request, and the school was opened in mid-1907, the same year the AIU established its Boys' School in Mosul. Nissim Albala, the director of the Albert Sassoon School in Baghdad, sent Heskel Nehama, formerly a monitor in Baghdad and an assistant in Basra, to direct the new school.[5] Although Daniel provided the school with a subvention, Soussa informed the Central Committee that it was already facing financial problems in August 1907.[6] These problems continued as the school admitted far more non–tuition-paying students than tuition-paying ones. For example, in 1910 the school had 173 students, only 30 of whom paid tuition.[7]

Although the school suffered financial problems, in March 1910, Menahem Daniel visited the school and was impressed with what he found. In fact, he was so pleased that he told Nehama:

> I could never express to you my great satisfaction for the solid education and instruction of these poor children who, without the school, would be plunged into ignorance and destitution like their forefathers. The intelligent manner in which you are marvelously directing the school and all the community obliges me to tell you that the Alliance should be proud to have such an experienced and devoted director who puts all of his effort into regenerating our unfortunate co-religionists. What I have just ascertained has persuaded me to write to the Alliance to send my gratitude and promise to lend it the necessary support for the creation of a girls' school in this city.[8]

It is unclear whether Nehama had hoped that Daniel would offer such assistance, but from this point forward the AIU clearly began making plans to open a girls' school in Hilla. Meanwhile, Daniel kept his promise, and less than a year later purchased a small building to be used by a future girls' school.[9]

By June 1911 Nehama had received governmental approval to open the school, which subsequently took place on the morning of Thursday June 29, 1911.[10] He mentioned that Daniel had placed the building under his own provisional control but would officially hand the property over to the AIU only once a permanent director arrived in the city.[11] The school opened with seventy-seven registered students, though seven of these girls were absent on the first day of class.[12] Although the school lacked a director, Nehama employed his wife, free of charge to the AIU, to run the school and hired a local female Hebrew teacher to aid her.[13] While he did not mention it explicitly, it is likely that his wife, who knew French, taught this subject in the school.

It is interesting to note that Nehama contended that the school's establishment was important, as it would prevent Jewish girls from attending the local Muslim girls' school.[14] By attending this latter institution, girls, in order to maintain perfect attendance, would have to violate Jewish law, as the school was open on the Jewish Sabbath.[15] This contrasted with the Baghdad Girls' School, whose establishment was not linked to a fear of Jewish girls attending non-Jewish schools, as discussed in Chapter 1. Madame Nehama's main goal, like Danon's in Baghdad sixteen years earlier, was to transform girls under her charge into what she perceived to be modern students. As was true for Danon, Nehama's first task was to ensure that her students maintained proper hygiene and adopted appropriate dress.[16] According to her husband, the thirty-five girls in the school's First Class quickly adapted to her orders.[17] The Nehamas, however, were soon ordered to leave Hilla in order to move to Kirkuk and establish yet another AIU school.[18]

Alice Abrevaya and the Hilla Girls' School, 1911–1913

Just before the Nehamas left Hilla for Kirkuk, Moïse Abrevaya and Alice Abrevaya (formerly Picciotto) were transferred from Basra to Hilla to direct the city's Boys' and Girls' Schools. Neither Moïse nor Alice had previously directed a school, though both had significant experience as assistants in AIU institutions in Ottoman Iraq. The Abrevayas were not pleased to find that Nehama had left them with much less money than they had expected to find, which forced them to borrow funds from Menahem Daniel in order to rent an adequate home.[19]

In his first letter on the state of the Boys' School, Moïse noted that it was clearly the best school in the city, though in his opinion it was only a mediocre school.[20] Meanwhile, Alice stated that she found the Girls' School's building to be in great disrepair.[21] However, she also noted that Daniel immediately ordered work done on the building, which slightly improved its condition.[22] The school had apparently lost students in the months since its establishment, as Abrevaya found only 40 students enrolled.[23] She claimed that the community probably had 100 girls who could attend the school, but many parents either preferred to keep their daughters at home or did not want to pay tuition for their education.[24] Still, she expressed confidence that student enrollment would increase.[25]

Abrevaya divided her forty students into two distinct classes and created a curriculum for them that included French, Hebrew, Arabic, and sewing[26]—a curriculum identical to that which Danon had created in Baghdad in 1895. She also mentioned that she wanted her students to spend at least two hours per day learning to sew, but since she did not have a capable monitor, the students in the First Class received only nine hours per week of instruction in this subject instead of ten.[27] It is also worth mentioning that Abrevaya lacked adequate supplies and requested that these be sent to her immediately.[28]

The students did not make a positive first impression on their new headmistress, though she seems to have expected this would be the case.[29] Abrevaya claimed that the students showed up barefoot, in torn and dirty dresses, and without having done their hair.[30] She initially sent them back to their homes to bathe and find proper clothing, but the girls returned with their parents, who informed Abrevaya that they lacked the means to provide proper school clothes for their children.[31] Abrevaya then turned to Daniel who, it seems, purchased modest but appropriate uniforms for the girls.[32] The realization that the vast majority of the community lived in poverty appears to have surprised the new director. Interestingly, the school still received high marks from the city's mayor, Hadji Namek Effendi. Abrevaya informed the Central Committee that during his visit she had tried to explain that the school was not yet in fine order, but he still asked her to admit his daughter.[33] Perhaps because of the Laura Kadoorie School's reputation, Effendi clearly believed his daughter could get a better education at an AIU school than at the local Muslim girls' school.

Although the mayor apparently thought highly of the school, in March 1912 Abrevaya lamented its lack of progress:

> Contrary to my hopes, the number of students has not increased. This had astonished me at first. I had been convinced in advance that the population would be excited about the opening of the school and would have hastened to send all of their daughters there. The brilliant results obtained in Baghdad could not fail to positively influence our coreligionists in Hilla. I needed a little time to be disabused of this idea. In spite of the deep roots that your work has planted in Baghdad, our work here still falls on deaf ears. So great are the distances and so difficult are the means of communication between the towns in this area that many of the people in Hilla, a town only 120 kilometers from Baghdad, completely ignore your school for girls in this town and still think that having girls educated is to willingly turn over their hearts to perdition.[34]

Abrevaya's letter highlights the fact that some teachers believed their tasks working on behalf of the AIU outside of Baghdad would be made easier by the strong reputation the AIU had built for itself over nearly fifty years of work. In this case, however, she realized that Hilla presented challenges that Baghdad, and likely other medium- to large-sized cities, did not. She noted that the school also suffered from rabbinical opposition and reiterated that most members of the Jewish community lived in poverty.[35]

While the school's population had not increased in late 1911 and early 1912, Abrevaya informed Bigart that her students had made great progress in reading and handicrafts.[36] She stated that the latter was important, as it would pay immediate dividends for students once they left the school.[37] Abrevaya, however, mentioned that students were struggling in language courses.[38] Interestingly, she also wrote that she had to replace an incapable monitor with a male monitor from the Boys' School.[39] Although, like her colleagues in Baghdad, she wanted to maintain an all-female staff, she was, unlike her aforementioned colleagues, unable to do so because of a complete lack of suitable candidates. It is also worth noting that Ali Reza Bey, the commander of the Thirteenth Army Corps, and J. Lorimer, the British Consul in Baghdad, visited the school in early 1912 and congratulated Abrevaya on her students' progress.[40] Perhaps these men were pleased to see any kind of modern school functioning in the city, even if it did not compare favorably with similar institutions in larger cities.

Unfortunately, Abrevaya penned only a few letters in 1912. It is clear that students in her First Class continued to make excellent progress, while those in the Second Class lagged behind, even with the help of the new male monitor.[41] Abrevaya once again emphasized the students' great progress in sewing, and even mentioned that some of the girls wanted to learn how to make their own clothes, modeled after European fashions.[42] To facilitate this task, she requested that the AIU send fashion magazines to the school.[43] Meanwhile, the school's population declined in the middle of the year to twenty-five, before once again reaching forty by November.[44] Abrevaya informed the Central Committee that the AIU needed to rethink its approach to female education in Hilla if they wanted the school to succeed. Because of widespread poverty among the Jewish community, which was exacerbated by community members moving away from the city to look for better work and opportunities in Baghdad and Basra, she advised the Central Committee to provide free tuition, materials, and clothes to students.[45] She claimed that doing this would convince most fathers to send their daughters to the school.[46]

In early 1913 Abrevaya introduced the students in her First Class to the study of basic arithmetic but, claiming they had trouble understanding even the simplest concepts, she did not expose members of the Second Class to this subject.[47] At the same time, she had divided the First Class into two divisions and mentioned that students in the second division were struggling with French pronunciation.[48] Finally, she once again lamented her inability to find suitable teachers and claimed that since it was very hard to find a mediocre female monitor in Baghdad, it would be even more difficult to do so in Hilla.[49]

The Central Committee realized that Abrevaya was struggling to manage her school and recommended that she cut down, by five hours per week, the amount of time the Second Class devoted to Hebrew lessons and instead use these hours to increase sewing instruction and introduce students to Jewish history.[50] While Abrevaya did not state that this was a bad idea in the abstract, she replied it would be impossible because it would require her to teach even more classes.[51] Such was the case even though in the early months of 1913 the school's enrollment was stagnant at forty students.[52] Abrevaya did, however, express some optimism, predicting that the school would gain new students after the Passover holiday break.[53]

Unfortunately, the Abrevayas left Hilla shortly after the Passover holiday and ultimately were appointed to direct the Boys' and Girls' Schools in Hamadan, Iran. Alice Abrevaya's time in Hilla had not been pleasant. She had spent much of it pleading for a 200 franc salary increase, lamenting the town's poverty, and trying to find ways to attract more students to her school.[54] Although she succeeded in creating a stable curriculum, she was unable to replicate in Hilla the success of the organization's work in Baghdad.

Rosa Farhi and the Hilla Girls' School, 1913–1914

In May 1913, Noury and Rosa Farhi, who were brother and sister, replaced Moïse and Alice Abrevaya as directors of the city's Boys' and Girls' Schools. Like her predecessor, Rosa Farhi noted the poor first impression her new students made on her. She claimed that Jewish girls in Hilla lacked energy and confidence, in contrast to the young Jewish girls in Baghdad, who were lively.[55] Farhi stated that in previous generations Jewish girls in Baghdad had been totally controlled by their parents but, thanks to the AIU's work, they had become emancipated from tyrannical parental control.[56] In contrast, Jewish girls in Hilla, aged eight to ten, were not permitted even to walk the street unless fully covered, and she complained that she had met an eleven-year-old girl who had been forced to marry a forty-five-year-old man.[57] She claimed that in Baghdad most Jewish girls married at eighteen to twenty-two, though it is unclear if this had become the norm for all girls or only those who graduated from the Laura Kadoorie School.[58] Unsurprisingly, Farhi immediately came to view Jewish society in Hilla as backward, especially when compared to Baghdad.

Farhi retained Abrevaya's class organization structure and, like her predecessor, noted the progress in French among students in the top division in the First Class, though she stated that they struggled to pronounce the language.[59] However, she appears to have struggled to get the First Class's second-division students to stop speaking Arabic to one another during French lessons.[60] Further, she claimed that she had made very little progress, especially with the second division, with regard to arithmetic.[61] One bright spot Farhi identified was student cleanliness and appearance, which she proudly informed the Central Committee had greatly improved during her first six weeks at the school.[62]

As had also been the case for her predecessor, Farhi struggled to increase the school's enrollment. However, in one of her letters she shed some light on this issue, noting that poverty had led many families to send their daughters, at a very young age, to work alongside local seamstresses to earn extra money for their families.[63] Farhi expressed optimism that with time this would fade, and claimed that if, in Baghdad, the community's economic prosperity was because of the Albert Sassoon School, then that community's moral regeneration was a result of the work of the Laura Kadoorie School.[64] She thus believed that the Hilla Girls' School would, like its sister institution in Baghdad, eventually change local culture, leading to an increase in the school's popularity. She was also pleased to note, in November 1913, that she had replaced her male monitor with a former student from the Laura Kadoorie School, whom she hoped would be able to more capably instruct the school's Second Class.[65]

At the start of the 1914 school year, Farhi altered her school's class organization by fusing the two divisions in the First Class and creating two divisions in the Second Class.[66] She stated that this reorganization resulted from her inability to devote equal time to the students in the First Class's divisions and the need to create separate divisions in the Second Class because of newly admitted students.[67] Farhi also explained that because of the poor first impression they had made on her, she had been trying to help her students become more intellectually active.[68] However, she was failing in this effort, for which she blamed local customs that forced girls to remain secluded at home or veiled when in public.[69] She hypothesized that such treatment limited her students' public interactions and hindered the development of their observational abilities.[70]

Farhi reported great progress in all fields of study over the course of the first three months of 1914, part of which she attributed to greater funding from the Central Committee.[71] At the same time, she stated that the city was still experiencing an exodus of Jewish residents because of the city's lack of water.[72] Unfortunately, Noury Farhi had fallen ill in March and had left Hilla for Baghdad.[73] Although Rosa remained in Hilla for a short time thereafter, she eventually joined her brother, leaving the Girls' School in the hands of her monitor.[74] Jewish notables in the city made a plea to the AIU to send new directors to the city, but the Central Committee was apparently unable to do so.[75] It is unknown exactly when the schools closed, but it is clear from a later letter that they were shut down either just prior to or during World War I. Unlike the schools in Baghdad, the schools did not reopen when the British captured Hilla.[76]

During its nearly three years of existence, the Hilla Girls' School impressed some local notables, both Jewish and non-Jewish, but the school ultimately failed to attract significant numbers of students. Beginning with seventy-seven students in June 1911, at the end of 1912, the school counted only forty students, seven of whom paid tuition; at the end of 1913, the school counted forty-eight students, four of whom paid tuition.[77] The school also struggled to retain directors, who despised living in Hilla. It is impossible to predict what would have happened had Noury Farhi not come down with an illness or had the Ottoman government not entered World War I. However, although the school appears to have been functioning at its best in early 1914, it is doubtful that it would have ever experienced the kind of growth in enrollment or reputation that the Laura Kadoorie School in Baghdad experienced.

The AIU's Arrival in Mosul, 1906–1908

The province of late Ottoman Mosul housed multiple small Jewish communities.[78] Within the city of Mosul, located well north of Baghdad, the Jewish population numbered a little more than 2,000 in the late nineteenth and early twentieth centuries.[79] This was twice the size of Hilla's population but a tiny fraction of Baghdad's. The modern educational landscape in Mosul was dominated by Christian, mostly Catholic, institutions that included both boys' and girls' schools.[80] Although the Jewish community had a large Talmud Torah, it lacked a modern school until the arrival of the AIU.[81]

Sometime in 1906, Elyahu Sayegh, the Chief Rabbi of Mosul, used his contacts at the French Consulate in Mosul to contact the AIU's Central Committee to request the organization consider establishing a school in his city.[82] After writing to the AIU, Sayegh began collecting money for this project and also rallied local notables to back his plan.[83] Although it took nearly a year, in August 1907, the Central Committee agreed to send a director to establish an AIU Boys' School in Mosul.[84]

The Central Committee chose to send Maurice Sidi, who had previously served as an assistant at the Boys' Schools in Tunis and Soussa (Tunisia). Sidi immediately encountered problems with the local governor, Mustapha Bey, who informed him he did not have permission to establish a new school.[85] In response, Sidi claimed he had been sent to take over a Midrash school that had existed for 200 years, though the governor retorted that the government did not recognize that school either.[86] Although Sidi mentioned that he enjoyed the support of the local French consul, he predicted the school would experience difficulties with the governor.[87]

Indeed, although on January 2, 1908, the school opened with 258 students to a great communal celebration, including women, Sidi soon faced governmental opposition to the AIU's presence.[88] On January 13, 1908, Bey warned local Jews not to send their children to the school.[89] Sidi believed Bey wanted to close the school, but Bey told him he merely wanted Sidi to provide a document from Istanbul certifying the school had a right to exist.[90]

In addition to issues with the government, the school also faced disappointment from local community members. Sidi stated that when he was rallying support for the school prior to its opening, Sayegh had promised the community that the institution would not only feed and clothe all of its students, but that its presence would also immediately enrich the mostly impoverished community.[91] Because the school had not lived up to their expectations, many community members had apparently become disillusioned; at the same time, they felt pressured by the local government to have nothing to do with the school.[92]

Bey continued to speak out against the school's existence throughout the winter and early spring. Sidi claimed that Bey opposed the school because he considered it to be a "French organization" dispensing money to Ottoman citizens.[93] The governor's views appear to have been consistent with those of his colleagues, though the AIU had not faced such strong governmental opposition in Baghdad or Hilla. However, as will be discussed, it faced similar, though brief, problems in Basra. Fortunately for Sidi, the French consul continued to be a stalwart defender of his institution.[94] Meanwhile, the school lost sixty impoverished students in March, as they, or more likely their parents, concluded that a modern education would not pay immediate dividends.

Less than two weeks later, Governor Bey placed notices on roads and in synagogues prohibiting Jews from sending their sons to the Boys' School.[95] According to these notices, violators would face a month in prison and a fine equivalent to twenty-three francs.[96] Although the school appears not to have closed, even temporarily, during this period, in May Sidi noted that government officials in Mosul were displeased to see Jewish boys walking in the street and in shops reciting French phrases.[97]

Tensions soon died down, and for a time the school's work proceeded without harassment.[98] By early September, clearly in the immediate aftermath of the CUP Revolution, a new governor, Zeki Pasha, had arrived who was supportive of the school.[99] Unfortunately, less than a week later local police came to the school, closed it down, and arrested Sidi.[100] The new governor immediately had Sidi released, claiming to have received a document from Istanbul recognizing the school's right to exist.[101] After less than three weeks, Sidi reopened the school on September 22.[102] Pasha later visited the school, alongside the local Minister of Education and a few civil servants, and during his visit he urged local Jewish notables, who also attended the ceremony, to provide the school with economic assistance.[103]

Pasha's clear support for the school raises the question of why local police had arrested Sidi for operating the school. Unfortunately, the letters in the AIU archive do not answer this question. Although not specifically addressing this issue, in her book *Mosul before Iraq*, Sarah Shields contends that in the aftermath of the CUP Revolution of July 1908 Mosul was thrown into confusion, with local officials unsure of which orders to follow.[104] Based on her findings, it likely that the local police were carrying out the orders, or perhaps the wishes, of the previous governor. In any case, from mid-September 1908 onward, the AIU enjoyed the support of the local Ottoman governors.

The Founding of the Mosul Girls' School, 1908–1912

As with the Boys' School, Rabbi Sayegh appears to have been instrumental in at least making a future girls' school a subject of discussion. As early as July 1908, he mentioned in an interview with the newspaper *Israel's Messenger* that he hoped the AIU would soon establish such a school in his city:

> But the idea soon struck me that my proposition to the Alliance to open a school to teach the young boys was incomplete and ineffective as long as the girls' tuition was left unprovided for. I at once wrote to the Alliance on the subject and pointed out to them the great necessity of providing

> means by which to educate the female sex as well, inasmuch as the training of the young ones depended mainly upon the training they receive in their girlhood. The President of the Alliance, Marcus Leven, has sent a very courteous reply to my letter saying that he is quite with me that we must educate the girls also; but as the account for the past year was closed, he regretted that he could not sanction further grants until the next year.[105]

In this interview Sayegh was clearly implying that girls' education was the necessary complement to boys' education in order to effect real social change among his city's Jewish community. By making this link, even implicitly, Sayegh was voicing similar opinions as male teachers at the Albert Sassoon Boys' School in Baghdad in the late 1880s and early 1890s.

Sayegh's letter failed to generate any serious discussion of opening a girls' school in Mosul, even though Leven responded by voicing his approval for the future creation of such an institution. The issue arose again in late 1909 in a letter Sidi wrote to the Central Committee. In this letter Sidi argued that Mosul was the most backward of all the towns in which the AIU operated a school and, partly because of that, was not yet ready for a girls' school.[106] However, he also mentioned that he had succeeded in gaining the trust of the local government and some local Jewish notables and planned to return to the matter shortly.[107] He ended his letter by imploring the Central Committee to consider constructing a school in the future, as he believed only an AIU school could rescue the city's girls from their deplorable conditions.[108]

In 1910 Sidi traveled to Baghdad, where he met and married Joya Simhon. Simhon, now Joya Sidi, moved back to Mosul and took up a provisional position teaching Hebrew in the Boys' School.[109] With an experienced female AIU teacher in the city it was only a matter of time until the Central Committee ordered the establishment of a girls' school. Although neither Maurice nor Joya Sidi's correspondence throughout 1911 mentioned plans to open such an institution, on February 21, 1912, the Central Committee informed Joya that she had been tasked with opening a Girls' School.[110]

Sidi did not mention when the school opened, but based on the date of her letter announcing its establishment, the first day of classes took place in late April.[111] Sidi informed the Central Committee that the school had opened with about thirty students, but an additional sixty-six had showed up the second day.[112] She claimed it had been difficult to recruit students because most families did not understand the benefits of educating their daughters.[113] Further, she stated she had stopped trying to convince mothers to send their daughters to the school, as mothers' opinions counted for nothing in Mosul. She instead focused all her efforts on lobbying fathers.[114] The school opened with three teachers, including Sidi. Sidi had hired two young local female Christian instructors to teach sewing and embroidering, while she taught Hebrew and French.[115] Interestingly, the initial curriculum did not include Arabic, likely because Sidi could not find an adequate local teacher. Indeed, she mentioned that the only indigenous women in the city capable of teaching on their own in a classroom setting were Christian.[116] She also claimed that, unfortunately, most of these women were afraid to enter the Jewish quarter and thus would not consider accepting a job at her school.[117] Sidi divided the school's students into two classes, one of forty students and another of fifty-six.[118] It is worth mentioning that, for financial reasons, the Girls' School did not have its own building but instead occupied two rooms in the Boys' School, though the rooms were completed separated from the rest of the building.[119] Also, the Girls' School opened without chairs or desks, so students had to sit on mats on the floor.[120]

While Sidi had previously mentioned how difficult it had been to convince parents to enroll students in her school, at least before it opened, by mid-May she had begun refusing to admit students because she lacked the room to accommodate new enrollees.[121] She informed her superiors that the students were making excellent progress in terms of their dress and cleanliness, though she stated that her two hires required constant supervision.[122] In addition to her teachers' struggles, she asserted that her students were so backward that they had trouble counting. For example, she wrote, "In order to say 12, they say 10 and 2; for 15 they say 10 and 5, etc."[123] According to Sidi this was just one example of her students' need for significant AIU support, though she also claimed that the Jewish community of Mosul was the most backward of any of the Jewish communities in Mesopotamia.[124]

By mid-June, Sidi asserted her students were making great progress, especially with regard to sewing and embroidering.[125] Indeed, the governor had visited the school earlier in the month and been impressed by the students' abilities in these pursuits, and also by their proper appearance.[126] This, however, was the last report Sidi submitted, as she and Maurice left Mosul in early July. They transferred to Beirut in order to take over as directors at the AIU Girls' and Boys' Schools in that city.[127]

Rachel Sasson and the Mosul Girls' School, 1912–1915

The Sidis were replaced as directors of the Mosul Boys' and Girls' Schools by David and Rachel Sassoon. David was born in Tehran in 1887, and after receiving his education had worked as an assistant at the Cairo and Tantah Boys'

Schools.[128] Rachel was born in Istanbul in 1890 and had worked as an assistant in Tantah, where she met and married David.[129]

Following the Sidis' departure, the Girls' School was closed for several months.[130] The Sassons arrived in Mosul in November 1912, at which point the correspondence trail picks up again. Rachel Sasson noted in her inaugural letter from Mosul that the Girls' School occupied one room in the Boys' School and had 110 students, though about 40 more girls wanted to enroll.[131] As they had under Sidi, the girls still lacked furniture and sat on the floor while in class.[132] Sasson also mentioned that the two instructors Sidi had previously hired had accepted employment from the AIU only because they were on break from the Protestant girls' school in which they worked and, thus, no longer worked for the organization.[133] Sasson had tried to find capable indigenous teachers, but to no avail. She also requested that the Central Committee order Marie Albala, at the Laura Kadoorie School in Baghdad, to send her an AIU-trained assistant.[134] Finally, Sasson mentioned that she had located a suitable building a couple of minutes from the Boys' School that could serve as a temporary home for her school, but she needed approval before entering into rental negotiations.[135]

Throughout the remainder of 1912, Sasson struggled to get the Girls' School into decent working order. In late November she mentioned she had reached out to some local Christian girls regarding monitorial positions at the school, but everyone had turned down her offer because of the distance between the Christian and Jewish quarters, and the need to travel through the Muslim quarter.[136] At the same time, the school had closed for a short time because the temperature in the building had become too cold to hold classes.[137] By late December, Sasson had finally managed to hire a sixteen-year-old monitor from a British missionary school, though her new hire required constant supervision.[138] This girl, however, allowed Sasson to divide the students into two workable classes.[139] The First Class consisted of girls aged twelve to fourteen, and the Second Class consisted of girls aged seven to eleven.[140] These two classes continued to share one room. During this time, the Central Committee had ordered Sasson to incorporate Arabic into the curriculum and to spend her entire day teaching in the classroom, which had begun to take its toll.[141]

It appears that the Central Committee took issue with the tone of Sasson's letter from December 29, 1912, as her husband explained that although she had showed some inexperience in writing the letter, she was devoted to her work and to the AIU.[142] David Sasson also informed the Central Committee that he had engaged in negotiations to rent a four- to five-room house but would require 920 francs to pay the year's rent, which was required in advance.[143]

Although space remained an issue, the school's population had declined markedly in late 1912 and early 1913. In early January, enrollment had dipped to fifty, though it increased to seventy-six by the middle of the month.[144] The BAIU for 1912 stated that by the end of the year sixty students were enrolled in the Girls' School, none of them paying tuition.[145] Rachel Sasson attributed this drop to two factors. First, she claimed that many older girls had entered the school out of curiosity but had not re-enrolled after the winter break.[146] Second, many poor girls had enrolled in the school believing they would receive free food and clothing, as poor boys in the Boys' School did.[147] When this did not happen, they stopped attending.[148]

As a result of losing so many poor students, Sasson implored her superiors to consider sending extra money to Mosul to help feed and clothe impoverished students at the Girls' School. She linked the organization's refusal to clothe students to the students' continued lack of cleanliness and, as a result, hired a woman to come each morning to help wash and groom some of the students.[149] By February, the Girls' School's enrollment had increased again to ninety-nine: twenty-seven in the First Class, and seventy-two in the Second Class, which was divided into two divisions.[150] As a result of the school's growth it once again occupied two rooms in the Boys' School's building.[151] Sasson noted that she had hired a second monitor and that students were making solid progress in counting numbers and in learning the Hebrew, Arabic, and French alphabets.[152] It was also during this time, in January and February 1913, that the Girls' School finally ordered the construction of chairs and desks for its students.[153] By this time, however, the lack of an adequate building had badly injured the school's reputation and was hindering students' academic progress.[154]

By early May the Central Committee had voted to send a small sum to Mosul to feed and clothe poor students, though it had not settled on a specific amount. Sasson requested 500 to 600 francs annually to help feed and clothe 50 to 60 students.[155] She mentioned that she had raised 40 francs in tuition, as 30 of the 100 girls had begun paying a token amount to attend.[156] Bigart, on behalf of the Central Committee, later ordered Sasson to raise 100 francs via tuition and local donations, but still did not state the exact sum the Committee's members were willing to send.[157] Sasson made one more attempt to secure this money in August but appears never to have been able to induce her superiors to send her a significant contribution.[158]

By mid-May David Sasson had succeeded in renting a small building for the Girls' School.[159] The school moved to this new building in mid-June, allowing Rachel Sasson to divide her students into three groups of twenty each, in addition to overseeing a forty-five child preschool.[160] During the move, the school finally received the furniture Sasson had ordered.[161] As a result of these positive developments, Sasson noted that the school experienced an increase in prestige.[162] Further, she claimed her students had made great progress in terms of their cleanliness and discipline and stated that these traits, once acquired, tended to make it easier for girls to achieve academic goals.[163] Sasson, however, was still struggling to run the school and once again requested the Central Committee to send her an assistant.[164] In addition to her Christian monitors lacking adequate training and experience, Sasson lamented that they were absent each Sunday because of the Christian Sabbath.[165]

Although she did not discuss it in her letters, Sasson experienced a tragedy in the summer of 1913. In July she gave birth to a son, who passed away shortly afterward.[166] Even so, Sasson continued to focus on improving her school. In August, in response to her request for an assistant being rejected by the Central Committee, she wrote to her superiors asking if the Girls' School could share a female assistant with the Boys' School.[167] This request was clearly out of desperation, as the Central Committee was not likely to approve a female assistant working even part time at the Boys' School. Meanwhile, David Sasson had apparently reached out to Maurice Sidi, now in Beirut, to find a suitable monitor for the Mosul Girls' School.[168] It is unclear why Sasson had not looked to Baghdad instead. In any case, Sidi located someone he believed to be an ideal candidate.[169]

Unfortunately, the Central Committee refused to provide funds for a new monitor, as evidenced by Rachel Sasson's letters in November and December requesting eighty francs per year to hire Sidi's candidate.[170] Even without further support from Paris, the school's students continued to progress, and its reputation continued to increase in late 1913. For instance, Sasson proudly noted that the local community had provided the school with a rabbi to teach Hebrew.[171] She stated this was important because it showed the kind of trust community members placed in her administration, as a male teacher in a girls' school would previously have been unthinkable.[172]

Another indication of the school's solid progress was its enrollment. By the end of 1913, Sasson stated that the school had 120 to 130 students, though the number in the BAIU for the year was 115.[173] The BAIU was perhaps inaccurate, or did not include all students who attended the attached preschool. It is also worth noting that the BAIU stated that ninety of the school's students paid tuition.[174] While this number may have been technically accurate, Sasson wrote that she collected only sixty francs in tuition, which means parents of paying students contributed only two-thirds of one franc per year, on average.[175] These data suggest that the BAIU's numbers cannot be accepted at face value, and that Sasson, like Danon in Baghdad in the mid- to late 1890s, was more concerned with nurturing a culture of payment for education than in using such payments as a key way to fund the school's operations.

Over the first half of 1914, the school experienced further success. Most notably, it attracted about a dozen new Muslim students, one of whom was the daughter of the city's mayor, Amine Effendi.[176] Interestingly, Sasson informed the Central Committee that Amine Effendi was very impressed with the AIU's concept of Jewish solidarity and held the organization's work in the highest of esteem.[177] Further, the local government had offered to provide funds for the school to recruit and employ a professionally trained Arabic teacher and a master seamstress from either Baghdad or Ottoman Syria.[178]

Unfortunately, it is impossible to know what kind of progress the school continued to make in mid- to late 1914 or whether the local government ultimately followed through in providing financial support. Little of Sasson's correspondence from the first part of the year discussed academic developments, though in her last letter, from July, she stated that her students had made progress in all three languages and in sewing.[179] It appears from David Sasson's letters that the schools remained open through at least early 1916, though in late 1915 they suffered a loss of students.[180] What is clear is that, like the Laura Kadoorie School, the Mosul Girls' School was functioning well on the eve of World War I. Indeed, as already described, the school had even managed to gain the support of the local government, a remarkable achievement considering the Boys' School's initial struggles with local authorities.

Late Ottoman Basra and Its Jewish Community

Basra was arguably the Ottoman Iraqi city most transformed by profound international economic changes that took place in the nineteenth century. Partly as a result of the formal British takeover of India in the 1850s and the completion of the Suez Canal in 1869, in the mid– to late nineteenth century Basra transformed from a regional Arab market town into a conduit for international trade between the Ottoman and British empires.[181] Most important, it was the only Ottoman Iraqi port city and so facilitated sea-borne import and export traffic in the region. Like Baghdad, it had a large expatriate community and also housed an important Jewish community.

While Basra's Jewish community had been influential in the eighteenth century, at least in local affairs, its importance, and population, dipped a bit in the first half of the nineteenth century before rebounding in the 1860s.[182] As the city became a more important regional trade center, the Jewish community in the city both grew and prospered. By 1913, about 5,000 Jews lived in Basra, not counting foreigners, and the community included some of the most prosperous merchants in the region.[183] Although Ottoman Jewish traders in Basra prospered as a result of the rise of British commercial and military power in the Indian Ocean, the historian Hana Batatu cautions against attributing the group's success to British policy.[184] In fact, Jewish and British merchants were often chief rivals in this region throughout this period.[185]

Founding the Basra Girls' School

Increasing prosperity as well as interaction with both Ottoman and foreign officials, and businessmen, influenced the community's leadership to establish two Talmud Torahs between 1880 and 1888.[186] Additionally, a modern Boys' School opened in 1890. From the school's inception, the city's leadership looked to both the AIU and AJA for support, though neither organization was willing to provide consistent financial or material backing in terms of personnel. Although the school enjoyed strong governmental support, in the eyes of the Jewish community it struggled to overcome an early scandal and, in order to gain rabbinical support, came to employ multiple rabbis as instructors.[187] By the end of the 1890s, the school had become a hybrid religious and secular institution with no clear direction.[188] At this point, however, the AIU began to take a more active interest in the city's Jewish community's fortunes. Hoping to increase its own prestige throughout Ottoman Iraq outside of Baghdad, the AIU, when invited, agreed to take over control of the school.[189] Thus, in late 1903, the AIU established its first school in Basra, under the direction of Jacques Behar, formerly an assistant at the Albert Sassoon School in Baghdad.[190] After having operated for nearly forty years in Baghdad, the AIU had finally begun to spread its influence to other parts of Ottoman Iraq.

Interestingly, while Basra received an AIU Boys' School in 1903, its Girls' School would not be established until 1913. Why this took so long remains unclear. In a letter from mid-1905, Behar mentioned that he had established a provisional girls' school for reading and writing Hebrew and for simple handicraft training under the direction of a young Baghdadi Jewish woman who had moved to Basra to escape the cholera epidemic in Baghdad the previous year.[191] About fifty students met in a synagogue for instruction. However, Behar did not refer to this letter again until a year and a half later, and never discussed what happened to the provisional school.[192] He had asked the Central Committee to help fund the construction of a building for a girls' school, but its members must have rejected this idea and refused to consider converting his provisional school into a formal AIU institution.[193] Based on a later letter, the AIU may have balked at providing support, as the Ottoman government in Basra had, for a period of time, questioned the legality of the Basra Boys' School's existence.[194]

Although the Boys' School in Basra consistently attracted students from 1903 to 1913, it appears that the community's financial troubles ruled out establishing a girls' school. According to Moïse Abrevaya, who succeeded Behar as the school's director, the community had suffered a major shortfall of revenue starting in 1906 as a result of tribal revolts in and around Basra, which had hurt commerce.[195] When, in mid-1911, the Central Committee expressed interest in establishing a girls' school, as long as it received significant support from the local community, Basra's Jewish community's leadership voted against doing so because of the community's financial distress.[196] The Kadoorie family also reached out to the Central Committee in 1909, offering assistance to create a school for 500 to 600 girls in the city, but this plan appears to have failed to gain any traction.[197]

At some point, likely in 1912, the Boys' School had begun accepting female students to study in a girls' class taught by a former male student.[198] By February 1913, the class had sixty students.[199] Moïse Ittah, Abrevaya's successor as director, stated that a great demand existed in the Jewish community for a girls' school, and since one did not exist many Jewish girls had enrolled in local Christian girls' schools.[200] Thus, unlike in Baghdad, Hilla, and even Mosul, with its strong missionary presence, it appears that one factor that influenced the AIU to consider establishing a girls' school in Basra was that Christian educational institutions were attracting significant numbers of Jewish girls.

By early 1913 the community's finances had improved, leading Ittah to conclude that its members would be willing and able to provide significant support to a girls' school.[201] At this time, Ittah described two possible ways in which a school could be founded. The first, and in his opinion the easiest way, would be for the Central Committee to fund a journey for Ittah to travel to AIU girls' schools throughout the Levant in search of a wife who could return to the city with him to act as a school's founder and director.[202] A second option would be to somehow find a suitable director elsewhere and send her to Basra.[203] The Central Committee ultimately went with the latter option.

Ittah spent much of the summer searching for a suitable building and a director to establish the school. Meanwhile, because of the community's relative wealth, at least compared with Hilla and Mosul, the Central Committee demanded, and received, a promise from the local Jewish community's leadership that the latter would not only pay the director's salary but also cover additional school expenses.[204] Immediately after the Basra Jewish community's leadership accepted the Central Committee's demands, Ittah drafted a letter to the Grand Rabbi in Istanbul requesting that the latter use his connections to gain Ottoman approval for the establishment of a girls' school.[205]

Although the school's legality seems to have still been in question, Rebecca Zilberstein, a nineteen-year-old woman from Haifa, arrived in the city in November 1913 to take over the girls' class in preparation for the establishment of the Girls' School.[206] Ittah noted that in addition to Jewish families, several notable Muslim families were waiting with anticipation for the establishment of a girls' school and hoped to have their daughters admitted to the new institution.[207] It is unclear whether Zilberstein was to be, and ultimately ended up being, the school's director, though evidence points in that direction. In a letter, Ittah stated he had hired a Christian woman who had experience running a Protestant girls' school in Mosul as the director, but Zilberstein's salary of 1,600 francs per month matches the number Ittah mentioned for the school's leader.[208] Additionally, prior to the end of World War I, Zilberstein is the only woman to write letters regarding the school's activities.

The Girls' School's opening was unfortunately delayed by several weeks as Ittah struggled to find a suitable building to rent. The building he had planned to lease turned out to be rented out to a local Protestant school, the director of which paid twice the amount Ittah had offered.[209] Since they were competing for some of the same students, the director of the Protestant school may have been hoping to delay the opening of a new AIU institution.

The Basra Girls' School, 1913–1915

The Girls' School ultimately opened on either December 25 or, more likely, December 24, 1913. The school was initially housed in a small building, so only 120 students were initially enrolled, although, according to Ittah, 300 had requested admission.[210] Students were initially divided into three classes. The First Class had fifteen students, all of whom had either studied at the Laura Kadoorie School in Baghdad or at a Catholic school and were thus conversant in basic French.[211] These students studied French, Arabic, Hebrew, sewing, geography, history, and Jewish history.[212] The Second Class had forty students, all of whom had spent the previous year in the girls' class at the Boys' School. The Third Class had sixty-five students, none of whom had any previous academic experience.[213]

According to Zilberstein, the school's opening was met with great excitement from the community:

> Everyone in the city greeted the opening of the school with great enthusiasm. All the Jewish families took their daughters out of Christian schools in order to send them to us. Others have recalled their daughters from Baghdad. Everyone, rich and poor, is rushing to attend the school.[214]

Further, she noted that the girls made a great impression on her but required guidance:

> The new students give me a lot of satisfaction. They are calm, obedient, and are avid learners. But they have some very bizarre habits. Their dress is bizarre, their hairstyles extraordinary, and so I have concerned myself with simplifying all of this.
>
> I have ordered them to wear black overalls and to style their hair properly. Almost half of my students have already adopted this uniform and I hope that after one or two weeks I will have achieved my goal. But they are especially lacking in manners. They are little savages that must be subjected to kindness and leniency.
>
> With a lot of work and patience they will certainly become a new enlightened and polite generation that is very different from the previous generation in Basra. This is my greatest desire.[215]

Like other female teachers at AIU girls' schools, Zilberstein was both impressed and shocked by her initial interactions with local Jewish girls in Ottoman Iraq. But, like her colleagues, rather than despair she set out to change both their appearance and mindset, with a goal of effecting generational change.

Although the school's establishment appears to have proceeded smoothly, it immediately faced two key obstacles. In February, the school was ordered to close by the local Minister of Education because it lacked permission to exist, though the local administrative council delayed this order until the matter could be examined.[216] It appears that the matter was resolved in the AIU's favor, as the school remained open. While the investigation was taking place, Ittah attempted to find a permanent home for the school, but he was unable to rent the building he found most suitable. It turns out the French government had provided funds to French Catholic priests to rent the locale for their own school.[217] Thus, the AIU was undermined, at least in this instance, by its own home government's support for a Christian school in Basra. It appears, however, that the Central Committee blamed Ittah for failing to finalize negotiations before the Catholic priests became involved.[218] Unfortunately, the archival record does not mention which building the school ended up renting during this period.

The lack of an adequate building explains why, by May, the school's enrollment had grown by only two, to 122.[219] By this time, Zilberstein had modified the classes a little, slightly decreasing the size of the First Class and increasing the size of the Second.[220] She noted that the school's greatest success to this point was that its curriculum, and her direction, had helped students become more lively and extroverted.[221] Zilberstein also claimed that her emphasis on cleanliness and proper attire had not only resonated with her students but also with many of their mothers.[222] Finally, she informed the Central Committee that while at first many students skipped school on Friday to help their mothers prepare for the Sabbath, nearly all students now attended class regularly on Friday.[223]

By July, the school was functioning well, though Zilberstein wrote of her students' struggles to learn to sew properly. The school had initially hired a native Baghdadi woman to teach both sewing and Arabic. This woman had spent time in Bombay and had a reputation as a capable seamstress and excellent speaker of English and Arabic.[224] She was paid a high initial salary, equivalent to what an assistant would make, which was likely close to the 1,600 francs that Zilberstein earned.[225] Unfortunately, the teacher turned out to be ill suited to working in a classroom and was fired, at which point Zilberstein and the school's Hebrew teacher, a local woman, worked jointly to teach sewing.[226] Zilberstein asserted that she planned to look for former graduates of the Laura Kadoorie School who could move to Basra to teach sewing and Arabic.[227]

But no additional letters were penned in 1914. A letter from August 1915 discussed the school's fate following the Ottoman entry into World War I and the subsequent British occupation of Basra. According to Zilberstein, upon the Ottoman entry into the war the city's Boys' School was transformed into a military hospital, while the Girls' School was turned into a workshop where she and her students made items for the hospital.[228] She also noted that the Jewish community suffered greatly, as some men were called into service and others took their families and fled the city.[229]

This all changed on November 22, 1914, when the British arrived in the city. From this point forward the Jewish community, which welcomed the arrival of the British, prospered, and the schools reverted back to AIU educational institutions with full enrollments.[230] In fact, Zilberstein claimed that students' progress in 1915 exceeded that of 1914. She also advised her superiors to introduce English into the school's curriculum now that the British were in charge of the area.[231] Toward the end of her letter she expressed optimism about the school's future work in the city:

> This new generation of women, thanks to our school and the arrival of the British, will be very advanced. Our great hope is to transform these girls into future mothers of model families, into women with attractive and kind interiors, into women able to provide good advice to their husbands and, especially, able to provide education to their children.[232]

Unlike what occurred in other parts of Ottoman Iraq, World War I had only a limited and short-lived negative impact on the Basra Girls' School's progress. Zilberstein's last letter indicates she felt energized by the arrival of the British and believed that the school's, and the community's, best days were ahead.

Conclusion

The expansion of AIU girls' schools beyond Baghdad to the cities of Ottoman Iraq took place sporadically between 1907 and 1913, with mixed results. In Hilla, a poor town near Baghdad with a declining Jewish population, the Girls' School struggled to attract and retain both students and teachers. The school ultimately closed at some point in 1914 and was never reopened. The experience in Mosul was different, as after struggling initially the Girls' School succeeded in creating a market for education. This institution faced significant obstacles during the war but appears to have continued to function. The Girls' School in Basra is, in some ways, the most interesting case study. As the second most important Jewish community in Ottoman Iraq, at least in terms of wealth and influence, one might think that Basra would have been the first city outside of Baghdad to receive a girls' school. In fact, it was the third, although once established the school gained immediate support from the community, which provided it with far more financial support than the communities in Hilla and Mosul had been able to do.

Despite the mixed results, the AIU's expansion can be considered successful overall. On the eve of World War I, the organization looked poised to continue to act as the most significant cultural and educational influence on Jewish girls and women in this region, especially those from the middle and upper classes.

CONCLUSION

In this book I have attempted to tell a recuperative yet analytical history of the AIU's girls' schools in Ottoman Iraq. Although I have tried to provide adequate historical context throughout this work, as this is the first study on this topic I have focused intensively on discussing specific developments within the schools in this area. This final chapter, then, presents an excellent opportunity to concisely place some of these developments in broader Ottoman and Arab Jewish context before concluding with some final thoughts about the organization's work in Ottoman Iraq.

Some Comparative Notes on the AIU Girls' School in Baghdad

One of the key themes throughout this book's chapters has been tuition. As discussed in Chapter 2, in its first five years of existence, the AIU Girls' School in Baghdad was notable for its director's unwillingness to accept non–tuition-paying students. However, as the school expanded, future directors became far more willing to accept nonpaying students. By 1908 nonpaying students had almost reached parity with tuition-paying students, and by 1911 the former had surpassed the latter. Interestingly, the schools' experience in this regard differed sharply from its sister institution in the Galata section of Istanbul. Esther Benbassa has found that while the Galata Girls' School, founded in 1877, had more nonpaying than paying students in its first twenty years of existence, by the first decade of the twentieth century the situation has dramatically changed. In fact, by 1912, around 82 percent of the school's expenses were covered by student tuition.[1] This differed markedly from the Laura Kadoorie School in Baghdad, where tuition in 1913 covered just over 40 percent of total expenses.[2]

Why did the Galata and Baghdad Girls' Schools have differing experiences? One possible part of the explanation is that while Istanbul's Jewish community was only slightly larger than Baghdad's Jewish community, its members were wealthier. Furthermore, Istanbul housed numerous quality girls' schools during this period, including government-run institutions. While Baghdad did experience an increase in the total number of girls' schools during this period, the Laura Kadoorie School in Baghdad remained the top such institution in the city and appears to have been the only one to which Jewish parents, even poor ones, would consider sending their daughters.

Shifting the focus to social change, one must remember that as an AIU institution, the Laura Kadoorie School was tasked with working toward the "moral regeneration" of the local Jewish community. As discussed in several chapters, one key way the school's staff contributed to this goal was in their fight against child marriage. It does appear that they succeeded in increasing the average age of brides, at least for girls who attended the school. The evidence on the impact of AIU schools on this issue in other parts of the Arab world is mixed. According to Rachel Simon, improved access to education appeared to make little difference for marriage ages in Libya during this period.[3] However, Aron Rodrigue's analytical sourcebook includes a letter from a female teacher in Fez, Morocco, who informs Bigart that several of her students' mothers had refused to marry their daughters off at young ages because they wanted them to attend her school.[4]

An issue that the directors in Baghdad clearly linked to child marriage was that of a woman's right to move freely in public. Rachel Danon, the school's first director, worked to make the school into a trusted safe-space for girls in the Jewish community. As we saw in Chapter 3, Oro Sémach built on Danon's work and created a lending library and a women's society in order to maintain students' attachment to the school even after they had graduated or married. Although it is unclear just how many girls and women continued to frequent the school after graduating, it is evident that some did. In any case, the school's directors' efforts in this regard were consistent with those of their colleagues' in other schools.[5] Indeed, Benbassa notes that the AIU subsidized a library for graduates at the Galata School.[6] Such actions by the AIU also illustrate its importance in creating a culture of reading among its female students and graduates.

Other important ways directors in Baghdad aimed to change their students included dress, hygiene, manners, and confidence. Students at the Laura Kadoorie School were quick to adapt to their directors' expectations and, as was discussed in Chapters 2 and 3, soon differentiated from other Jewish girls in the city in terms of dress, appearance, and self-advocacy. This was clearly a common occurrence in cities in which the AIU operated. Rena Molho, for example, mentions that students at Salonica's Girls' School stood out to observers because of their dress and manners.[7] A report from Marrakesh included in Rodrigue's sourcebook highlights this same development.[8] The organization appears to have been wildly successful in cultivating Parisian-Jewish bourgeois manners and fashion to girls throughout its educational network.

Vocational Training in the Ottoman and Arab Jewish World

Another major theme in this study has been the expansion of vocational education for Jewish girls in Baghdad from 1891, which was four years before the AIU Girls' School in the city was established, up to the eve of World War I. How did such training of and work by Baghdadi Jewish girls compare to that of other Jewish women in the Ottoman Empire and the broader Arab world? To answer this question it is necessary to briefly discuss developments in these regions.

The AIU's vocational programs for Jewish girls in the major cities of Ottoman Europe and Anatolia preceded the organization's work in Baghdad, sometimes by as much as twenty years.[9] Although wealthier students learned needlework in AIU schools in these areas, dedicated vocational training was reserved for girls from poor families. For instance, the vocational program in Salonica, home of the largest Jewish community in the Ottoman Empire, was opened in 1880 and focused on training lower-class students in "sewing, embroidery, millinery, and the manufacture of bras and dresses."[10] As in Baghdad, girls from wealthy families in other Ottoman and Arab cities were expected to become homemakers.[11]

Vocational training for Jewish girls in Ottoman Palestine was undertaken by several foreign organizations, although both Sephardic and Ashkenazi women in this area had long histories of knowledge in handicrafts.[12] According to Margalit Shilo, the first group to attempt to promote large-scale textile production among Jewish women in this area was the Jewish Colonization Association.[13] Both Zionist organizations and the AJA-run Evelina de Rothschild School established vocational training for girls in the first decade of the twentieth century.[14] In fact, Annie Landau, the headmistress at the latter institution, was so dedicated to the idea of using vocational training to improve the lives of her lower-class students that she provided them with jobs for a few years after they graduated if they were unable to find employment elsewhere.[15]

In Tripoli, Libya, it was an Italian school, which predated the establishment of an AIU girls' school, that introduced the formal study of needlework to upper-class Jewish girls in the 1870s and 1880s.[16] When the AIU Girls' School opened in the city in 1896 it focused largely on vocational training, partly, it seems, because the AIU wanted to differentiate its new institution from its Italian competitor.[17] This also may explain why the school initially attracted poorer students than the Italian school.[18] In this regard the school differed markedly from the Laura Kadoorie School, as the latter had attracted a largely middle- to upper-class student body, especially during its first decade. Rachel Simon contends that the establishment of the AIU Girls' School in Tripoli marked the arrival of formal vocational education for Libyan women as a whole.[19] Again, this is slightly different from what happened in Baghdad, where it was a Catholic school that first introduced vocational education for girls in the 1880s.

As a result of French colonial and missionary activities, the major cities of the Maghreb, in contrast to those of Libya and Ottoman Iraq, witnessed the arrival of modern girls' schools in the 1830s and 1840s. In Tunis, Jewish girls were exposed to formal needlework training in the 1860s.[20] Joy Land notes that when the AIU began establishing vocational workshops for Jewish girls in the city in the 1880s and 1890s these institutions struggled to even survive.[21] Land mentions intense local competition as on the chief reason for the AIU's workshops' problems.[22] Such competition was surely a result of the work of earlier schools in training Muslim and Jewish women starting in the mid–nineteenth century. Even in Morocco, where the AIU first established a workshop for dressmaking, in Tangiers, at the early date of 1873, the situation was similar, as the organization's workshops failed to make significant progress.[23]

When placed in comparative perspective, the vocational program in Baghdad appears to have followed a unique path. Following an abortive attempt to introduce female vocational education in 1885–1886, the program was slow to take off in the 1890s, and received very little support from the Central Committee, which appears to have been more concerned with supporting struggling workshops in other Ottoman cities and in the Maghreb. Part of the problem was that the general Girls' School in Baghdad lacked a suitable building. This certainly slowed Sémach's progress vis-à-vis vocational training at the turn of the twentieth century. Yet when Marie Albala arrived in 1905 and made vocational education the cornerstone of her reforms, the school became a hotbed of such activity, which included the creation of a successful carpet-weaving workshop. In fact, this workshop appears to have, at least partly, challenged the Shiite monopoly in the carpet-weaving industry in Baghdad. At the same time, the school's sewing workshop successfully competed with the one housed at the local Catholic school, even forcing the latter to lower its prices.

What, then, accounts for the success of the AIU's vocational program in Baghdad, especially during Albala's tenure from 1905 to 1913? First, although Baghdad was home to a large expatriate European community, the city lacked a colonial presence and colonial schools. Second, it had a smaller missionary presence than eastern Arab cities situated along the Mediterranean or in the Maghreb, which meant that it lacked numerous missionary schools seeking to educate girls. Third, it was relatively far away from more cosmopolitan Ottoman cities, where girls' primary schools were opened starting in the 1870s and 1880s. In fact, only one modern girls' school predated the opening of the Girls' School in Baghdad, and it does not seem to have made a major impact on girls' education in the city. As a result, the AIU's female directors were able to chart their own path and introduce formal vocational training to girls in the city's Jewish community.

Finally, it is worth noting that Sémach and Albala clearly recognized that their institution had an opportunity to assume what those in the business world sometimes refer to as a "first-mover" advantage. Since Baghdad housed a large, wealthy expatriate community, and since many indigenous Baghdadi Jewish and Christian women were adopting new, European fashions, Sémach foresaw a future in which the school's trainees would be the first local women who could truly service this clientele. Ultimately, Albala put Sémach's plan into motion and showed that with solid planning, capable instructors, and an understanding of changing economic conditions, the school could help Jewish girls adapt to a globalizing economy. It is worth noting that Albala did this with what appears to have been less direct support from her superiors than her colleagues in other cities enjoyed. Ultimately, Baghdad, with its consulates, foreign residents, lack of colonial history, and relative lack of missionary schools, proved fertile ground for vocational programs directed by a determined director.

Final Thoughts

This book has aimed to shed light on the AIU's network of girls' schools in Ottoman Iraq in the late nineteenth and early twentieth century, with an emphasis on the Girls' School in Baghdad. The impetus for this project came from my realization that although scholars have often pointed to Baghdadi Jews as being among the, if not *the*, most well-integrated Jewish community in the Arab world, and have also mentioned the AIU's major impact on this community, little scholarship is available on the AIU's activities in this city or its surrounding areas.[24] As I have shown throughout this work, this is especially the case with the AIU Girls' Schools in Baghdad, Mosul, Basra, and Hilla.

It is important to emphasize that the AIU's girls' schools and its staff faced area- and era-specific challenges in Ottoman Iraq. The Girls' School in Baghdad, established in 1895, achieved by far the greatest success during this period, but its first several directors had the unenviable tasks of creating a market for formal girls' education in the Baghdadi Jewish community. This institution did, however, have the advantage of being founded in a large and growing community with a wealthy upper class and expanding middle class.

In contrast to the school in Baghdad, the girls' schools in Hilla and Mosul struggled to gain traction at first. Because of widespread poverty among the Jewish community in Hilla, the Girls' School there was not able to attract a significant number of students during its three years of operation. In Mosul, the situation was not quite as dire, though the Girls' School's lack of funds and the relative poverty of the city's Jewish community slowed its progress and forced students and administrators to make do without adequate furniture or facilities.

Basra differed from Hilla and Mosul in that, like Baghdad, its community included a wealthy elite that could afford to make significant contributions to local, modern academic institutions. However, the Central Committee's expectation that this community would provide far more local funding for a school than did the Baghdadi Jewish community for its school appears to have delayed the founding of the Basra Girls' School by several years. This led to Jewish families sending their daughters, at least in the early twentieth century, to Christian schools.

The schools, however, did have some commonalities. In all four communities the AIU established the first formal educational institutions for Jewish girls. Additionally, in Baghdad, Mosul, and Basra, the demand for such institutions came, initially, from men, whether members of the local community or teachers at the local AIU boys' schools, who believed that Jewish societies could be regenerated only if both boys and girls received formal, secular educations.

One of the limitations in writing a book about these schools, and Jewish girls' education in Ottoman Iraq, is that it is difficult to identify what kind of impact these institutions had on Ottoman Jewish society in Iraq and Jewish girls' and women's places in society in this region. Unlike during the interwar and post–World War I periods, the cities of Ottoman Iraq lacked active Jewish presses, and foreign presses provide only snapshots of social change during this period. The letters of AIU teachers and administrators do shed light on this issue, but scholars should not take their accounts at face value.

In her recent book, *New Babylonians*, Orit Bashkin discusses social changes experienced by Iraqi Jewish women in the post-Ottoman, interwar, and post–World War II periods and also the politicization of the "women question" during this era.[25] Bashkin highlights the proliferation of girls' schools, associations, philanthropic activities, and women's work as teachers during this period.[26] Although the scope of girls' and women's activities and opportunities had increased in the period Bashkin's work covers, it was the AIU's work in late Ottoman Iraq that provided the foundation for these later developments. Indeed, as I have shown in this book, the AIU schools created the first educational opportunities for Jewish girls in these areas, sanctioned the first philanthropic society for Baghdadi Jewish women, helped increase the age of marriage for many Jewish girls, and even contributed to women's economic opportunities through vocational education. Thus, while it is impossible to definitively assess the AIU's impact on social change for Jewish girls and women in Ottoman Iraq, it is clear that the organization's schools and activities altered at least segments of local Jewish communities with regard to the proper roles of girls and women in society.

NOTES

Introduction

1. Archives of the Alliance Israélite Universelle (AAIU) Irak III.E.8, N. Albala's speech, November 15, 1911.
2. While the term "Ottoman Iraq" may seem anachronistic to some, recent scholarship has highlighted its suitability. See Hala Fattah, "The Question of the 'Artificiality,'" in *Iraq: Its History, People, and Politics*, edited by Shams C. Inati (New York: Humanity Books, 2003): 49–60; Nabil al-Tikriti, "Was There an Iraq before Iraq?" *International Journal of Contemporary Iraqi Studies* 3, no. 2. (2009): 133–142; and Reidar Visser, "Proto-Political Conceptions of 'Iraq' in late Ottoman Times," *International Journal of Contemporary Iraqi Studies* 3, no. 2. (2009): 143–154.
3. The literature on the AIU's activities in the Ottoman Iraqi provinces and in independent Iraq is limited. The most widely cited study for Baghdad is Maurice Sawdayee, *The Baghdad Connection* (Self-published: Locust Valley, NY, 1991). An article that touches on AIU female education in Baghdad is Nilly Gabbay, "The Education of Girls in the Jewish Community of Baghdad, 1894–1951" [In Hebrew], *Pe'amim* 82 (2003): 94–118. For a general overview of the AIU's activities in the these cities and provinces see Zvi Yehuda's, "Iraqi Jewry and Cultural Change in the Educational Activity of the Alliance Israélite Universelle" in *Sephardi and Middle Eastern Jewries*, edited by Harvey E. Goldberg (Bloomington & Indianapolis: Indiana University Press, 1996), 134–145. For an overview of Basra see David Sagiv, *The Jewish Community in Basra, 1914–1952* [In Hebrew] (Jerusalem: Karmel, 2004), 143–164. For an in-depth analysis of the AIU's arrival in Basra see Jonathan Sciarcon, "Expanding the Mission: The Alliance Israélite Universelle, the Anglo-Jewish Association, and the Jewish Boys' School in Basra, 1890–1903," *The International Journal of Contemporary Iraqi Studies* 9, no. 3 (2015): 191–207. For an overview of Mosul see Ezra Lanaido, *The Jews of Mosul: From Exile to "Operation Ezra and Nehemia"* [In Hebrew] (Tirat-Carmel: Center for Research of the Jews of Mosul, 1981), 180–220.
4. See Abraham Ben-Jacob, *History of the Jews of Iraq from the Gaonic Period to the Present* [In Hebrew] (Jerusalem: Ben-Zvi Institute, 1965); Sylvia Kedourie, "Aspects of Jewish life in Baghdad under the Monarchy," *Middle East Studies* 12 (1976): 188–208; Nissim Rejwan, *The Jews of Iraq: 3000 Years of History and Culture* (Boulder, CO: Westview Press, 1985); Elie Kedourie, "The Break between Muslims and Jews in

Iraq," in *Jews among Arabs: Contacts and Boundaries*, edited by Mark R. Cohen and Abraham L. Udovitch (Princeton, NJ: Darwin Press, 1989), 21–63; Nissim Kazzaz, *The Jews of Iraq in the Twentieth Century* [In Hebrew] (Jerusalem: Ben-Zvi Institute, 1991). A notable exception to Israeli Jewish work on this topic is the Palestinian historian Abbas Shiblak's book, *Iraqi Jews: A History* (London: Saqi, 2005).

5. See Yosef Meir, *Socio-Cultural Development of Iraqi Jews, 1830 to the Present* [In Hebrew] (Tel Aviv: Naharayim, 1989). For a less academic and purely descriptive look at Jewish educational institutions in Iraq see Abraham Twena, *Jewish Education in Baghdad* (Ramla: Geoula Synagogue Committee, 1975).
6. Yehuda, "Iraqi Jewry and Cultural Change in the Educational Activity of the Alliance Israélite Universelle," 145.
7. See Reuven Snir, "'My Heart Beats with Love of the Arabs': Iraqi Jews Writing in Arabic in the Twentieth Century," *Journal of Modern Jewish Studies* 1, no. 2 (2002): 182–203; Idem., "'We Are Arabs Before We Are Jews': The Emergence and Demise of Arab-Jewish Culture in Modern Times," *Electronic Journal of Oriental Studies* VIII, no. 9 (2005): 1–47; Idem., "'My Adherence to the Creed of Moses Has not Diminished My Love for Muhammad's Nation': The Emergence of Iraqi-Jewish Modern Literary Discourse," *Jewish Quarterly Review* 98, no. 1 (2008): 62–87; Lital Levy, "'From Baghdad to Bialik with Love': A Reappropriation of Modern Hebrew Poetry, 1933," *Comparative Literature Studies* 32, no. 3 (2005):125–154; Idem., "Historicizing the Concept of Arab Jews in the *Mashriq*," *Jewish Quarterly Review* 98, no. 4 (2008): 452–469; Orit Bashkin, *New Babylonians: A History of Jews in Modern Iraq* (Stanford, CA: Stanford University Press, 2012).
8. See Orit Bashkin, "Why Did Baghdadi Jews Stop Writing to Their Brethren in Mainz? Some Comments about the Reading Practices of Iraqi Jews in the 19th Century," *Journal of Semitic Studies* (2005): 95–110; Idem., "'Religious Hatred Shall Disappear from the Land': Iraqi-Jews as Ottoman Subjects, 1864–1913," *International Journal of Contemporary Iraqi Studies* 4, no. 3 (2010): 305–323; and Yaron Harel, *Intrigue and Revolution: Chief Rabbis in Aleppo, Baghdad, and Damascus, 1744–1914* (Portland: Littman Library of Jewish Civilization, 2015). Translated by Yehonatan Chipman.
9. Bashkin, *New Babylonians*, 24–25.
10. Although I have taken care not to employ excessive academic jargon, my approaches to sources have been informed by my readings of scholars of postmodern historical theory and gender studies. These works include but are not limited to Richard Jenkins, *Re-thinking History* (New York: Routledge Classics, 2003); Alan Munslow, *Deconstructing History*, 2nd edition (London and New York: Routledge, 2006); Joan Wallach Scott, *Gender and the Politics of History* (New York: Columbia University Press, 1999); Joan Kelly, "The Social Relation of the Sexes: Methodological Implications of Women's History," in *Women, History, & Theory: The Essays of Joan Kelly* (Chicago: The University of Chicago Press, 1984), 1–18; and Merry E. Wiesner-Hanks, *Gender in History: Global Perspectives*, 2nd edition (Chichester: Wiley-Blackwell, 2011), 1–10.
11. For a critical analysis of women's travel writing see Sara Mills, *Discourses of Difference: An Analysis of Women's Travel Writing and Colonialism* (London: Routledge, 1991).
12. A large body of scholarship exists on the background and founding of the AIU. See Michael M. Laskier, *The Alliance Israélite Universelle and the Jewish Communities of Morocco, 1862–1962* (Albany: State University of New York Press, 1983), 31–37; Aron Rodrigue, *French Jews, Turkish Jews: The Alliance Israélite Universelle and the Politics*

of Jewish Schooling in Turkey, 1860–1925 (Bloomington & Indianapolis: Indiana University Press, 1990), 17–24; Michael Graetz, *The Jews in Nineteenth-Century France: From the French Revolution to the Alliance Israélite Universelle*, translated by Jane Marie Todd (Stanford, CA: Stanford University Press, 1996); Lisa Moses Leff, *Sacred Bonds of Solidarity: The Rise of Jewish Internationalism in Nineteenth-Century France* (Stanford, CA: Stanford University Press, 2006); Paula Hyman, *The Jews of Modern France* (Berkeley: University of California Press, 1998), 77–90; Esther Benbassa, *The Jews of France: A History From Antiquity To The Present*, translated by M.B. DeBevoise (Princeton, NJ: Princeton University Press, 1999), 114–133; André Chouraqui, *Cent ans d'histoire: L'Alliance Israélite Universelle et la renaissance juive contemporaine (1860–1960)* (Paris: Press universitaires de France, 1965); Narcisse Leven, *Cinquante ans d'histoire: L'alliance Israélite Universelle (1860–1910)* (Paris: F. Lacan, 1911). On the issue of regeneration see Jay R. Berkovitz, *The Shaping of Jewish Identity in Nineteenth-century France* (Detroit: Wayne State University Press, 1989), 128–149. For the Damascus Affair see Jonathan Frankel, *The Damascus Affair: "Ritual Murder," Politics, and the Jews in 1940* (Cambridge: Cambridge University Press, 1997).

13. For an overview of this vast network see Paul Silberman, "An Investigation of the Schools of the Alliance Israélite Universelle from 1862–1940" (New York: New York University, 1973) PhD dissertation. For an accessible and brief first-hand account of the AIU's background, goals, and operations see Jacques Bigart, "The Alliance Israélite Universelle," *American Jewish Yearbook* 2 (1900–1901): 45–65.
14. For an analytical discussion of Jewish international movements in the mid- to late nineteenth century see Abigail Green, "Nationalism and the 'Jewish International': Religious Internationalism in Europe and the Middle East c. 1840–c. 1880," *Comparative Studies in Society and History* 50, no. 2 (2008): 535–558.
15. See Zosa Szajkowski, "Conflicts in the Alliance Israélite Universelle and the Founding of the Anglo-Jewish Association, the Vienna Allianz and the Hilfsverein," *Jewish Social Studies* 19, nos. 1–2 (1957): 29–50.
16. For a look at Jewish philanthropists in this period see Abigail Green, "Rethinking Sir Moses Montefiore: Religion, Nationhood and International Philanthropy in the Nineteenth Century" *American Historical Review* 110, no. 3 (2005): 631–658.
17. On the relationship between the AIU and the Zionism movement see Catherine Nicault, "Face au sionisme (1897–1940)" in *Histoire de l'Alliance Israélite Universelle de 1860 à nos jours*, edited by D'André Kaspi (Paris: Armand Colin, 2010), 189–226.
18. Szajkowski, "Conflicts in the Alliance Israélite Universelle," 29–30.
19. Ibid.
20. Rodrigue, *Jews and Muslims: Images of Sephardi and Eastern Jewries in Modern Times* (Seattle: University of Washington Press, 2003), 25.
21. Frances Malino, "The Women Teachers of the Alliance Israélite Universelle, 1872–1940," in *Jewish Women in Historical Perspective*, 2nd edition, edited by Judith Baskin (Detroit: Wayne State University Press, 1998), 253.
22. For a succinct overview of the establishment of the AIU's network see Rodrigue, *Jews and Muslims*, 13–21.
23. For the Tanzimat reforms see Carter Vaughn Findley, "The Tanzimat," in The *Cambridge History of Turkey Volume 4: Turkey in the Modern World*, edited by Resat Kasaba (Cambridge: Cambridge University Press, 2008), 11–37; Roderic H. Davison, *Reform in the Ottoman Empire, 1856–1876* (Princeton, NJ: Princeton University Press, 1963); Donald Quataert, *The Ottoman Empire: 1700–1922*, 2nd edition (Cambridge:

Cambridge University Press, 2005), 65–68; M. Sükrü Hanioglu, *A Brief History of the Late Ottoman Empire* (Princeton, NJ: Princeton University Press, 2008), 72–108; and Caroline Finkel, *Osman's Dream: The History of the Ottoman Empire* (New York: Basic Books, 2005), 447–487. For educational reforms during the Tanzimat and Hamidic periods see Benjamin C. Fortna, "The Reign of Abdülhamid II," in *The Cambridge History of Turkey Volume 4*, 38–61. For studies on educational reform in the Tanzimat and Hamidic periods see Selim Deringil, *The Well-Protected Domains: Ideology and the Legitimation of Power in the Ottoman Empire, 1876–1909* (London & New York: I.B. Tauris, 1998), 93–111; Selcuk Aksin Somel, *The Modernization of Public Education in the Ottoman Empire, 1839–1908: Islamization, Autocracy, and Discipline* (Leiden: Brill, 2001); and Benjamin C. Fortna, *Imperial Classroom: Islam, the State and Education in the late Ottoman Empire* (Oxford: Oxford University Press, 2002).

24. For brief overviews on Christian missionary work in the Ottoman Empire, Middle East, and North Africa during this period see Heleen Murre-van den Berg, "Nineteenth-Century Protestant Missions and Middle-Eastern Women: An Overview," in *Gender, Religion, and Change in the Middle East: Two Hundred Years of History*, edited by Inger Marie Okkenhaug and Ingvild Flaskerud (New York: Berg, 2005), 103–122; Heleen Murre-van den Berg, "The Middle East: Western Missions and the Eastern Churches, Islam and Judaism," in *The Cambridge History of Christianity Volume 9: World Christianities C. 1815– C. 1914*, edited by Sheridan Gilley and Brian Stanley (Cambridge: Cambridge University Press, 2006), 458–472; and Heleen Murre-van den Berg, "The Study of Western Missions in the Middle East (1820–1920): An Annotated Bibliography," in *The Social Dimension of Christian Missions in the Middle East: Historical Studies of the 19th and 20th Centuries*, edited by Norbert Friedrich, Uwe Kaminsky, and Roland Löffler (Stuttgart: Franz Steiner Verlag, 2010), 35–54.
25. On Ottoman views of missionary activity see Deringil, *The Well-Protected Domains*, 112–119.
26. Frances Malino, "L'émancipation des femmes," in *Histoire de l'Alliance Israélite Universelle de 1860 à nos jours*, edited by D'André Kaspi (Paris: Armand Colin, 2010), 263–294, esp. 263–264.
27. Ibid.
28. Ibid., 264.
29. Rachel Simon, "Jewish Female Education in the Ottoman Empire," in *Jews, Turks, Ottomans: A Shared History, Fifteenth Through the Twentieth Century*, edited by Avigdor Levy (Syracuse, NY: Syracuse University Press, 2002), 127–152, esp. 133.
30. Margalit Shilo, *Princess or Prisoner? Jewish Women in Jerusalem, 1840–1914* (Waltham, MA: Brandeis University Press, 2005), 151–164. For a continuation of this school's history see the recent important monograph by Laura S. Schor, *The Best School in Jerusalem: Annie Landau's School for Girls, 1900–1960* (Waltham, MA: Brandeis University Press, 2013). For an overview on missionary activity in the service of female education in Ottoman Palestine see Nancy L. Stockdale, *Colonial Encounters among English and Palestinian women, 1800–1948* (Gainesville: University of Florida Press, 2007), 113–135; Ela Greenberg, *Preparing The Mothers of Tomorrow: Education and Islam in Mandate Palestine* (Austin: University of Texas Press, 2010), 18–32; Inger Marie Okkenhaug, *The Quality of Heroic Living, of High Endeavour and Adventure: Anglican Mission, Women and Education in Palestine, 1888–1948* (Leiden: Brill, 2002), 1–49; Billie Melman, *Women's Orients: English*

Women and the Middle East, 1718–1918 (Ann Arbor: University of Michigan Press, 1992), 175–190;

31. Rebecca Rogers, *A Frenchwoman's Imperial Story: Madame Luce in Nineteenth-Century Algeria* (Stanford, CA: Stanford University Press, 2013), 44.
32. There is a large and growing body of scholarship, especially dealing with American and European protestant groups, detailing missionary goals of using girls and women to transform families and society. Some representative examples are Ellen Fleischmann, "'Our Moslem Sisters': Women of Greater Syria in the Eyes of American Protestant Missionary Women," in *Islam and Christian-Muslim Relations* 9, no. 3 (1998): 307–325; Gulnar Eleanor Francis-Dehqani, "CMS Women Missionaries in Iran, 1891–1934: Attitudes Towards Islam and Muslim Women," in *Women, Religion and Culture in Iran*, edited by Sarah Ansari and Vanessa Martin (Richmond, Surrey: Curzon, 2002), 27–50; Jeanne-Marie Warzeski, "'Women's Work for Women': American Presbyterian Missionary Women in Egypt, 1854–1914," in *Women Travellers in the Near East*, edited by Sarah Searight (Cambridge: ASTENE and Oxbow Books, 2005), 79–91; Barbara Reeves-Ellington, "Embracing Domesticity: Women, Mission, and Nation Building in Ottoman Europe, 1832–1872," in *Competing Kingdoms: Women, Mission, Nation, and the American Protestant Empire, 1812–1960*, edited by Barbara Reeves-Ellington, Kathryn Kish Sklar, and Connie A. Shemo (Durham, NC & London: Duke University Press, 2010), 269–292; and K. Pelin Basci, "Shadows in the Missionary Garden of Roses: Women of Turkey in American Missionary texts," in *Deconstructing Images of "The Turkish Woman,"* edited by Zehra F. Arat (New York: St. Martin's Press, 1998), 101–123. For a discussion of the impact of Enlightenment era views of education on nineteenth-century French education see Jennifer J. Popiel, *Rousseau's Daughters: Domesticity, Education, and Autonomy in Modern France* (Durham: University of New Hampshire Press, 2008).
33. Murre-van den Berg, "Nineteenth-Century Protestant Missions and Middle Eastern Women," 103. On the concept of "getting" the girls see, for example, Carol Devens, "'If We Get the Girls We Get the Race': Missionary Education of Native American Girls," in *American Nations: Encounters in Indian Country: 1850 to the Present*, edited by Frederick E. Hoxie, Peter C. Mancall, and James H. Merrell (New York: Routledge, 2001), 157–171.
34. See Elizabeth Antébi, "Changer la femme pour changer l'homme: le modèle des institutrices de L'Alliance Israélite Universelle," in *Femmes et judaïsme aujourd'hui*, edited by Sonia Sarah Lipsyc (Paris: Museum of Jewish Art and History, 2008), 257–267.
35. For goals of missionary women see Fleischmann, "'Our Moslem Sisters,'" 309–310. As Fleischmann notes, the initial goal of converting Muslims soon faded.
36. On this issue for missionary women see Okkenhaug, *The Quality of Heroic Living*, 12–13. For a brief discussion of AIU goals linked to notions of domesticity see Rodrigue, *Jews and Muslims*, 80–81.
37. For an overview of general AIU vocational training see Esther Benbassa, "L'artisanat juif en Turquie à la fin du 19e siècle: l'Alliance Israélite Universelle et ses oeuvres d'apprentissage," *Turcica* 17 (1985): 113–126.
38. Hygiene, propriety, and proper manners were key themes in women's education in Europe in this period and both missionaries and other European and American agents attempted to spread these ideas to girls and women in the Ottoman Empire and Middle East. For some representative studies of these themes in European

women's education during this period see Linda Clark, *Schooling the Daughters of Marianne: Textbooks and the Socialization of Girls in Modern French Primary Schools* (Albany: State University of New York Press, 1984), 5–25; Patricia A. Tilburg, *Colette's Republic: Work, Gender, and Popular Culture in France, 1870–1914* (New York: Bergham Books, 2009), 46–74.

39. On the "civilizing mission" see Alice L. Conklin, "The Civilizing Mission," in *The French Republic: History, Values, Debates*, edited by Edward Berenson, Vincent Duclert, and Christophe Prochasson (Ithaca, NY: Cornell University Press, 2009), 173–181; and Matthew Burrows, "'Mission Civilisatrice': French Cultural Policy in the Middle East, 1860–1914," *The Historical Journal* 29, no. 1 (1986): 109–135.
40. On the links between the AIU and the civilizing mission see Rodrigue, *French Jews, Turkish Jews*, 71–80; Malino, "'Institutrices' in the Metropole and the Maghreb: A Comparative Perspective," *Historical Reflections* 32, no. 1 (2006): 129–142; esp. 133.
41. Perhaps the most well-known stand-alone article on a girls' school is Esther Benbassa's "Education for Jewish girls in the East: A Portrait of the Galata School in Istanbul, 1879–1912," *Studies in Contemporary Jewry* 9 (1993): 163–173. In some cases books on AIU activities or Jewish communities in specific cities, regions, or countries have included chapters, or subsections within chapters, on girls' education. See Erol Hacker, *Edirne, Its Jewish Community, and Alliance Schools: 1867–1937* (Istanbul: The Isis Press, 2006), 151–162; Rena Molho, "Female Jewish Education in Salonica at the End of the 19th Century," in *Salonica and Istanbul: Social, Political and Cultural Aspects of Jewish Life* (Istanbul: The Isis Press, 2005), 139–150; Lanaido, *Jews of Mosul*, 188, 206–209; Dario Miccoli, *Histories of the Jews of Egypt: An imagined Bourgeoisie, 1882–1950s* (London: Routledge, 2015), 32–43. On the lives, work, and writings of female teachers see Malino, "The Women Teachers of the Alliance Israélite Universelle"; Idem., "'Institutrices' in the Metropole and the Maghreb"; Idem., "Prophets in Their Own Land? Mothers and Daughters of the Alliance Israélite Universelle," *Nashim* no. 3 (2000): 56–73; Sylvie Fogiel-Bijaoui, "Un Chemin D'Émanicpation: L'Alliance Israélite Universelle Et Les Femmes Juives De Palestine (1872–1939)," *Archives Juives* 46, no. 1 (2013): 107–119; Joy Land, "Corresponding Women: Female Educators of the Alliance Israélite Universelle in Tunisia, 1882–1914," in *Jewish Culture and Society in North Africa*, edited by Emily Benichou Gottreich and Daniel J. Schroeter (Bloomington and Indianapolis: Indiana University Press, 2011), 239–256; Rachel Simon, *Change within Tradition among Jewish Women in Libya* (Seattle: University of Washington Press, 1992), 114–126; Annie Benveniste, "Le rôle des Institutrices de l'Alliance Israélite Universelle à Salonique," *Combat pour la Diaspora* 8 (1982): 13–26.
42. Susan G. Miller, "Gender and the Poetics of Emancipation: *The Alliance Israélite Universelle* in Northern Morocco, 1890–1912," in *Franco-Arab Encounters: Studies in Memory of David C. Gordon*, edited by L. Carl Brown and Matthew S. Gordon (Beirut: American University of Beirut, 1996), 229–252; and Shalom Bar-Asher, "The Emancipation of North-African Jewish Women: The Alliance Israélite Universelle," in *Jews and Muslims in the Islamic World*, edited by Bernard Dov Cooperman and Zvi Zohar (Bethesda: University Press of Maryland, 2013), 33–50.
43. Joy Land, "Corresponding Lives: Women Educators of the *Alliance Israélite Universelle* School for Girls in the City of Tunis, 1882–1914" (UCLA, 2006) PhD dissertation.
44. For examples of the general discussions see Tomer Levi, *The Jews of Beirut: The Rise of a Levantine Community, 18602–1930s* (New York: Peter Lang, 2012), 88–91;

Kristen E. Schulze, *The Jews of Lebanon: Between Coexistence and Conflict* (Brighton, England: Sussex Academic Press, 2001), 25–30; Harel, *Intrigue and Revolution*, 84–85, 121–122, 174–175; and Bruce Masters, *Christians and Jews in the Ottoman Arab World: The Roots of Sectarianism* (Cambridge: Cambridge University Press, 2001), 154–156.

45. Some important studies that have furthered my understanding of the broad field of general nineteenth- and early twentieth-century Middle Eastern Women's histories include but are in no way limited to Judith Tucker, *Women in Nineteenth-Century Egypt* (Cambridge: Cambridge University Press, 1985); Donald Quaetart, "Ottoman Women, Households, and Textile Manufacturing, 1800–1914" in *Women in Middle Eastern History: Shifting Boundaries in Sex and Gender*, edited by Nikki R. Keddie and Beth Baron (New Haven, CT: Yale University Press, 1991), 161–176; Leila Ahmed, *Women and Gender in Islam: Historical Roots of a Modern Debate* (New Haven, CT: Yale University Press, 1992), 127–168; Guity Nashat and Judith E. Tucker, *Women in the Middle East and North Africa* (Bloomington and Indianapolis: Indiana University Press, 1998), 73–101; Ellen L. Fleischmann, "The Other "Awakening": The Emergence of Women's Movements in the Modern Middle East, 1900–1940," in *Social History of Women and Gender in the Modern Middle East*, edited by Margaret L. Meriwether and Judith E. Tucker (Boulder, CO: Westview Press, 1999), 89–140; Julia Clancy-Smith, "Envisioning Knowledge: Educating the Muslim Woman in Colonial North Africa, c.1850–1918," in *Iran and Beyond: Essays in Middle Eastern History in Honor of Nikki R. Keddie*, edited by Rudi Matthee and Beth Baron (Costa Mesa: Mazda Publishers, Inc., 2000), 99–120; Nikki R. Keddie, *Women in the Middle East: Past and Present* (Princeton, NJ: Princeton University Press, 2007), 60–101.

46. On women's history in Iraq in the late nineteenth and early twentieth centuries see Noga Efrati, "The Other 'Awakening' in Iraq: The Women's Movement in the First Half of the Twentieth Century," *British Journal of Middle Eastern Studies* 31, no. 2 (2004): 153–173; and Idem., "Competing Narratives: Histories of the Women's Movement in Iraq, 1910–1958" *International Journal of Middle East Studies* 40, no. 3 (2008): 445–466. Efrati's work builds on and supersedes Doreen Ingram's, *The Awakened: Women in Iraq* (London: Third World, 1983).

47. See, for example, a discussion of one such educator's struggles in Edirne in the late 1860s in Rodrigue, *French Jews, Turkish Jews*, 59.

48. Rodrigue, *Jews and Muslims*, 105.

49. Rodrigue, *French Jews, Turkish Jews*, 80.

50. Ibid., 68–69.

51. Rodrigue, *Jews and Muslims*, 135.

52. Malino, ""Institutrices,"" 132–134.

53. Rodrigue, *Jews and Muslims*, 80–82.

54. Ibid., 201–205.

55. Somel, *Modernization of Public Education in the Ottoman Empire*, 16–23.

56. Ibid., 3–11; Emine Ö. Evered, *Empire and Education under the Ottomans: Politics, Reform, and Resistance from the Tanzimat to the Young Turks* (London: I.B. Tauris, 2012), 1–9.

57. Evered, *Empire and Education under the Ottomans*, 4–9, 19–21; Somel, *Modernization of Public Education in the Ottoman Empire*, 8–12.

58. Somel, *Modernization of Public Education in the Ottoman Empire*, 42–44.

59. Fortna, *Imperial Classroom*, 12.

60. Ibid., 76–77.

61. Somel, *Modernization of Public Education in the Ottoman Empire*, 10–11.

62. Ibid., 84.
63. Ibid., 56–57.
64. See Elizabeth B. Frierson, "Unimagined Communities: Women and Education in the Late-Ottoman Empire, 1876–1909," *Critical Matrix* 9, no. 2 (1995): 55–90.
65. Somel, *Modernization of Public Education in the Ottoman Empire*, 10–11.
66. For a brief overview of general political, social, and economic developments in Baghdad in the nineteenth century see Charles Tripp, *A History of Iraq*, 2nd edition (New York: Cambridge University Press, 2005), 8–20.
67. See Ebubekir Ceylan, *The Ottoman Origins of Modern Iraq: Political Reforms, Modernization and Development in the Nineteenth-Century Middle East* (London: I.B. Tauris, 2011), 35–37.
68. Charles Issawi, *The Fertile Crescent, 1800–1914: A Documentary Economic History* (Oxford: Oxford University Press, 1988), 124.
69. These are some of the main issues dealt with in Gokhan Çetinsaya, *Ottoman Administration of Iraq* (London: Routledge, 2006). See especially chapter 2.
70. Somel, *Modernization of Public Education in the Ottoman Empire*, 114–115.
71. Ceylan, *Ottoman Origins of Modern Iraq*, 205.
72. Ibid., 211.
73. On educational institutions in Ottoman Iraq see Abbas Kadhim, "Iraqi Education In The Ottoman Era," *Kufa Review* no. 2, issue 3 (2013): 25–53.
74. Çetinsaya lists the school's founding as having taken place in 1898. See Çetinsaya, *Ottoman Administration of Iraq*, 17. However, Abdul Wahhab Abbas Al-Qaysi claims the school was opened in 1899. See Abdul-Wahhab Abbas Al-Qaysi, "The Impact of Modernization on Iraqi Society during the Ottoman Era" (Ann Arbor, 1958) PhD dissertation, 69.
75. Somel, *Modernization of Public Education in the Ottoman Empire*, 226–230; Çetinsaya, *Ottoman Administration of Iraq*, 125–126; Deringil, *The Well-Protected Domains*, 100–101; Evered, *Empire and Education Under the Ottomans*, 161–166.

Pioneering Female Jewish Education

1. *Bulletin de L'Alliance Israéllite Universelle* (Henceforth BAIU) (July 1863), 9.
2. Hayyim J. Cohen, *The Jews of the Middle East, 1860–1972* (New York: John Wiley & Sons, 1973), 72–73.
3. Elie Kedourie, *Arabic Political Memoirs and Other Studies* (London: Frank Cass, 1974), 267.
4. Ibid.
5. Ibid., 268.
6. Shlomo Deshen, "Baghdad Jewry in Late Ottoman Times: The Emergence of Social Classes and Secularization," in *Jews among Muslims: Communities in the Precolonial Middle East*, edited by Shlomo Deshen and Walter P. Zenner (New York: New York University Press, 1996), 189.
7. See Hanna Batatu, *The Old Social Classes and the Revolutionary Movements of Iraq: A Study of Iraq's Old Landed and Commercial Classes and of Its Communists, Ba'thissts, and Free Officers* (Princeton, NJ: Princeton University Press, 1978), 247–249.
8. See chapters 3 and 4 in Harel, *Intrigue and Revolution*.
9. Ibid., 58–59; 79–86.
10. Ibid., 84–85.

11. Ibid.
12. See Lital Levy, "Jewish Writers in the Arab East: Literature, History, and the Politics of Enlightenment, 1863–1914" (University of California, Berkeley, 2007) PhD dissertation. For a discussion of the Jewish press in Baghdad in the late nineteenth century see chapter 6 of the dissertation.
13. Bashkin, "Why Did Baghdadi Jews Stop Writing to Their Brethren in Mainz?" 101–102.
14. A brief overview of religious, secular, and governmental education for Jews in nineteenth-century Baghdad can be found in Reeva S. Simon, "Jewish Communal Education in Baghdad to 1914," *Pe'anim: Studies in Oriental Jewry* 36 [In Hebrew] (1988): 52–63.
15. See Meir, *Socio-Cultural Development of Iraqi Jews*, 23–29; David Solomon Sassoon, *The History of the Jews in Baghdad* (Letchworth, UK: The Alcuin Press, 1949), 170–172. Sassoon's book includes information on education in Baghdad in the nineteenth and early twentieth centuries, but based on some errors the book contains regarding the founding of the AIU's schools, note that other errors may be present as well.
16. Cohen, *Jews of the Middle East*, 114.
17. Ibid.
18. Ibid.
19. Norman Stillman, *The Jews of Arab Lands: A History and Source Book* (Philadelphia: Jewish Publication Society of America, 1979), 377–383, includes informative primary source documents from the British Foreign Office that shed light on one Baghdadi Jewish encounter with Christian missionaries in the 1840s.
20. For a brief discussion of the role of mothers in educating Jewish girls in Baghdad in this period see Shaul Sehayek, "Changes in the Status of Urban Jewish Women in Iraq as the Nineteenth Century Turned," in *Women in Judaism* 3, no. 2 (Winter, 2003), translated by Dina Ripsman Eylon and Dalia Maishlish: 1–24.
21. AAIU Irak I.C.2, J. Valadjj to AIU, March 10, 1889. See also Nilly Gabbay, *The Jewish Woman in Baghdad: Processes of Change in her Social Status during the First Half of the Twentieth Century* [In Hebrew]. (Jerusalem: Association of the Jewish Academics from Iraq, 2006), 48–50. Gabbay also mentions that girls and boys were studying together in this period.
22. AAIU Irak I.C.2., J. Valadji to AIU, March 10, 1889; Sehayek, "Changes in the Status of Urban Jewish Women in Iraq as the Nineteenth Century Turned," 7–8.
23. Harel, *Intrigue and Revolution*, 110.
24. See, for example, Rogers, *A Frenchwoman's Imperial* Story, chapter 3; Lisa Pollard, "Learning Gendered Modernity: The Home, the Family, and the Classroom in the Construction of Egyptian National Identity (1885–1919)," in *Beyond the Exotic: Women's Histories in Islamic Societies*, edited by Amira El-Azhary Sonbol (Syracuse, NY: Syracuse University Press 2005), 249–269.
25. The most notable study of the school's activities is Sawdayee, *The Baghdad Connection*.
26. Leven, *Cinquante ans d'histoire*, 54.
27. Derek Frenette, "L'Alliance Israélite Universelle and the Politics of Modern Jewish Education in Baghdad: 1864–1914" (Simon Fraser University, 2005) Master's thesis, 24–25.
28. Rodrigue, *French Jews, Turkish Jews*, 40–42.

29. AAIU Irak I.E.3 J. Muattar to AIU, August 17, 1866.
30. Ibid.
31. On increasing British influence in the Persian Gulf see Batatu, *The Old Social Classes and the Revolutionary Movements of Iraq*, 247–249; Frederick F. Anscombe, *The Ottoman Gulf: The Creation of Kuwait, Saudi Arabia, and Qatar* (New York: Columbia University Press, 1997), 21–29; Stuart Cohen, *British Policy in Mesopotamia, 1903–1914* (Reading: Ithaca Press, 2008), 4–10; Charles Issawi, *The Fertile Crescent 1800–1914*, 142–143; and Hala Fattah, *The Politics of Regional Trade in Iraq, Arabia, and the Gulf, 1745–1900* (Albany: State University of New York Press, 1997), 113–122.
32. AAIU Irak I.C.1, French Consul in Baghdad to AIU, June 23, 1868.
33. Ibid.
34. Ibid.
35. For an overview of the changing nature of Ottoman state relations with Ottoman Jewish communities during the Tanzimat and Hamidic periods see Daniel J. Schroeter, "The Changing Relationship between the Jews of the Arab Middle East and the Ottoman State in the Nineteenth Century," in *Jews, Turks, Ottomans: A Shared History, Fifteenth through the Twentieth Century*, edited by Avigdor Levy (Syracuse, NY: Syracuse University Press, 2002), 88–107
36. AAIU Irak I.C.1, AIU Students to French Consul in Baghdad, June 16, 1868.
37. Leven, *Cinquante ans d'histoire*, 54–55.
38. "The Alliance Israélite Universelle: Half-Yearly Report," *The Jewish Chronicle*, April 4, 1873.
39. See Morris Cohen's "English Education at the Baghdad School" in *Anglo-Jewish Association Twenty-Second Annual Report (1892–1893)*, 64–66. Henceforth the *Anglo-Jewish Association's Annual Report* will be referenced as AJAR. Please note that I have accessed some of these reports in printed, published form, and others have been accessed from the University of Southampton's online archives. When citing the latter I have followed the University of Southampton's recommended guidelines.
40. BAIU (1875 2nd Semester), 33; BAIU No. 5 (1882 2nd Semester), 27.
41. BAIU (1886 2nd Semester), 32.
42. BAIU (1895 1st and 2nd Semesters), 85.
43. Frenette, "L'Alliance Israélite Universelle," 19. On Jewish perceptions of Midhat Pasha's time as governor of Baghdad see also Orit Bashkin, "'Religious Hatred Shall Disappear from the Land,'" 312–314.
44. BAIU (1869 2nd Semester), 64.
45. Paul Dumont, "Jews, Muslims, and Cholera: Intercommunal Relations in Baghdad at the End of the Nineteenth Century," in *The Jews of the Ottoman Empire*, edited by Avidgor Levy (Princeton, NJ: Darwin Press, 1994), 353–372.
46. AAIU Irak I.C.1, French Consul (Name slightly unclear) to AIU, December 4, 1867.
47. Yusuf Rizk-Allah Ghanimah, *A Nostalgic Trip into The History of the Jews of Iraq*, translated by A. Dallal (Lanham, MD: University Press of America, 1998), 140–142.
48. Two key sources that highlight some of these issues are AIU Boys' School English Teacher Morris Cohen's report from 1880 on the AIU and the Jews in Baghdad and Director Jacques Louria's report on the AIU School in 1886. AJA Archives (University of Southampton) AJ95/150/4/AJAR (1879–1880), 92–98; and BAIU (1886 2nd Semester), 56–59.
49. Meer S. Basri, *Eminent Jewish Men of Modern Iraq* [In Arabic] (Jerusalem: Association for Jewish Academics from Iraq, 1983), 28–33.
50. Ibid.; See also Bashkin, "'Religious Hatred Shall Disappear from the Land,'" 319–320.

51. BAIU (1st Semester 1874), 10.
52. Ibid.
53. AJA Archives (University of Southampton), AJ95/150/7 AJAR (1882–1883), 30–31
54. BAIU (1883 2nd Semester), 32.
55. AAIU Irak VII.E.75, J. Louria to AIU, June 7, 1885.
56. AAIU Irak VII.E.75, J. Louria to AIU, November 25, 1885.
57. AAIU Irak VII.E.75, J. Louria to AIU, March 28, 1886.
58. Ibid.; see also Meir, *Socio-cultural development of Iraqi Jews*, 393 & 398–399 on rabbinical opposition to the girls' workshop.
59. AAIU Irak VII.E.75, J. Louria to AIU, April 19, 1886
60. AAIU Irak I.B.7, S. Sassoon to Louria, August 19, 1886.
61. Ibid.
62. AAIU Irak VII.E.75, J. Louria to AIU, August 20, 1886.
63. AAIU Irak XII.E.112, S. Somekh to AIU, March 24, 1890.
64. AJAR (1895–1896), 50–51.
65. Advocates of women's education in Iran advanced a similar argument. See Firoozeh Kashani-Sabet, *Conceiving Citizens: Women and the Politics of Motherhood in Iran* (Oxford: Oxford University Press, 2011), 121–125.
66. Rachel G. Fuchs and Victoria E. Thompson, *Women in Nineteenth-Century Europe* (New York: Palgrave Macmillan, 2005), 84; Rebecca Rogers, "Learning to be Good Girls and Women: Education, Training and Schools," in *The Routledge History of Women in Europe since 1700*, edited by Deborah Simonton (London and New York: Routledge, 2006), 93–133.
67. Afsaneh Najmabadi, "Crafting an Educated Housewife," in *Remaking Women: Feminism and Modernity in the Middle East*, edited by Lila Abu-Lughod (Princeton, NJ: Princeton University Press, 1998), 91–125, esp. 94–95.
68. Pollard, "Learning Gendered Modernity," 260–261.
69. Antébi, "Changer la femme pour changer l'homme."
70. AAIU Irak XII.E.112 S. Somekh to AIU, May 19, 1890.
71. AAIU Irak XII.E.112 Somekh to AIU, April 16, 1891.
72. Ibid.
73. Harel, *Intrigue and Revolution*, 102–103.
74. AAIU Irak XII.E.112 S. Somekh to AIU, May 19, 1890.
75. Ibid.
76. AAIU Irak XII.E.112 S. Somekh to AIU, July 22, 1890.
77. Ibid.
78. Ibid.
79. Ibid.
80. Ibid.
81. Ibid.
82. Ibid.
83. Ibid.
84. AAIU Irak XII.E.112 S. Somekh to AIU, April 16, 1891.
85. Ibid.
86. Ibid.
87. Ibid.
88. Ibid.
89. Ibid.
90. Ibid.

91. Ibid.
92. Ibid.
93. On cultural expectations of Jewish women in the Ottoman Empire and Middle East see Sezgin, "Jewish Women in the Ottoman Empire," 223–224; Rachel Simon, "Between the Family and the Outside World: Jewish Girls in the Modern Middle East and North Africa," *Jewish Social Studies* 7, no. 1 (2001): 81–108; Sara Reguer, "The World of Women," in *The Jews of the Middle East and North Africa in Modern Times*, edited by Reeva Spector Simon, Michael Menachem Laskier, and Sara Reguer (New York: Columbia University Press, 2003), 235–250.
94. AAIU Irak XII.E.112 S. Somekh to AIU, June 18, 1891.
95. Ibid.
96. AAIU Irak V.E.34, J. Danon to AIU, June 21, 1894.
97. Pollard, "Learning Gendered Modernity," 260–261.
98. AAIU Irak V.E.34, J. Danon to AIU, June 21, 1894.
99. AAIU Irak V.E.35, R. Danon to AIU, December 13, 1894.
100. AAIU Irak V.E.34, J. Danon to AIU, November 15, 1894.
101. AAIU Irak V.E.35, R. Danon to AIU, December 13, 1894.
102. Ibid.
103. Ibid.
104. Shilo, *Princess or Prisoner?* 158.
105. Habīb K. Chiha, *La province de Bagdad, son passé, son present, son avenir* (Cairo: El-Maaref, 1908), 104.
106. FO 195/1509. The report is discussed in Issawi, *The Fertile Crescent 1800–1914*, 33. I also consulted the original document, which mentions the employment of a seamstress. On Christian female educational institutions in Ottoman Baghdad see also Hilali Abdul-Razzak, *History of Education in Iraq during the Ottoman Times, 1638–1917* [In Arabic] (Baghdad: The National Printing & Publishing Company, 1959), 202–203.
107. Jean-Baptiste Piolet, *Les missions catholiques francaises au XIXe siècle Vol. 1* (Paris: A. Colin, 1901), 243–244
108. FO 195/1509
109. AAIU Irak V.E.35, R. Danon to AIU, January 24, 1895.
110. "Anglo-Jewish Association" in *The Jewish Chronicle*, December 7, 1894.
111. AAIU Irak V.E.35, R. Danon to AIU, January 24, 1895.
112. Ibid.
113. Simon, *Change within Tradition*, 110–115.
114. Ibid.
115. AAIU Irak V.E.35, R. Danon to AIU, January 24, 1895.
116. Ibid.
117. Rodrigue, *French Jews, Turkish Jews*, 80–81.
118. AAIU Irak V.E.35, R. Danon to AIU, January 24, 1895.
119. Ibid.
120. Benbassa, "Education for Jewish Girls in the East," 166.
121. Molho, "Female Jewish Education in Salonica,"142–143.
122. Hacker, *Edirne, Its Jewish Community, and Alliance Schools*, 155.
123. AAIU Irak V.E.35, R. Danon to AIU, February 7, 1895.
124. Ibid.
125. Ibid.

126. Ibid.
127. AJA Archives (University of Southampton) AJ95/ADD/6, June 4, 1895.
128. Ibid.
129. AJA Archives (University of Southampton) AJ95/ADD/6, February 26, 1895.
130. AAIU Irak V.E.35, R. Danon to AIU, May 16, 1895.
131. AAIU Irak V.E.35, R. Danon to AIU, July 11, 1895.
132. BAIU (1895 1st and 2nd Semesters), 85.
133. Ibid.
134. Ibid. Although the financial summary for 1895 does not include a specific mention of rent, "loyer," when comparing the numbers for school furniture with the combined numbers for rent and school furniture from 1896 it is clear that rent is for 1895 is subsumed under the category of "mobilier scolaire."
135. Ibid.
136. Sciarcon, "Expanding the Mission," 194–195.
137. Shilo, *Princess or Prisoner?* 152–153.
138. AAIU Irak V.E.35, R. Danon to AIU, May 16, 1895.
139. Ibid.
140. AAIU Irak V.E.35, R. Danon to AIU, July 11, 1895.
141. AAIU Irak V.E.35, R. Danon to AIU, date missing. My best guess is that this letter is from March 28, 1895. I have come to this conclusion based on three observations. First, the letter notes that it covers the period from February 22 to March 27. Second, the previous letter was dated March 14, and Danon consistently wrote her letters on the same day of the week and normally wrote once every two weeks. Third, the letter appears to have been placed in the mail at the same time as the letter from March 14, as both include postal stamps from April 18.
142. Ibid.
143. Ibid.
144. AAIU Irak V.E.35, R. Danon to AIU, January 24, 1895.
145. AAIU Irak V.E.35, R. Danon to AIU, February 7, 1895.
146. Ibid.
147. Ibid.
148. Ibid.
149. Ibid.
150. Ibid.
151. AAIU Irak V.E.35, R. Danon to AIU, March 14, 1895.
152. AAIU Irak V.E.35, R. Danon to AIU, November 7, 1895.
153. AAIU Irak V.E.35, R. Danon to AIU, January 9, 1896.
154. Ibid.
155. AAIU Irak V.E.35, R. Danon to AIU, November 7, 1895.
156. AAIU Irak V.E.35, R. Danon to AIU, May 16, 1895.
157. AAIU Irak V.E.35, R. Danon to AIU, March 14, 1895.
158. Ibid.
159. Malino, "The Women Teachers of the Alliance Israélite Universelle, 1872–1940," 248–249.
160. This was a common belief among foreign teachers in girls' schools in the Arab world. For example, see Rebecca Rogers, *A Frenchwoman's Imperial Story*, 97–99.
161. AAIU Irak V.E.35, R. Danon to AIU, November 7, 1895.

162. Ibid.
163. Ibid.
164. Najmabadi, "Crafting an Educated Housewife," 102–103.
165. Benbassa, "Education for Jewish Girls in the East," 166–168.
166. Ibid.
167. Okkenhaug, *The Quality of Heroic Living*, 21–28.
168. Malino, "L'émancipation des femmes," 274–276.
169. Ibid.
170. AAIU Irak V.E.34., J. Danon to AIU March (specific date uncertain), 1894.
171. BAIU (1895 1st and 2nd Semesters), 100; AAIU Irak V.E.35, J. Danon to AIU, October 21, 1895. Note that this letter appears in Rachel Danon's file although it was written by Joseph Danon.
172. Ibid.
173. Ibid.
174. For a discussion of AIU female vocational training in Tangiers, Morocco, during this period see Susan G. Miller, "Gender and the Poetics of Emancipation," 240–244.
175. AAIU Irak V.E.35, J. Danon to AIU, October 21, 1895.
176. Miller, "Gender and the Poetics of Emancipation," 237.
177. Fleischmann, "'Our Moslem Sisters,'" 308.
178. AAIU Irak V.E.35, R. Danon to AIU, March 14, 1895.
179. Ibid.
180. Ibid.
181. Ibid.
182. Ibid.
183. Ibid.
184. AAIU Irak V.E.35, R. Danon to AIU, July 11, 1895.
185. For a discussion of corporate identity in French schools see Anne T. Quartararo, *Women Teachers and Popular Education in Nineteenth-Century France* (Newark: University of Delaware Press, 1995), chapter 7.
186. AJAR (1895–1896), 31.
187. AAIU Irak V.E.35, R. Danon to AIU, July 11, 1895. Danon's letter from May 16, 1895, also discusses opposition to girls learning to do handicrafts.
188. AAIU Irak V.E.35, R. Danon to AIU, July 11, 1895.
189. Quataert, "Ottoman Women, Households, and Textile Manufacturing," 164.
190. AAIU Irak V.E.35, R. Danon to AIU, March 1895 (most likely March 28).
191. Ibid.
192. AJA Archives (University of Southampton), AJ95/ADD/2, December 2, 1894.
193. AAIU Irak V.E.35, R. Danon to AIU, June 6, 1895.
194. Ibid.
195. AAIU Irak V.E.35, R. Danon to AIU, May 16, 1895.
196. Ibid.
197. Ibid.
198. Ibid.
199. Ibid.
200. Ibid.
201. Ibid.
202. AAIU Irak V.E.35, R. Danon to AIU, June 6, 1895.
203. AAIU Irak V.E.35, R. Danon to AIU, January 9, 1896.

Chapter 2: From Danon to Sutton

1. Schor, *Best School in Jerusalem*, 55–57.
2. AAIU Irak V.E.35, R. Danon to AIU, April 9, 1896.
3. AAIU Irak V.E.35, R. Danon to AIU, April 23, 1896.
4. Ibid.
5. Ibid.
6. Ibid.
7. AAIU Irak V.E.35, R. Danon to AIU, June 18, 1896.
8. Ibid.
9. AAIU Irak V.E.35, R. Danon to AIU, July 9, 1896.
10. AAIU Irak V.E.35, R. Danon to AIU, December 17, 1896.
11. Ibid.
12. AAIU Irak V.E.35, R. Danon to AIU, January 7, 1897.
13. AAIU Irak V.E.35, R. Danon to AIU, June 3, 1897.
14. AAIU Irak V.E.35, R. Danon to AIU, May 5, 1898.
15. Ibid.
16. AAIU Irak V.E.35, R. Danon to AIU, November 30, 1898.
17. AAIU Irak V.E.35, R. Danon to AIU, March 7, 1899.
18. AAIU Irak V.E.35, R. Danon to AIU, April 23, 1896.
19. AAIU Irak V.E.35, R. Danon to AIU, September 3, 1896.
20. Ibid.
21. Ibid.
22. Ibid.
23. Ibid.
24. AAIU Irak V.E.35, R. Danon to AIU, October 8, 1896; October 22, 1896.
25. AAIU Irak V.E.35, R. Danon to AIU, October 22, 1896.
26. AAIU Irak V.E.35, R. Danon to AIU, January 7, 1897.
27. AAIU Irak V.E.35, R. Danon to AIU, June 3, 1897.
28. AAIU Irak V.E.35, R. Danon to AIU, August 12, 1897.
29. AAIU Irak V.E.35, R. Danon to AIU, October 21, 1897.
30. AAIU Irak V.E.35, R. Danon to AIU, November 4, 1897.
31. Ibid.
32. Ibid.
33. AAIU Irak V.E.35, R. Danon to AIU, February 26, 1896.
34. Ibid.
35. Malino, "The Women Teachers of the Alliance Israélite Universelle," 256.
36. AAIU Irak V.E.35, R. Danon to AIU, April 23, 1896.
37. Ibid.
38. Ibid.
39. AAIU Irak V.E.35, R. Danon to AIU, February 26, 1896.
40. AAIU Irak V.E.35, R. Danon to AIU, July 9, 1896.
41. Ibid.
42. Malino, "The Women Teachers of the Alliance Israélite Universelle," 250.
43. Ibid.
44. AAIU Irak V.E.35, R. Danon to AIU, September 10, 1896.
45. AAIU Irak V.E.35, R. Danon to AIU, October 8, 1896.
46. AAIU Irak V.E.35, R. Danon to AIU, September 21, 1896.
47. AAIU Irak V.E.35, R. Danon to AIU, January 7, 1897.

48. AAIU Irak V.E.35, R. Danon to AIU, March 31, 1897.
49. Ibid.
50. Ibid.
51. Ibid.
52. Ibid.
53. Ibid.
54. Ibid.
55. AAIU Irak V.E.35, R. Danon to AIU, January 13, 1898.
56. AAIU Irak V.E.35, R. Danon to AIU, March 24, 1898.
57. AAIU Irak V.E.35, R. Danon to AIU, April 6, 1898.
58. Ibid.
59. Ibid.
60. AAIU Irak V.E.35, R. Danon to AIU, September 8, 1898.
61. AAIU Irak V.E.35, R. Danon to AIU, March 7, 1899.
62. AAIU Irak V.E.35, R. Danon to AIU, January 5, 1899; March 7, 1899.
63. AAIU Irak V.E.35, R. Danon to AIU, November 24, 1898.
64. AAIU Irak V.E.35, R. Danon to AIU, August 26, 1897.
65. Ibid.
66. AAIU Irak XII.E.113, F. Sutton to AIU, April 1, 1897.
67. Ibid.
68. Ibid.
69. Ibid.
70. AAIU Irak V.E.35, R. Danon to AIU, March 31, 1897.
71. Ibid.
72. Ibid.
73. Ibid.
74. AAIU Irak XII.E.113, F. Sutton to AIU, January 13, 1898.
75. Ibid.
76. AAIU Irak V.E.35, R. Danon to AIU, March 12, 1896.
77. AAIU Irak V.E.35, R. Danon to AIU, July 9, 1896.
78. AAIU Irak V.E.35, R. Danon to AIU, August 12, 1897.
79. AAIU Irak V.E.35, R. Danon to AIU, January 13, 1898.
80. AAIU Irak V.E.35, R. Danon to AIU, September 8, 1898.
81. AAIU Irak V.E.35, R. Danon to AIU, December 17, 1896.
82. Ibid.
83. For an overview of the process of becoming a schoolgirl in France and England in the nineteenth century see Christina De Bellaigue, *Educating Women: Schooling and Identity in England and France, 1800–1867* (New York: Oxford University Press, 2007), 138–165.
84. For similar developments in other schools focusing on girls' education in the Arab world see Shilo, *Princess or Prisoner?* 158–170; and Rogers, *A Frenchwoman's Imperial Story*, 92–103.
85. Schor, *Best School in Jerusalem*, 62; Okkenhaug, *Quality of Heroic Living*, 23–25. For a discussion of how learning to adhere to rules and regulations helps create schoolgirl culture see also Rogers, "Schools, Discipline, and Community: Diary Writing and Schoolgirl Culture in Late Nineteenth-Century France," *Women's History Review* 4, no. 4 (1995): 525–555.
86. AAIU Irak V.E.35, R. Danon to AIU, January 13, 1898.
87. AAIU Irak XII.E.113, F. Sutton to AIU, March 9, 1899.

88. AAIU Irak V.E.35, R. Danon to AIU, April 6, 1899.
89. Ibid.
90. For letters by AIU teachers in Morocco that mention child marriage see Rodrigue, *Jews and Muslims*, 82–91.
91. See Schor, *Best School in Jerusalem*, 62; and Shilo, *Princess of Prisoner?* 170–171; Fleischman, "'Our Moslem Sisters,'" 315; and Beth Baron, *The Women's Awakening in Egypt* (New Haven: Yale University Press, 1994), 163–166.
92. Simon, "Between the Family and the Outside World," 82–83.
93. Cohen, *Jews of the Middle East*, 170.
94. Sehayek, "Changes in the Social Status of Urban Jewish Women in Iraq as the Nineteenth Century Turned," 8–9.
95. AAIU Irak V.E.35, R. Danon to AIU, June 2, 1898.
96. Shilo, *Princess of Prisoner?* 172–173. My mention of the classroom as a contested space is influenced by Lisa Pollard's article, "Learning Gendered Modernity." However, unlike the subject of Pollard's study, the AIU classroom in Baghdad was not a site of contestation between political colonizers and a subject population.
97. Malino, "The Women Teachers of the Alliance Israélite Universelle," 257.
98. AAIU Irak V.E.35, R. Danon to AIU, June 16, 1898.
99. Ibid.
100. Ibid.
101. Ibid.
102. Schor, *Best School in Jerusalem*, 61–62.
103. Rodrigue, *French Jews, Turkish Jews*, 108–109.
104. AAIU Irak V.E.35, R. Danon to AIU, June 16, 1898.
105. Ibid.
106. Ibid.; R. Danon to AIU, September 8, 1898.
107. AAIU Irak V.E.35, R. Danon to AIU, September 8, 1898.
108. Ibid.
109. Ibid.
110. Ibid. At this point Danon had not yet requested permission to leave Baghdad, so the future departure she mentions in this letter is unspecified.
111. AAIU Irak V.E.35, R. Danon to AIU, November 24, 1898.
112. Ibid.
113. Ibid.
114. Ibid.
115. Ibid.
116. AAIU Irak V.E.35, R. Danon to AIU, January 10, 1899.
117. AAIU Irak V.E.35, R. Danon to AIU, April 6, 1899.
118. Two important works on this topic are Malino, "The Women Teachers of the Alliance Israélite Universelle" and Land, "Corresponding Women: Female Educators of the Alliance Israélite Universelle in Tunisia, 1882–1914."
119. AAIU Irak V.E.35, Danon to AIU, March 4, 1897.
120. Ibid.
121. Ibid.
122. Ibid.
123. AAIU Irak V.E.35, R. Danon to AIU, May 6, 1897.
124. AAIU Irak V.E.35, R. Danon to AIU, March 10, 1898.
125. Ibid.
126. Ibid.

127. Rodrigue, *Jews and Muslims*, 57–62.
128. Malino, "The Women Teachers of the Alliance Israélite Universelle," 264; Land, "Corresponding Women," 67.
129. AAIU Irak V.E.35, R. Danon to AIU, November 30, 1898.
130. Ibid.
131. Miller, "Gender and the Poetics of Emancipation," 238–239.
132. Rodrigue, *Jews and Muslims*, 57–62.
133. Malino, "'Institutrices,'" 135.
134. AAIU Irak V.E.35, R. Danon to AIU, April 6, 1899.
135. Ibid.
136. AAIU Irak XII.E.113, F. Sutton to AIU, March 24, 1899
137. AAIU Irak XII.E.113, F. Sutton to AIU, April 13, 1899.
138. AAIU Irak XII.E.113, F. Sutton to AIU, May 4, 1899.
139. Ibid.
140. Ibid.
141. See Chapter 3.
142. AAIU Irak XII.E.113, F. Sutton to AIU, May 4, 1899.
143. AAIU Irak XII.E.113, F. Sutton to AIU, June 1, 1899.
144. Ibid.
145. Ibid.
146. AAIU Irak V.E.34, J. Danon to AIU, June 1, 1899.
147. Ibid.
148. Ibid.
149. AAIU Irak V.E.34, J. Danon to AIU, June 8, 1899.
150. Ibid; J. Danon to AIU, November 23, 1899.
151. AAIU Irak XII.E.113, Sutton to AIU, July 6, 1899.
152. Ibid.
153. Ibid.
154. Ibid.
155. AAIU Irak V.E.34, J. Danon to AIU, August 24, 1899.
156. AAIU Irak V.E.34, J. Danon to AIU, November 9, 1899.
157. AAIU Irak XII.E.113, F. Sutton to AIU, November 9, 1899.
158. Ibid.
159. Ibid.
160. Ibid.
161. BAIU (1st and 2nd Semesters 1899), 136–137.

Chapter 3: Making Adjustments

1. For a brief biography of Sémach see Ariel Danan, "Une institutrice de l'Alliance Israélite Universelle, Oro Sémach," *Les Cahiers du Judaïsme* 12 (2002): 58–62.
2. AAIU Irak XI.E.105, O. Sémach to AIU, December 14, 1899. This letter is located in Yomtob Sémach's file.
3. Ibid.
4. AAIU Irak XI.E.106, O. Sémach to AIU, December 21, 1899.
5. Ibid.
6. Ibid.
7. AAIU Irak XI.E.106, O. Sémach to AIU, January 11, 1900.
8. Ibid.

9. AAIU Irak XI.E.106, O. Sémach to AIU, January 9, 1900.
10. Ibid.
11. AAIU Irak XI.E.106, O. Sémach to AIU, January 25, 1900.
12. Ibid.
13. AAIU Irak XI.E.106, O. Sémach to AIU, April 6, 1900.
14. Ibid.
15. AAIU Irak XI.E.106, O. Sémach to AIU, May 17, 1900.
16. Ibid.
17. Ibid.
18. AAIU Irak XI.E.105, O. Sémach to AIU, December 14, 1899; BAIU (1st and 2nd Semester 1899), 136–137.
19. AAIU Irak XI.E.106, O. Sémach to AIU, March 8, 1900.
20. AAIU Irak XI.E.106, O. Sémach to AIU, June 7, 1900.
21. AAIU Irak XI.E.106, O. Sémach to AIU, March 7, 1901.
22. AAIU Irak XI.E.106, O. Sémach to AIU, June 6, 1901.
23. Ibid.
24. AAIU Irak XI.E.106, O Sémach to AIU, October 17, 1901.
25. AAIU Irak XI.E.106, O. Sémach to AIU, January 8, 1902.
26. Ibid.
27. Ibid.
28. Ibid.
29. Ibid.
30. AAIU Irak XI.E.106, O. Sémach to AIU, August 21, 1902.
31. Ibid.
32. Ibid.
33. Ibid.
34. AAIU Irak XI.E.106, O. Sémach to AIU, November 6, 1902.
35. AAIU Irak XI.E.106, O. Sémach to AIU, January 8, 1903.
36. Ibid.
37. AAIU Irak XI.E.106, O. Sémach to AIU, July 16, 1903.
38. Ibid.
39. AAIU Irak XI.E.106, O. Sémach to AIU, September 3, 1903.
40. AAIU Irak XI.E.106, O. Sémach to AIU, October 29, 1903.
41. Ibid.
42. Ibid.
43. AAIU Irak XI.E.106, O. Sémach to AIU, December 17, 1903.
44. AAIU Irak XI.E.106, O. Sémach to AIU. The date for this letter is listed as October 24, 1903, but it refers to a letter from November 25, 1903, and is included with correspondence for December 24, 1903. Thus it appears that this letter is from December 24, 1903.
45. AAIU Irak XI.E.106, O. Sémach to AIU, February 25, 1904.
46. Ibid.
47. Both Yomtob and Oro Sémach mentioned this child's death in 1904, but neither stated when it occurred. See AAIU Irak XI.E.105, Y. Sémach to AIU, July 31, 1904; and AAIU Irak XI.E.106, O. Sémach to AIU, October 4, 1904.
48. AAIU Irak VI.E.57, S. Halfon to AIU, April 14, 1904. The wedding took place March 29, 1904.
49. AAIU Irak VI.E.57, S. Halfon to AIU, September 5, 1904.
50. AAIU Irak XI.E.106, O. Sémach to AIU, October 4, 1904.

51. AAIU Irak V.E.040, J. Douec to AIU, November 3, 1904.
52. AAIU Irak III.E.8, N. Albala to AIU, February 15, 1905.
53. See Chapter 4
54. AAIU Irak XI.E.105, Y. Sémach to AIU, January 18, 1900.
55. Ibid.
56. AAIU Irak XI.E.105, Y. Sémach to AIU, March 22, 1900.
57. Ibid.
58. AAIU Irak XI.E.105, Y. Sémach to AIU, May 3, 1900.
59. Ibid.
60. AAIU Irak XI.E.105, Y. Sémach to AIU, July 19, 1900.
61. Ibid.
62. AAIU Irak XI.E.105, Y. Sémach to AIU, September 6, 1900.
63. Ibid.
64. For discussions of the Baghdadi Jewish diaspora in China in this period see Chiara Betta, "The Baghdadi Jewish Diaspora in Shanghai: Community, Commerce, and Identities," in *Sino-Judaica*, edited by Chiara Betta (Menlo-Park, CA: Sino-Judaica Institute, 2003), 81–104; Caroline Plüss, "Assimilation versus Idiosyncrasy: Strategic Constructions of Sephardic Identities in Hong Kong," *Jewish Culture and History* 5.2 (2002), 48–69; and Idem., "Baghdadi Jews in Hong Kong: Converting Cultural, Social and Economic Capital among Three Transregional Networks," *Global Networks* 11, no. 1 (2011), 82–96.
65. AAIU Irak XI.E.105, Y. Sémach to AIU, May 2, 1901.
66. AAIU Irak XI.E.105, Y. Sémach to AIU, July 24, 1901.
67. AAIU Irak XI.E.106, O. Sémach to AIU, October 17, 1901.
68. AJA Archives (University of Southampton) AJ95/ADD/6 November 25, 1901.
69. AAIU Irak XI.E.105, Y. Sémach to AIU, February 13, 1902.
70. AAIU Irak XI.E.106, O. Sémach to AIU, February 20, 1902.
71. AAIU Irak XI.E.106, O. Sémach to AIU, June 5, 1902.
72. AAIU Irak XI.E.105, Y. Sémach to AIU May 8, 1902; June 26, 1902.
73. AAIU Irak XI.E.106, O. Sémach to AIU, August 21, 1902.
74. AAIU Irak XI.E.105, Y. Sémach to AIU, December 11, 1902.
75. Ibid.
76. Ibid.
77. Ibid.
78. AAIU Irak XI.E.105, Y. Sémach to AIU, March 5, 1903.
79. Ibid.
80. AAIU Irak XI.E.105, Y. Sémach to AIU, May 14, 1903.
81. Ibid.
82. AAIU Irak XI.E.105, Y. Sémach to AIU, June 11, 1903.
83. AAIU Irak XI.E.105, Y. Sémach to AIU, July 9, 1903.
84. AAIU Irak XI.E.105, Y. Sémach to AIU, July 23, 1903.
85. AAIU Irak XI.E.105, Y. Sémach to AIU, August 20, 1903.
86. Ibid.
87. Ibid.
88. Ibid.
89. Ibid.
90. AAIU Irak XI.E.105, Y. Sémach to AIU, September 3, 1903.
91. AAIU Irak XI.E.105, Y. Sémach to AIU, August 20, 1903.
92. AAIU Irak XI.E.105, Y. Sémach to AIU, September 3, 1903.

93. AAIU Irak XI.E.106, O. Sémach to AIU, October 8, 1903.
94. AAIU Irak XI.E.106, O. Sémach to AIU, October 29, 1903.
95. Ibid.
96. Ibid.
97. Ibid.
98. AAIU Irak XI.E.105, Y. Sémach to AIU, October 29, 1903; December 31, 1903.
99. Ibid.
100. AAIU Irak XI.E.105, Y. Sémach to AIU, December 31, 1903.
101. Ibid.
102. Ibid.
103. Ibid.
104. AAIU Irak XI.E.105, Y. Sémach to AIU, February 25, 1904.
105. Ibid.
106. AAIU Irak XI.E.105, Y. Sémach to AIU, March 3, 1904; March 30, 1904.
107. AAIU Irak XI.E.105, Y. Sémach to AIU, April 21, 1904.
108. Ibid.
109. Ibid.
110. AAIU Irak XI.E.106, O. Sémach to AIU, March 6, 1902. Yomtob Sémach's correspondence includes earlier, more frequent, and more detailed discussions of the outbreak but does not discuss its impacts on the Girls' School.
111. Ibid.
112. AAIU Irak XI.E.106, O. Sémach to AIU, March 6, 1902.
113. Ibid.
114. AAIU Irak XI.E.106, O. Sémach to AIU, June 5, 1902.
115. AAIU Irak XI.E.106, O. Sémach to AIU, March 6, 1902.
116. Ibid.
117. Ibid.
118. Ibid.
119. Ibid.
120. AAIU Irak, XI.E.106, O. Sémach to AIU, August 21, 1902.
121. AAIU Irak XI.E.106, O. Sémach to AIU, March 10, 1904. This outbreak also spread to Iran, but its origins were in the Ottoman Iraqi provinces. See R.M. Burrell, "The 1904 Epidemic of Cholera in Persia: Some Aspects of Qājār Society," *Bulletin of the School of Oriental and African Studies, University of London* 51, no. 2 (1988): 258–259. For a brief overview of cholera outbreaks in the region see M.H. Azizi and F. Azizi, "History of Cholera Outbreaks in Iran during the 19th and 20th Centuries," *Middle East Journal of Digestive Diseases* 2, no. 1 (2010): 51–55. The cholera outbreak of 1904 in Iran, which began in Iraq, was, according to Ahmed Seyf, one of the two most damaging in the nineteenth and early twentieth centuries. See also Seyf, "Iran and Cholera in the Nineteenth Century" *Middle Eastern Studies* 38, no. 1 (2002): 173–174.
122. AAIU Irak XI.E.106, O. Sémach to AIU, March 10, 1904.
123. Schor, *Best School in Jerusalem*, 52–53.
124. AAIU Irak V.E.40, J. Douec to AIU, August 10, 1904.
125. AAIU Irak V.E.40, J. Douec to AIU, September 22, 1904.
126. AAIU Irak V.E.40, J. Douec to AIU, November 3, 1904.
127. Ibid; also see J. Douec to AIU, September 22, 1904.
128. AAIU Irak XII.E.113, F. Sutton to AIU, March 8, 1900.
129. Ibid.

130. For a discussion of intrinsic versus extrinsic motivation in education see Roland Bénabou and Jean Tirole, "Intrinsic and Extrinsic Motivation," *The Review of Economic Studies* 70, No. 3 (2003): 489–520.
131. AAIU Irak XI.E.106, O. Sémach to AIU, January 3, 1901.
132. Ibid.
133. AAIU Irak XI.E.106, O. Sémach to AIU, March 7, 1901.
134. AAIU Irak XI.E.106, O. Sémach to AIU, March 21, 1901.
135. Ibid.
136. AAIU Irak XI.E.106, O. Sémach to AIU, January 7, 1904.
137. AAIU Irak XI.E.106, O. Sémach to AIU, November 6, 1902.
138. AAIU Irak XI.E.106, O. Sémach to AIU, December 11, 1902.
139. Ibid.
140. Ibid.
141. AAIU Irak XI.E.106, O. Sémach to AIU, June 7, 1900.
142. Ibid.
143. Ibid.
144. Ibid.
145. AAIU Irak XI.E.106, O. Sémach to AIU, January 8, 1902.
146. Ibid.
147. AAIU Irak XI.E.106, O. Sémach to AIU, January 8, 1903.
148. Ibid.
149. Ibid.
150. Ibid.
151. AAIU Irak XI.E.106, O. Sémach to AIU, March 5, 1903.
152. AAIU Irak XI.E.106, O. Sémach to AIU, July 16, 1903.
153. For a discussion on key aspects of the monitorial system see Neville F. Newman, "Shapes and Spaces: Inside Joseph Lancaster's Monitorial 'Laboratory,'" *The Journal of Educational Thought* 32, no. 2 (1998): 139–168.
154. AAIU Irak XI.E.105B, Y. Sémach to AIU, May 7, 1903; AAIU Irak XI.E.106, O. Sémach to AIU, October 29, 1903.
155. AAIU Irak V.E.40, J. Douec to AIU, November 10, 1904.
156. AAIU Irak XI.E.106, O. Sémach to AIU, March 5, 1903.
157. AAIU Irak XI.E.106, O. Sémach to AIU, January 7, 1904.
158. Ibid.
159. Ibid.
160. Schor, *Best School in Jerusalem*, 46–47.
161. Ibid.
162. Fleischmann, "The Other 'Awakening,'" 102.
163. Ibid., 102–103.
164. Ibid.
165. Ibid., 104.
166. AAIU Irak XI.E.106, O. Sémach to AIU, January 9, 1900.
167. Ibid.
168. Ibid.
169. Ibid.
170. AAIU Irak XI.E.106, O. Sémach to AIU, April 5, 1900.
171. Ibid.
172. AAIU Irak XI.E.106, O. Sémach to AIU, June 7, 1900.
173. AAIU Irak XI.E.106, O. Sémach to AIU, April 5, 1900.
174. Ibid.

175. AAIU Irak XI.E.106, O. Sémach to AIU, March 7, 1901.
176. Ibid.
177. AAIU Irak XI.E.106, O. Sémach to AIU, August 8, 1901.
178. Ibid.
179. Ibid.
180. Ibid.
181. AAIU Irak XI.E.106, O. Sémach to AIU, January 8, 1902.
182. Ibid.
183. Ibid.
184. AAIU Irak XI.E.106, O. Sémach to AIU, October 29, 1903.
185. AAIU Irak XI.E.106, O. Sémach to AIU, March 24, 1904. On the history of the use of sewing machines in the region see Uri M. Kupferschmidt, "The Social History of the Sewing Machine in the Middle East," *Die Welt des Islams* 44, no. 2 (2004): 195–213.
186. AAIU Irak XI.E.106, O. Sémach to AIU, March 24, 1904.
187. Ibid.
188. AAIU Irak XI.E.106, O. Sémach to AIU, June 5, 1902.
189. Ibid.
190. AAIU Irak XI.E.106, O. Sémach to AIU, March 5, 1903.
191. Ibid.
192. Ibid. On Jewish women's mobility inside and outside of the home in Baghdad in this period see Sehayek, "Changes in the Social Status of Urban Jewish Women in Iraq as the Nineteenth Century Turned," 3–6. For a brief discussion of the impact of the AIU on various Jewish communities in the Arab world see Simon, "Between the Family and the Outside World," 83–85.
193. AAIU Irak XI.E.106, O. Sémach to AIU, March 5, 1903.
194. AAIU Irak XI.E.106, O. Sémach to AIU, August 27, 1903.
195. Ibid.
196. Ibid.
197. Ibid.
198. AAIU Irak XI.E.106, O. Sémach to AIU, June 5, 1902.
199. Sehayek, "Changes in the Social Status of Urban Jewish Women in Iraq as the Nineteenth Century Turned," 7–8.
200. Regeur, "The World of Women," 247.
201. AAIU Irak I.C.2, J. Douec to AIU, January 4, 1903. While I have accessed the original document, the translation is from Aron Rodrigue, *Jews and Muslims*, 91–93. Rodrigue's translation includes a minor mistake as it dates the letter as having been written on February, 4, 1903, when in fact it was written on January 4, 1903.
202. Rodrigue, *Jews and Muslims*, 91.
203. Sezgin, "Jewish Women in the Ottoman Empire," 227.
204. See also Simon, "Between the Family and the Outside World," 91–92.
205. For a description of Middle Eastern Jewish women's marriage attire and customs in this region in this period see Sara Reguer, "The World of Women," 236–237.
206. See Chapter 2.
207. Simon, "Between the Family and the Outside World," 91.
208. AAIU Irak XI.E.106, O. Sémach to AIU, October 4, 1904.
209. AAIU Irak XI.E.106, O. Sémach to AIU, February 25, 1904.
210. Ibid. Sémach did not provide her sister's annual salary but stated that she was now being paid 80 francs per month.
211. Ibid.

Chapter 4: From the Baghdad Girls' School to the Laura Kadoorie School for Girls

1. For a brief overview see, Hanioğlu, *A Brief History of the Late Ottoman Empire*, 150–157.
2. Bedross Der Matossian, *Shattered Dreams of Revolution: From Liberty to Violence in the Ottoman Empire* (Stanford, CA: Stanford University Press, 2014), 2–3.
3. Bashkin, "'Religious Hatred Shall Disappear from the Land,'" 315–316.
4. For a discussion of notions of trust in the government see Bashkin, "'Religious Hatred Shall Disappear from the Land,'" 310–312.
5. Harel, *Intrigue and Revolution*, 324–325.
6. Ibid., 329–330.
7. For a brief discussion of Zionism in Damascus in this period see Harel, *Intrigue and Revolution*, 267–271. On the links and battles between Zionist and non-Zionist Jews in Salonica see Cohen, *Becoming Ottomans*, chapter 4. For a discussion on Ottomanism and Zionism in Ottoman Palestine see Michelle U. Campos, *Ottoman Brothers: Muslims, Christians, and Jews in Early Twentieth-Century Palestine* (Stanford, CA: Stanford University Press, 2011), chapter 6.
8. Bashkin, "'Religious Hatred Shall Disappear from the Land,'" 320.
9. AAIU Irak III.E.9, M. Albala to AIU, February 23, 1905.
10. AAIU Irak II.E.8, N. Albala to AIU, February 13, 1905.
11. AAIU Irak III.E.9, M. Albala to AIU, February 23, 1905.
12. Ibid.
13. Ibid.
14. AAIU Irak III.E.9, M. Albala to AIU, March 9, 1905
15. AAIU Irak II.E.8, M. Albala to AIU, June 12, 1905. This letter is housed in Nissim Albala's letter file.
16. Ibid.
17. AAIU Irak III.E.9, M. Albala to AIU, September 7, 1905.
18. Ibid.
19. Ibid.
20. AAIU Irak III.E.9, M. Albala to AIU, November 9, 1905.
21. Ibid.
22. Ibid.
23. BAIU (1905), 124.
24. AAIU Irak III.E.9, M. Albala to AIU, May 21, 1906.
25. Ibid.
26. AAIU Irak III.E.9, M. Albala to AIU, Jul 30, 1906.
27. AAIU Irak III.E.9, M. Albala to AIU, October 28, 1906.
28. Ibid.
29. BAIU (1906), 124.
30. AAIU Irak III.E.9, M. Albala to AIU, January 15, 1907.
31. AJAR (1907–1908), 42.
32. BAIU (1908), 154.
33. AAIU Irak III.E.9, M. Albala to AIU, July 15, 1907.
34. AAIU Irak II.E.8, N. Albalta to AIU, December 16, 1907; AJAR 1907–1908, 21–22
35. BAIU (1909), 113.
36. AAIU Irak III.E.9, M. Albala to AIU, October 17, 1909.
37. AAIU Irak III.E.9, M. Albala to AIU, November 1, 1909.

38. Ibid.
39. Ibid.
40. AAIU Irak III.E.9, M. Albala to AIU, January 17, 1910.
41. BAIU (1910), 224.
42. AAIU Irak III.E.9, M. Albala to AIU, December 4, 1910.
43. AAIU Irak III.E.9, M. Albala to AIU, December 16, 1910; AAIU Irak III.E.9, M. Albala to AIU, December 4, 1910.
44. AAIU Irak III.E.9, M. Albala to AIU, May 1, 1911.
45. AAIU Irak III.E.9, M. Albala to AIU, June 19, 1911.
46. Ibid.
47. AJAR (1911–1912), 24.
48. AAIU Irak II.E.8, N. Albala's speech, November 15, 1911.
49. Ibid.
50. AAIU Irak II.E.8, N. Albala's speech, November 15, 1911.
51. Ibid.
52. Ibid.
53. Fleischmann, "The Other 'Awakening,'" 99–100; Baron, *Women's Awakening in Egypt*, 124–125.
54. Efrati, "Competing Narratives," 448–449.
55. Ibid.
56. For an insightful discussion of Moyal's life and career see Levy, "Jewish Writers in the Arab East," chapter 4.
57. This speech, along with a brief biographical introduction of Moyal, is found in translation from Arabic in Moshe Behar and Zvi Ben-Dor Benite, eds., *Modern Middle Eastern Jewish Thought: Writings on Identity, Politics, & Culture, 1893–1958* (Waltham, MA: Brandeis University Press, 2013), 30–37.
58. Ibid.
59. AAIU Irak III.E.9, M. Albala to AIU, January 15, 1912.
60. Ibid.
61. Ibid.
62. Ibid.
63. Ibid.
64. Ibid.
65. AAIU Irak, III.E.9, M. Albala to AIU, May 8, 1912.
66. Ibid.
67. Ibid.
68. Ibid.
69. Ibid.
70. AAIU Irak VIII.E.92, L. Policar to AIU, November 25, 1912.
71. AAIU Irak III.E.9, M. Albala to AIU, January 16, 1913.
72. Ibid.
73. Ibid. For a brief description of the Menahem Daniel Kindergarten see Twena, *Dispersion & Liberation Part Five*, 60–61.
74. AAIU Irak III.E.9, M. Albala to AIU, January 16, 1913.
75. Ibid.
76. AAIU Irak III.E.9, M. Albala to AIU, September 5, 1913.
77. Ibid.
78. Ibid.
79. Ibid.

80. Ibid.
81. Ibid.
82. Ibid.
83. AAIU Irak III.E.9, M. Albala to AIU, March 8, 1906.
84. Ibid.
85. AAIU Irak III.E.9, M. Albala to AIU, July 30, 1906.
86. AAIU Irak III.E.9, M. Albala to AIU, July 19, 1907.
87. Ibid.
88. Ibid.; M. Albala to AIU, October 8, 1907.
89. AAIU Irak III.E.9, J. Bigart to M. Albala, undated. This letter appears to have been in response to M. Albala's letter from March 8, 1908.
90. AAIU Irak III.E.9, M. Albala to AIU, August 8, 1908.
91. AAIU Irak III.E.9, M. Albala to AIU, January 5, 1909.
92. Ibid.
93. AAIU Irak III.E.9, M. Albala to AIU, April 22, 1909.
94. AAIU Irak III.E.9, M. Albala to AIU, June 7, 1909.
95. Ibid.
96. Ibid.
97. Ibid.
98. AAIU Irak III.E.9, M. Albala to AIU, October 17, 1909.
99. AAIU Irak III.E.9, M. Albala to AIU, November 1, 1909.
100. AAIU Irak III.E.9, M. Albala to AIU, November 15, 1909.
101. AAIU Irak III.E.9, M. Albala to AIU, April 7, 1910.
102. AAIU Irak III.E.9, M. Albala to AIU, December 4, 1910.
103. AAIU Irak III.E.9, M. Albala to AIU, December 10, 1910.
104. AAIU Irak VIII.E.91, A. Picciotto to AIU, February 9, 1911.
105. AAIU Irak VIII.E.91, A. Picciotto to AIU, May 1, 1911.
106. AAIU Irak III.E.9, M. Albala to AIU, February 9, 1911.
107. AAIU Irak III.E.9, M. Albala to AIU, June 19, 1911.
108. AAIU Irak III.E.9, M. Albala to AIU, April 20, 1912.
109. Ibid.
110. Ibid.
111. Ibid.
112. AAIU Irak III.E.9, M. Albala to AIU, May 6, 1912; AAIU Irak XII.E.115, R. Termin to AIU, May 2, 1912.
113. AAIU Irak III.E.9, M. Albala to AIU, February 14, 1913.
114. AAIU Irak III.E.9, M. Albala to AIU, June 29, 1913.
115. Ibid.
116. AAIU Irak III.E.9, M. Albala to AIU, April 14, 1905.
117. Ibid.
118. Ibid.
119. Ibid.
120. AAIU Irak III.E.9, M. Albala to AIU, July 6, 1905.
121. Ibid.
122. Ibid.
123. Ibid.
124. Ibid.
125. Ibid.
126. Ibid.

127. AAIU Irak III.E.9, M. Albala to AIU, September 7, 1905.
128. Ibid.
129. AAIU Irak III.E.9, M. Albala to AIU, October 26, 1905.
130. AAIU Irak III.E.9, M. Albala to AIU, January 18, 1906.
131. Ibid.
132. Ibid.
133. AAIU Irak III.E.9, M. Albala to AIU, October 26, 1905.
134. AAIU Irak III.E.9, M. Albala to AIU, January 18, 1906.
135. AAIU Irak III.E.9, M. Albala to AIU, October 28, 1906.
136. AAIU Irak III.E.9, M. Albala to AIU, April 15, 1907.
137. Ibid.
138. Ibid.
139. Ibid.
140. Ibid.
141. Ibid.
142. Ibid.
143. AAIU Irak III.E.9, M. Albala to AIU, July 10, 1907.
144. Ibid.
145. AAIU Irak III.E.9, M. Albala to AIU, February 4, 1908.
146. Ibid.
147. Ibid.
148. Ibid.
149. Ibid.
150. Ibid.
151. Ibid.
152. Ibid.
153. AAIU Irak III.E.9, M. Albala to AIU, January 5, 1909.
154. Ibid.
155. Ibid.
156. AAIU Irak III.E.9, M. Albala to AIU, April 22, 1909.
157. AAIU Irak III.E.9, M. Albala to AIU, May 19, 1909.
158. Ibid.
159. Ibid.
160. AAIU Irak III.E.9, M. Albala to AIU, April 22, 1909.
161. AAIU Irak III.E.9, M. Albala to AIU, May 19, 1909.
162. AAIU Irak III.E.9, M. Albala to AIU, July 19, 1910.
163. Ibid.
164. Ibid.
165. Ibid.
166. Ibid.; M. Albala to AIU, December 26, 1910.
167. AAIU Irak III.E.9, M. Albala to AIU, July 19, 1910.
168. Ibid.
169. AAIU Irak VIII.E.91, A. Piccioto to AIU, July 8, 1910.
170. AAIU Irak III.E.9, M. Albala to AIU, March 12, 1911.
171. Ibid.
172. Ibid.
173. Ibid.
174. AAIU Irak III.E.9, M. Albala to AIU, May 15, 1911.
175. Ibid.

176. Ibid.
177. AAIU Irak III.E.9, M. Albala to AIU, July 22, 1911.
178. AAIU Irak III.E.9, M. Albala to AIU February 19, 1912.
179. AAIU Irak III.E.9, M. Albala to AIU, January 15, 1912.
180. AAIU Irak IV.E.22, L. Chalom to AIU, March 14, 1912; AAIU Irak VI.E.47, R. Farhi to AIU, January 14, 1912.
181. AAIU Irak III.E.9, M. Albala to AIU, October 24, 1912.
182. AAIU Irak III.E.9, M. Albala to AIU, January 16, 1913.
183. AAIU Irak III.E.9, M. Albala to AIU, February 23, 1905.
184. Ibid.
185. AAIU Irak II.E.8, N. Albala to AIU, February 23, 1905.
186. AAIU Irak II.E.8, M. Albala to AIU, November 16, 1905. This letter is housed in Nissim's letter file.
187. AAIU Irak II.E.8, N. Albala to AIU, February 15, 1906.
188. Ibid.
189. AAIU Irak III.E.9, M. Albala to AIU, October 30, 1906.
190. Ibid.
191. AAIU Irak III.E.9, M. Albala to AIU, November 19, 1908.
192. AAIU Irak III.E.9, M. Albala to AIU, December 1, 1910.
193. AAIU Irak III.E.9, M. Albala to AIU, February 6, 1911.
194. AAIU Irak III.E.9, M. Albala to AIU, February 19, 1912.
195. AAIU Irak III.E.9, J. Bigart to M. Albala, 1912. The exact date is unknown, but the letter is postmarked March 20, 1912.
196. AAIU Irak III.E.9, M. Albala to AIU, November 28, 1912.
197. AAIU Irak III.E.9, M. Albala to AIU, February 14, 1913.
198. AAIU Irak II.E.8, N. Albala to AIU, November 26, 1913.
199. Ibid.
200. AAIU Irak II.E.8, J. Bigart to N. Albala, March 5, 1914.
201. AAIU Irak III.E.13, I. Bassan to AIU, November 20, 1913.
202. AAIU Irak IV.E.14, R. Bassan to AIU, February 8, 1914.
203. Ibid.
204. AAIU Irak IV.E.14, R. Bassan to AIU, February 23, 1914.
205. AAIU Irak IV.E.14, R. Bassan to AIU, February 8, 1914.
206. Ibid.
207. Ibid.; R. Bassan to AIU, February 23, 1914.
208. AAIU Irak IV.E.14, R. Bassan to AIU, March 29, 1914.
209. AAIU Irak IV.E.14, R. Bassan to AIU, February 8, 1914.
210. Ibid.
211. Ibid.
212. AAIU Irak IV.E.14, R. Bassan to AIU, May 4, 1914.
213. Ibid.
214. AAIU Irak III.E.13, R. Bassan to AIU, May 21, 1917. This letter is housed in Isaac Bassan's letter file. For a discussion of the war in Iraq see Mohammad Gholi Majd, *Iraq in World War I: From Ottoman Rule to British Conquest* (Lanham, MD: University Press of America, 2006); Peter Sluglett, *Britain in Iraq: Contriving King and Country, 1914–1932* (New York: Columbia University Press, 2007), 8–41. On Baghdad during the war see Reeva Spector Simon, "The View from Baghdad" in *The Creation of Iraq: 1914–1921* (New York: Columbia University Press, 2004), edited by Reeva Spector Simon and Eleanor H. Tejirian, 40–43.
215. AAIU Irak III.E.13, R. Bassan to AIU, May 21, 1917.

216. Ibid.
217. Ibid.
218. Ibid.
219. Ibid.
220. Ibid.
221. Ibid.
222. Ibid.
223. Ibid.
224. AAIU Irak VIII.E.85, Madame Nehama to AIU, 1918. The letter is not dated but is postmarked July 8, 1918. Nehama did not use her first name in the letter.
225. AAIU Irak III.E.13, R. Bassan to AIU, May 21, 1917

Chapter 5: The AIU Girls' Schools in Hilla, Mosul, and Basra

1. BAIU (1908), 163–164.
2. AAIU Irak II.B.12, M. Soussa to AIU, December 7, 1906. On changes in education, including the arrival of the AIU, in Hilla in this period see Zvi Yehuda, "Toward a Study of a Jewish Community in Iraq in the Period of Change: The Jewish Community in Hilla—Changes in Education (1900–1914)," [In Hebrew] *Miqqedem Umiyyam* 2 (1986): 187–207.
3. AAIU Irak II.B.12, M. Soussa to AIU, December 7, 1906; Yehuda, "The Jewish Community in Hilla," 189–190.
4. AAIU Irak II.B.12, M. Soussa to AIU, December 7, 1906.
5. AAIU Irak II.B.12, M. Soussa to AIU, August 6, 1907.
6. Ibid.
7. BAIU (1910), 239.
8. AAIU Irak XIV.E.142, H. Nehama to AIU, March 7, 1910.
9. AAIU Irak XIV.E.142, H. Nehama to AIU, January 15, 1911.
10. AAIU Irak XIV.E.142, H. Nehama to AIU, June 29, 1911.
11. Ibid.
12. Ibid.
13. Ibid.
14. Ibid.
15. Ibid.
16. AAIU Irak XIV.E.142, H. Nehama to AIU, August 4, 1911.
17. Ibid.
18. AAIU Irak XIV.E.142, H. Nehama to AIU, September 13, 1911.
19. AAIU Irak XIV.E.139, M. & A. Abrevaya to AIU, November 13, 1911. The Abrevayas' letters are housed in the same letter file, and the two cosigned some of their letters.
20. AAIU Irak XIV.E.139, M. Abrevaya to AIU, November 22, 1911.
21. AAIU Irak XIV.E.139, A. Abrevaya to AIU, November 25, 1911.
22. Ibid.
23. Ibid.
24. Ibid.
25. Ibid.
26. Ibid.
27. Ibid.
28. Ibid.
29. AAIU Irak XIV.E.139, A. Abrevaya to AIU, December 20, 1911.
30. Ibid.

31. Ibid.
32. Ibid.
33. Ibid.
34. AAIU Irak XIV.E.139, A. Abrevaya to AIU, March 3, 1912.
35. Ibid.
36. Ibid.
37. Ibid.
38. Ibid.
39. Ibid.
40. Ibid.
41. AAIU Irak XIV.E.139, A. Abrevaya to AIU, June 6, 1912.
42. Ibid.
43. Ibid.
44. AAIU Irak XIV.E.139, A. Abrevaya to AIU, November 1, 1912.
45. Ibid.
46. Ibid.
47. AAIU Irak XIV.E.139, A. Abrevaya to AIU, January 3, 1913.
48. Ibid.
49. Ibid.
50. AAIU Irak XIV.E.139, A. Abrevaya to AIU, February 7, 1913.
51. Ibid.
52. AAIU Irak XIV.E.139, A. Abrevaya to AIU, April 3, 1913.
53. Ibid.
54. For her initial salary request see AAIU Irak XIV.E.139, A. Abrevaya to AIU, May 17, 1912.
55. AAIU Irak XIV.E.141, R. Farhi to AIU, May 22, 1913.
56. Ibid.
57. Ibid.
58. Ibid.
59. AAIU Irak XIV.E.141, R. Farhi to AIU, July 3, 1913.
60. Ibid.
61. Ibid.
62. Ibid.
63. AAIU Irak XIV.E.141, R. Farhi to AIU, November 4, 1913.
64. Ibid.
65. Ibid.
66. AAIU Irak XIV.E.141, R. Farhi to AIU, January 1, 1914.
67. Ibid.
68. Ibid.
69. Ibid.
70. Ibid.
71. AAIU Irak XIV.E.141, R. Farhi to AIU, April 30, 1914.
72. Ibid.
73. AAIU Irak II.B.12, M. Soussa to AIU, April 3, 1914.
74. AAIU Irak II.B.12, M. Soussa to AIU, July 29, 1914.
75. Ibid.
76. AAIU Irak XIV.E.143, M. Zeloof to AIU, December 31, 1918.
77. BAIU (1912), 112; BAIU (1913), 142.

78. For an overview of economic and social life in nineteenth-century Mosul see Sarah Shields, *Mosul Before Iraq: Like Bees Making Five-Sided Cells* (Albany: State University of New York Press, 2000).
79. Shields, *Mosul Before Iraq*, 144. For a discussion of the Jewish community in late Ottoman Mosul see Lanaido, *The Jews of Mosul*, 87–91.
80. Shields, *Mosul before Iraq*, 47–49.
81. Lanaido, *Jews of Mosul*, 175–176; Meir, *Socio-cultural Development of Iraqi Jews*, 151.
82. AAIU Irak XV.E.146, July 24, 1908; interview with E. Sayegh in the newspaper *Israel's Messenger*. A copy of the article is included in this letter file.
83. AAIU Irak XV.E.146, E. Sayegh to AIU, September 9, 1906.
84. AAIU Irak XV.E.146, E. Sayegh to AIU, August 2, 1907.
85. AAIU Irak XVI.E.151, M. Sidi to AIU, December 27, 1907.
86. Ibid.
87. Ibid.
88. AAIU Irak XVI.E.151, M. Sidi to AIU, January 29, 1908; Lanaido, 182.
89. AAIU Irak XVI.E.151, M. Sidi to AIU, January 29, 1908.
90. Ibid.
91. AAIU Irak XVI.E.151, M. Sidi to AIU, February 28, 1908.
92. Ibid.
93. AAIU Irak XVI.E.151, M. Sidi to AIU, March 30, 1908.
94. Ibid.
95. AAIU Irak XVI.E.151, M. Sidi to AIU, April 11, 1908.
96. Ibid.
97. AAIU Irak XVI.E.151, M. Sidi to AIU, May 15, 1908.
98. AAIU Irak XVI.E.151, M. Sidi to AIU, June 22, 1908.
99. AAIU Irak XVI.E.151, M. Sidi to AIU, September 4, 1908.
100. AAIU Irak XVI.E.151, M. Sidi to AIU, September 11, 1908. Shields also mentions the school's closure in passing in her work on late Ottoman Mosul, though she provides no further details. See Shields, *Mosul before Iraq*, 48–49.
101. AAIU Irak XVI.E.151, M. Sidi to AIU, September 11, 1908.
102. AAIU Irak XVI.E.151, M. Sidi to AIU, September 26, 1908.
103. AAIU Irak XVI.E.151, M. Sidi to AIU, November 27, 1908.
104. Shields, *Mosul before Iraq*, 60.
105. AAIU Irak XV.E.146, July 24, 1908; interview with Sayegh in *Israel's Messenger*.
106. AAIU Irak XVI.E.151, M. Sidi to AIU, December 3, 1909.
107. Ibid.
108. Ibid.
109. AAIU Irak XVI.E.151, M. Sidi to AIU, May 17, 1911.
110. AAIU Irak XVI.E.152, J. Sidi to AIU, May 3, 1912.
111. Sidi's letter announcing the school's opening was written on May 3, 1912.
112. AAIU Irak XVI.E.152, J. Sidi to AIU, May 3, 1912.
113. Ibid.
114. Ibid.
115. Ibid.
116. Ibid.
117. Ibid.
118. Ibid.
119. Ibid.

120. Ibid.
121. AAIU Irak XVI.E.152, J. Sidi to AIU, May 17, 1912.
122. Ibid.
123. Ibid.
124. Ibid.
125. AAIU Irak XVI.E.152, J. Sidi to AIU, June 14, 1912.
126. Ibid.
127. AAIU Irak XVI.E.151, M. Sidi to AIU, June 22, 1912.
128. For a discussion of David's life see Monique Nahon, *Hussards de l'Alliance: Rachel & David Sasson* (Paris: Éditions du Palio, 2010), 19–28.
129. For Rachel's life see Nahon, *Hussards de l'Alliance*, 29–34.
130. AAIU Irak XV.E.150, R. Sasson to AIU, February 14, 1913.
131. AAIU Irak XV.E.150, R. Sasson to AIU, November 9, 1912.
132. Ibid.
133. Ibid.
134. Ibid.
135. Ibid.
136. AAIU Irak XV.E.150, R. Sasson to AIU, November 29, 1912.
137. Ibid.
138. AAIU Irak XV.E.150, R. Sasson to AIU, December 29, 1912.
139. Ibid.
140. Ibid.
141. Ibid.
142. AAIU Irak XV.E.149, D. Sasson to AIU, January 3, 1913.
143. Ibid.
144. AAIU Irak XV.E.150, R. Sasson to AIU, January 17, 1913.
145. BAIU (1912), 118.
146. AAIU Irak XV.E.150, R. Sasson to AIU, January 17, 1913.
147. Ibid.
148. Ibid.
149. Ibid.
150. AAIU Irak XV.E.150, R. Sasson to AIU, February 14, 1913.
151. Ibid.
152. Ibid.
153. Ibid.
154. Ibid.
155. AAIU Irak XV.E.150, R. Sasson to AIU, May 2, 1913.
156. Ibid.
157. AAIU Irak XV.E.150, R. Sasson to AIU, June 20, 1913.
158. AAIU Irak XV.E.150, R. Sasson to AIU, August 15, 1913.
159. AAIU Irak XV.E.149, D. Sasson to AIU, May 23, 1913.
160. AAIU Irak XV.E.150, R. Sasson to AIU, June 20, 1913.
161. Ibid.
162. Ibid.
163. Ibid.
164. Ibid.
165. Ibid.
166. Nahon, *Hussards de l'Alliance*, 42.

167. AAIU Irak XV.E.150, R. Sasson to AIU, August 15, 1913.
168. AAIU Irak XV.E.149, D. Sasson to AIU, September 19, 1913.
169. Ibid.
170. AAIU Irak XV.E.150, R Sasson to AIU, November 20, 1913; November 28, 1913; and December 20, 1913.
171. AAIU Irak XV.E.150, R. Sasson to AIU, November 28, 1913.
172. Ibid.
173. AAIU Irak XV.E.150, R. Sasson to AIU, December 20, 1913; BAIU (1913), 148–149.
174. BAIU (1913), 148–149.
175. AAIU Irak XV.E.150, R. Sasson to AIU, December 20, 1913.
176. AAIU Irak XV.E.150, R. Sasson to AIU, February 12, 1914.
177. Ibid.
178. Ibid.
179. AAIU Irak XV.E.150, R. Sasson to AIU, July 4, 1914.
180. AAIU Irak XV.E.149, D. Sasson to AIU, November 30, 1915; January 15, 1916.
181. See Fattah, *The Politics of Regional Trade*, 69–71, 102–113. On the region's integration into the world economy in this period see Thabit A.J. Abdullah, *A Short History of Iraq*, 2nd edition (New York: Longman, 2011), 77–78.
182. For a look at the influence of the city's Jewish community in the nineteenth century see Thabit J. Abdullah, *Merchants, Mamluks, and Murder: The Political Economy of Trade in Eighteenth Century Basra* (Albany: State University of New York Press, 2001), 1–3 & 110–112. For a brief overview of the community's history in the nineteenth and early twentieth century see David Sassoon, "The History of the Jews in Basra," *The Jewish Quarterly Review* 17, no. 4 (1927): 407–469.
183. BAIU (1913), 133.
184. Batatu, *Old Social Classes and the Revolutionary Movements of Iraq*, 247.
185. Ibid., 248.
186. Meir, *Socio-cultural Development of Iraqi Jews*, 141–142
187. Sciarcon, "Expanding the Mission," 194–196.
188. Ibid., 200–203.
189. Ibid., 203–204.
190. David Sagiv's *The Jewish Community in Basra* briefly discusses the establishment of this school but relies on the BAIU.
191. AAIU Irak XIII.E.123, J. Behar to AIU, July 20, 1905.
192. Ibid.
193. Ibid.
194. AAIU Irak XIII.E.123, J. Behar to AIU November 18, 1906.
195. AAIU Irak XIII.E.121, M. Abrevaya to AIU, July 7, 1911.
196. AAIU Irak XIII.E.121, M. Abrevaya to AIU, June 30, 1911.
197. AAIU Irak XIII.E.126, M. Ittah to AIU, June 8, 1912.
198. AAIU Irak XIII.E.126, M. Ittah to AIU, February 4, 1913.
199. Ibid.
200. Ibid.
201. Ibid.
202. AAIU Irak XIII.E.126, M. Ittah to AIU, May 9, 1913.
203. Ibid.
204. AAIU Irak XIII.E.126, M. Ittah to AIU, August 4, 1913
205. AAIU Irak XIII.E.126, M. Ittah to AIU, August 22, 1913.

206. AAIU Irak XIII.E.126, M. Ittah to AIU, December 5, 1913.
207. Ibid.
208. AAIU Irak XIII.E.126, M. Ittah to AIU, January 2, 1914.
209. AAIU Irak XIII.E.126, M. Ittah to AIU, November 8, 1913.
210. AAIU Irak XIII.E.126, M. Ittah to AIU, January 2, 1914; AAIU Irak XIV.E.133, R. Zilberstein to AIU, December 25, 1913.
211. AAIU Irak XIII.E.126, M. Ittah to AIU, January 2, 1914.
212. Ibid.
213. Ibid.
214. AAIU Irak XIV.E.133, R. Zilberstein to AIU, December 25, 1913.
215. Ibid.
216. AAIU Irak XIII.E.126, M. Ittah to AIU, February 6, 1914.
217. AAIU Irak XIII.E.126, M. Ittah to AIU, April 18, 1914.
218. AAIU Irak XIII.E.126, M. Ittah to AIU, May 29, 1914.
219. AAIU Irak XIV.E.133, R. Zilberstein to AIU, May 22, 1914.
220. Ibid.
221. Ibid.
222. Ibid.
223. Ibid.
224. AAIU Irak XIV.E.133, R. Zilberstein to AIU, July 25, 1914.
225. Ibid.
226. Ibid.
227. Ibid.
228. AAIU Irak XIV.E.133, R. Zilberstein to AIU, August 26, 1915.
229. Ibid.
230. Ibid.
231. Ibid.
232. Ibid.

Conclusion

1. Benbassa, "Education for Jewish Girls in the East," 166.
2. BAIU (1913), 132.
3. Simon, *Change Within Tradition*, 46–47.
4. Rodrigue, *Jews and Muslims*, 82–84.
5. Simon, "Between the Family and the Outside World," 84–85.
6. Benbassa, "Education for Jewish Girls in the East," 170.
7. Molho, "Female Jewish Education in Salonica," 148.
8. Rodrigue, *Jews and Muslims*, 88–89.
9. Rodrigue, *French Jews, Turkish Jews*, 108–110.
10. Molho, "Female Jewish Education in Salonica," 146.
11. Sezgin, "Jewish Women in the Ottoman Empire," 229.
12. Shilo, *Princess or Prisoner?* 120–121.
13. Ibid., 121–123.
14. Ibid.
15. Schor, *Best School in Jerusalem*, 62–63.
16. Simon, *Change Within Tradition*, 112.
17. Ibid., 114–115.
18. Ibid., 99.

19. Ibid.
20. Keith Walters, "Education for Jewish Girls in late nineteenth- and early twentieth-century Tunis and the spread of French in Tunisia," in *Jewish Culture and Society in North Africa*, edited by Emily Benichou Gottreich and Daniel J. Schroeter (Bloomington and Indianapolis: Indiana University Press, 2011), 257–281. On the origins of modern schooling for girls in Tunis see 263–265.
21. Land, "Corresponding Lives," 204–205.
22. Ibid.
23. Laskier, *Alliance Israélite Universelle and the Jewish Communities of Morocco*, 128.
24. For a discussion of the Jewish acculturation in Baghdad see Michel Abitbol, "From Coexistence to the Rise of Antagonisms," in *A History of Jewish-Muslim Relations: From the Origins to the Present Day* (Princeton, NJ: Princeton University Press, 2013), 297–311.
25. Bashkin, *New Babylonians*, 84–97.
26. Ibid.

BIBLIOGRAPHY

Archival Sources

Alliance Israélite Universelle Irak Files

Baghdad

I.C.1 General Reports
I.C.2 General Reports
I.E.3 Founding of the Boys' School
II.E.8 Letters of Nissim Albala (Boys' School), 1905–1914
III.E.9 Letters of Marie Albala (Girls' School), 1905–1913
III.E.13 Letters of Isaac Bassan (Boys' School), 1913–1917
IV.E.14 Letters of Rebecca Bassan (Girls' School), 1913–1917
IV.E.16 Letters of Jacques Behar (Boys' School), 1903
IV.E.20 Letters of Rosa Braun (Girls' School), 1906–1910
IV.E.22 Letters of Leila Chalom (Girls' School), 1912–1914
IV.E.28 Letters of Morris Cohen (Boys' School), 1885–1900
IV.E.32 Letters of Rebecca Confino (Girls' School), 1909–1911
V.E.34 Letters of Joseph Danon (Boys' School), 1893–1900
V.E.35 letters of Rachel Danon (Girls' School), 1894–1899
V.E.40 Letters of Jamilé Douec (Girls' School), 1900–1905
VI.E.47 Letters of Rosa Farhi (Girls' School), 1905–1906 & 1912–1913
VI.E.54 Letters of Régine Gueron (Girls' School), 1915
VI.E.57 Letters of Salomon Halfon (Boys' School), 1904–1904
VII.E.71 Letters of Claire Levy (Girls' School), 1915
VII.E.72 Letters of Dola Levy (No Affiliation), 1903
VII.E.74 Letters of Sultana Levy (Girls' School), 1915
VIII.E.84 Letters of Flora Nahon (Girls' School), 1912–1914

VIII.E.91 Letters of Alice Picciotto (Girls' School), 1909–1911

VIII.E.92 Letters of Léa Policar (Girls' School), 1910–1913

XI.E105 Letters of Yomtob Sémach (Boys' School), 1899–1904

XI.E.106 Letters of Oro Sémach (Girls' School), 1899–1904

XI.E.111Letters of Joya Simhon (Girls' School), 1909–1911

XII.E.112 Letters of Saul Somekh (Boys' School), 1888–1893

XII.E.113 Letters of Faridé Sutton (Girls' School), 1897–1900

XII.E.115 Letters of Rebecca Termin (Girls' School), 1912–1914

Basra

II.B.10 Committee Reports

XIII.E.120 General Reports

XIII.E.121 Letters of Moïse Abrevaya (Boys' School), 1908–1913

XIII.E.123 Letters of Jacques Behar (Boys' School), 1903–1908

XIII.E.126 Letters of Moïse Ittah (Boys' School), 1911–1917

XIV.E.132 Letters of Albert Zilberstein (Boys' School), 1913–1917

XIV.E.133 Letters of Rebecca Zilberstein (Girls' School), 1913–1917

Hilla

II.B.12 Committee Reports

XIV.E.139 Letters of Alice Abrevaya (Boys' & Girls' Schools), 1911–1913

XIV.E.140 Letters of Noury Farhi (Boys' School), 1913–1914

XIV.E.141 Letters of Rosa Farhi (Girls' School), 1913–1914

XIV.E.142 Letters of Heskel Nehama (Boys' School), 1907–1911

XIV.E.143 Letters of M. Zeloof (No Affiliation), 1918

Mosul

XV.E.146 Committee Reports

XV.E.149 Letters of David Sasson (Boys' School), 1912–1918

XV.E.50 Letters of Rachel Sasson (Girls' School), 1912–1915

XVI.E.151 Letters of Maurice Sidi (Boys' School), 1907–1912

XVI.E.152 Letters of Joya Sidi (Girls' School), 1911–1912

Anglo-Jewish Association Archives (Special Collections, University of Southampton)

MS137/AJ95/ADD2 Council Minutes, 1881–1895

MS137/AJ95/ADD3 Council Minutes, 1895–1909

MS137/AJ95/ADD6 Executive Committee, 1889–1909

British National Archives

Newspapers

London Jewish Chronicle

Published and Unpublished Material

Abdullah, Thabit J. *Merchants, Mamluks, and Murder: The Political Economy of Trade in Eighteenth Century Basra.* Albany: State University of New York Press, 2001

_______. *A Short History of Iraq,* 2nd edition. New York. Longman, 2011.

Abdul-Razzak, Hilali. *History of Education in Iraq During the Ottoman Times, 1638–1917.* Baghdad: The National Printing & Publishing Company, 1959. In Arabic.

Abu-Lughod, Leila (ed.). *Remaking Women: Feminism and Modernity in the Middle East.* Princeton, NJ: Princeton University Press, 1998.

Ahmed, Leila. *Women and Gender in Islam: Historical Roots of a Modern Debate.* New Haven, CT: Yale University Press, 1992.

Al-Qaysi, Abdul-Wahhab Abbas. The Impact of Modernization on Iraqi Society during the Ottoman Era. Ann Arbor: University of Michigan, 1958. Unpublished PhD dissertation.

Al-Tikriti, Nabil. "Was There an Iraq before Iraq?" *International Journal of Contemporary Iraqi Studies* 3, no. 2 (2009): 133–142.

Anglo-Jewish Association. *Anglo-Jewish Association Annual Reports,* 1871–1915. London.

Anscombe, Frederick S. *The Ottoman Gulf: The Creation of Kuwait, Saudi Arabia, and Qatar.* New York: Columbia University, 1997.

Antébi, Elizabeth. "Changer la femme pour changer l'homme: le modèle des institutrices de L'Alliance Israélite Universelle." In *Femmes et judaïsme aujourd'hui*: Edited by Sonia Sarah Lipsyc, 257–267. Paris: Museum of Jewish Art and History, 2008.

Ayalon, Yaron. *Natural Disasters in the Ottoman Empire: Plague, Famine, and Other Misfortunes.* Cambridge: Cambridge University Press, 2014.

Azizi, M.H., and F. Azizi. "History of Cholera Outbreaks in Iran during the 19th and 20th Centuries." *Middle East Journal of Digestive Diseases* 2, no. 1 (2010): 51–55.

Bar-Asher, Shalom. "The Emancipation of North-African Jewish Women: The Alliance Israélite Universelle." In *Jews and Muslims in the Islamic World*: Edited by Bernard Dov Cooperman and Zvi Zohar, 33–50. College Park: University of Maryland, 2013.

Baron, Beth. *The Women's Awakening in Egypt: Culture, Society, and the Press.* New Haven, CT: Yale University Press, 1994.

Basci, K. Pelin. "Shadows in the Missionary Garden of Roses: Women of Turkey in American Missionary texts." In *Deconstructing Images of "The Turkish Woman"*: Edited by Zehra F. Arat, 101–123. New York: St. Martin Press, 1998.

Bashkin, Orit. *New Babylonians: A History of Jews in Modern Iraq.* Stanford, CA: Stanford University Press, 2012.

_______. "'Religious Hatred Shall Disappear from the Land': Iraqi-Jews as Ottoman Subjects, 1864–1913." *International Journal of Contemporary Iraqi Studies* 4, no. 3 (2010): 305–323.

_______. "Why Did Baghdadi Jews Stop Writing to Their Brethren in Mainz? Some Comments about the Reading Practices of Iraqi Jews in the 19th Century." *Journal of Semitic Studies* (2005): 95–110.

Basri, Meer S. *Eminent Jewish Men of Modern Iraq.* Jerusalem: Association for Academics from Iraq, 1983. In Arabic.

Batatu, Hanna. *The Old Social Classes and the Revolutionary Movements of Iraq: A Study of Iraq's Old Landed and Commercial Classes and of its Communists, Ba'thissts, and Free Officers*. Princeton, NJ: Princeton University Press, 1978.

Behar, Moshe, and Zvi Ben-Dor Benite (eds.) *Modern Middle Eastern Jewish Thought: Writings on Identity, Politics, & Culture, 1893–1958*. Waltham, MA: Brandeis University Press, 2013.

Bénabou Roland, and Jean Tirole. "Intrinsic and Extrinsic Motivation." *The Review of Economic Studies* 70, no. 3 (2003): 489–520.

Benbassa, Esther. *The Jews of France: A History from Antiquity to the Present*. Princeton, NJ: Princeton University Press, 1999. Translated by M.B. DeBevoise.

_______. "Education for Jewish Girls in the East: A Portrait of the Galata School in Istanbul, 1879–1912." *Studies in Contemporary Jewry* 9 (1993): 163–173.

_______. "L'artisanat juif en Turquie à la fin du 19e siècle: l'Alliance Israélite Universelle et ses oeuvres d'apprentissage." *Turcica* 17 (1985): 113–126.

Ben-Jacob, Abraham. *History of the Jews of Iraq from the Gaonic Period to the Present*. Jerusalem: Ben-Zvi Institute, 1965. In Hebrew.

Benveniste, Annie. "Le rôle des Institutrices de l'Alliance Israélite Universelle à Salonique." *Combat pour la Diaspora* 8 (1982): 13–26.

Berkovitz, Jay R. *The Shaping of Jewish Identity in Nineteenth-Century France*. Detroit, MI: Wayne State University Press, 1989.

Betta, Chiara. "The Baghdadi Jewish Diaspora in Shanghai: Community, Commerce, and Identities." *Sino-Judaica* 4 (2003): 81–104.

Bigart, Jacques. "The Alliance Israélite Universelle." *American Jewish Yearbook* 2 (1900–1901): 45–65.

Bulletin de l'Alliance Israélite Universelle 1860–1913. Paris.

Burrell, R.M. "The 1904 Epidemic of Cholera in Persia. Some Aspects of Qājār Society." *Bulletin of the School of Oriental and African Studies* 51, no. 2 (1988): 258–270.

Burrows, Matthew. "'Mission Civilisatrice': French Cultural Policy in the Middle East, 1860–1914." *The Historical Journal* 29, no. 1 (1986): 109–135.

Campos, Michelle U. *Ottoman Brothers: Muslims, Christians, and Jews in Early Twentieth-Century Palestine*. Stanford, CA: Stanford University Press, 2011.

Ceylan, Ebubekir. *The Ottoman Origins of Modern Iraq: Political Reform, Modernization, and Development in the Nineteenth-Century Middle East*. London: I.B. Tauris, 2011.

Chiha, Habīb K. *La province de Bagdad, son passé, son present, son avenir*. Cairo: El Maaref, 1908.

Chouraqui, André. Cent ans d'histoire: L'Alliance Israélite Universelle et la renaissance *juive contemporaine (1860–1960)*. Paris: Press universitaires de France, 1965.

Clancy-Smith, Julia. "Envisioning Knowledge: Educating the Muslim Woman in Colonial North Africa, c.1850–1918." In *Iran and Beyond: Essays in Middle Eastern History in Honor of Nikki R. Keddie*: Edited by Rudi Matthee and Beth Baron, 99–120. Costa Mesa, CA: Mazda Publishers, Inc., 2000.

Clark, Linda. *Schooling the Daughters of Marianne: Textbooks and the Socialization of Girls in Modern French Primary Schools*. Albany: State University of New York Press, 1984.

Cohen, Hayyim J. *The Jews of the Middle East, 1860–1972*. New York: John Wiley & Sons, 1973.

Cohen, Julia Phillips. *Becoming Ottomans: Sephardi Jews and Imperial Citizenship in the Modern Era*. New York: Oxford University Press, 2014.

Cohen, Stuart. *British Policy in Mesopotamia, 1903–1914*. Reading: Ithaca Press, 2008.

Conklin, Alice L. "The Civilizing Mission." In *The French Republic: History, Values, Debates*: Edited by Edward Berenson, Vincent Duclert, and Christophe Prochasson, 173–181. Ithaca, NY: Cornell University Press, 2009.

Cooperman, Bernard Dov, and Zion Zohar (eds.) *Jews and Muslims in the Islamic World.* College Park: University of Maryland Press, 2013.

Danan, Ariel. "Une institutrice de l'Alliance Israélite Universelle, Oro Semach." *Cahiers du Judaïsme* 12 (2002): 58–62.

Davison, Roderic H. *Reform in the Ottoman Empire, 1856–1876.* Princeton, NJ: Princeton University Press, 1963.

De Bellaigue, Christina. *Educating Women: Schooling and Identity in England and France, 1800–1867.* New York: Oxford University Press, 2007.

Der Matossian, Bedross. *Shattered Dreams of Revolution: From Liberty to Violence in the Late Ottoman Empire.* Stanford, CA: Stanford University Press, 2014.

Deringil, Selim. *The Well-Protected Domains: Ideology and the Legitimation of Power in the Ottoman Empire, 1876–1909.* London: I.B. Tauris Press, 1998.

Deshen, Shlomo. "Baghdad Jewry in Late Ottoman Times: The Emergence of Social Classes and Secularization." In *Jews among Muslims: Communities in the Precolonial Middle East*: Edited by Shlomo Deshen and Walter P. Zenner, 187–196. London: Palgrave Macmillan, 1996.

Devens, Carol. "'If We Get The Girls We Get The Race': Missionary Education of Native American Girls." In *American Nations: Encounters in Indian Country: 1850 to the Present*: Edited by Frederick E. Hoxie, Peter C. Mancall, and James H. Merrell, 157–171. New York: Routledge, 2001.

Dumont, Paul. "Jews, Muslims, and Cholera: Intercommunal Relations in Baghdad at the End of the Nineteenth Century." In *The Jews of the Ottoman Empire*: Edited by Avigdor Levy, 353–372. Princeton, NJ: Darwin Press, 1994.

Efrati, Noga. "Competing Narratives: Histories of the Women's Movement in Iraq, 1910–1958." *International Journal of Middle East Studies* 40, no. 3 (2008): 445–466.

_______. "The Other 'Awakening' in Iraq: The Women's Movement in the First Half of the Twentieth Century." *British Journal of Middle Eastern Studies* 31, no. 2 (2004): 153–173.

Fattah, Hala. *The Politics of Regional Trade in Iraq, Arabia, and the Gulf, 1745–1900.* Albany: State University of New York Press, 1997.

_______. "The Question of "Artificiality." In *Iraq: Its History, People and Politics*: Edited by Shams C. Inati, 49–60. New York: Humanity Books, 2003.

Findley, Carter Vaughn. "The Tanzimat." In *The Cambridge History of Turkey Volume 4: Turkey in the Modern World*: Edited by Resat Kasaba, 11–37. Cambridge: Cambridge University Press, 2008.

Finkel, Caroline. *Osman's Dream: The History of the Ottoman Empire.* New York: Basic Books, 2005.

Fleischmann, Ellen. "The Other 'Awakening': The Emergence of Women's Movements in the Modern Middle East, 1900–1940." In *Social History of Women and Gender in the Modern Middle East*: Edited by Margaret L. Meriwether and Judith E. Tucker, 89–140. Boulder, CO: Westview Press, 1999.

_______. "'Our Moslem Sisters': Women of Greater Syria in the Eyes of American Protestant Missionary Women." *Islam and Christian-Muslim Relations* 9, no. 3 (1998): 307–325.

Fogiel-Bijaoui, Sylvie. "Un Chemin D'Émanicpation: L'Alliance Israélite Universelle Et Les Femmes Juives De Palestine (1872–1939)." *Archives Juives* 46, no. 1 (2013): 107–119.

Fortna, Benjamin C. "The Reign of Abdülhamid II." In *Cambridge History of Turkey Volume 4: Turkey in the Modern World*: Edited by Resat Kasaba, 38–61. Cambridge: Cambridge University Press, 2008.

_______. *Imperial Classroom: Islam, the State, and Education in the late Ottoman Empire.* Oxford: Oxford University Press, 2002.

Francis-Dehqani, Gulnar Eleanor. "CMS Women Missionaries in Iran, 1891–1934: Attitudes Towards Islam and Muslim Women." In *Women, Religion and Culture in Iran*: Edited by Sarah Ansari and Vanessa Martin, 27–50. Richmond, Surrey: Curzon, 2002.

Frankel, Jonathan. *The Damascus Affair: "Ritual Murder," Politics, and the Jews in 1940.* Cambridge: Cambridge University Press, 1997.

Frenette, Derek. L'Alliance Israélite Universelle and the Politics of Modern Jewish Education in Baghdad: 1864–1914. Burnaby, British Columbia: Simon Fraser University, 2005. Unpublished Master's thesis.

Frierson, Elizabeth B. "Unimagined Communities: Women and Education in the Late-Ottoman Empire, 1876–1909." *Critical Matrix* 9, no. 2 (1995), 55–90.

Fuchs, Rachel G., and Victoria E. Thompson. *Women in Nineteenth-Century Europe.* New York: Palgrave Macmillan, 2005.

Gabbay, Nilly. *The Jewish Woman in Baghdad: Processes of Change in her Social Status During the First Half of the Twentieth Century.* Jerusalem: Association of the Jewish Academic from Iraq, 2006. In Hebrew.

_______. "The Education of Girls in the Jewish Community of Baghdad, 1894–1951." *Pe'amim* 82 (2003): 94–118. In Hebrew.

Ghanimah, Yusuf Rizk-Allah. *A Nostalgic Trip into the History of the Jews of Iraq.* Lanham, MD: University Press of America, 1998. Translated by A. Dallal.

Goldberg, Harvey E. (ed.) *Sephardi and Middle Eastern Jewries: History and Culture in the Modern Era.* Bloomington: Indiana University Press, 1996.

Gottreich, Emily Benichou, and Daniel J. Schroeter (eds.) *Jewish Culture and Society in North Africa.* Bloomington: Indiana University Press, 2011.

Graetz, Michael. *The Jews in Nineteenth-Century France: From the French Revolution to the Alliance Israélite Universelle.* Stanford, CA: Stanford University Press, 1996. Translated by Jean Marie Todd.

Green, Abigail. "Nationalism and the 'Jewish International': Religious Internationalism in Europe and the Middle East c. 1840–c. 1880." *Comparative Studies in Society and History* 50, no. 2 (2008): 535–558.

_______. "Rethinking Sir Moses Montefiore: Religion, Nationhood and International Philanthropy in the Nineteenth Century." *American Historical Review* 110, no. 3 (2005): 631–658.

Greenberg, Ela. *Preparing the Mothers of Tomorrow: Education and Islam in Mandate Palestine.* Austin: University of Texas Press, 2010.

Hacker, Erol. *Edirne, Its Jewish Community, and Alliance Schools: 1867–1937.* Istanbul: Isis Press, 2006.

Hanioğlu, M. Sükrü. *A Brief History of the Late Ottoman Empire.* Princeton, NJ: Princeton University Press, 2008.

Harel, Yaron. *Intrigue and Revolution: Chief Rabbis in Aleppo, Baghdad, and Damascus, 1744–1914.* Portland: Littman Library of Jewish Civilization, 2015. Translated by Yehonatan Chipman.

Hyman, Paula. *The Jews of Modern France.* Berkeley: University of California Press, 1998.

Ingram, Doreen. *The Awakened: Women in Iraq.* London: Third World, 1983.

Issawi, Charles. *The Fertile Crescent 1800–1914: A Documentary Economic History.* Oxford: Oxford University Press, 1981.

Jenkins, Richard. *Re-thinking History.* New York: Routledge Classics, 2003.

Kadhim, Abbas. "Iraqi Education in the Ottoman Era." *Kufa Review* 2, no. 3 (2013): 25–53.

Kasaba, Resat (ed.). *The Cambridge History of Turkey Volume 4: Turkey in the Modern World.* Cambridge University Press, 2008.

Kashani-Sabet, Firoozeh. *Conceiving Citizens: Women and the Politics of Motherhood in Iran.* Oxford: Oxford University Press, 2011.

Kaspi, D'André (ed.). *Histoire de l'Alliance Israélite Universelle de 1860 à nos jours.* Paris: Armand Colin, 2010.

Kazzaz, Nissim. *The Jews of Iraq in the Twentieth Century.* Jerusalem: Ben-Zvi Institute, 1991. In Hebrew.

Keddie, Nikki R. *Women in the Middle East: Past and Present.* Princeton, NJ: Princeton University Press, 2007.

Keddie, Nikki R., and Beth Baron (eds.) *Women in Middle Eastern History: Shifting Boundaries in Sex and Gender.* New Haven, CT: Yale University Press, 1991.

Kedourie, Elie. *Arabic Political Memoirs and Other Studies.* London: Frank Cass, 1974.

_______. "The Break between Muslims and Jews in Iraq." In *Jews among Arabs: Contacts and Boundaries*: Edited by Mark R. Cohen & Abraham L. Udovitch, 21–63. Princeton, NJ: Darwin Press, 1989.

Kedourie, Sylvie. "Aspects of Jewish life in Baghdad under the Monarchy." *Middle East Studies* 12 (1976): 188–208.

Kelly, Joan. "The Social Relation of the Sexes: Methodological Implications of Women's History." In *Women, History, & Theory: The Essays of Joan Kelly.* Chicago: The University of Chicago Press, 1984.

Kupferschmidt, Uri M. "The Social History of the Sewing Machine in the Middle East." *Die Welt des Islams* 44, no. 2 (2004): 195–213.

Lanaido, Ezra. *The Jews of Mosul: From Exile to Operations Ezra and Nehemia.* Tirat-Carmel: Center for Research of the Jews of Mosul, 1981. In Hebrew.

Land, Joy. "Corresponding Women: Female Educators of the Alliance Israélite Universelle in Tunisia, 1882–1914." In *Jewish Culture and Society in North Africa*: Edited by Emily Benichou Gottreich and Daniel J. Schroeter, 239–256. Bloomington: Indiana University Press, 2011.

_______. *Corresponding Lives: Women Educators of the Alliance Israélite Universelle School for Girls in the City of Tunis, 1882–1914.* Los Angeles: UCLA, 2006. Unpublished PhD Dissertation.

Laskier, Michael M. *The Alliance Israélite Universelle and the Jewish Communities of Morocco*, 1862–1962. Albany: State University of New York Press, 1983.

Leff, Lisa Moses. *Sacred Bonds of Solidarity: The Rise of Jewish Internationalism in Nineteenth-Century France.* Stanford, CA: Stanford University Press, 2006.

Leven, Narcisse. *Cinquante ans d'histoire: L'alliance Israélite Universelle* (1860–1910). Paris: F. Lacan, 1911.

Levi, Tomer. *The Jews of Beirut: The Rise of a Levantine Community, 1860s–1930s.* New York: Peter Lang, 2012.

Levy, Avigdor (ed.). *Jews, Turks, Ottomans: A Shared History, Fifteenth through the Twentieth Century.* Syracuse, NY: Syracuse University Press, 2002.

_______. (ed.) *The Jews of the Ottoman Empire.* Princeton, NJ: Darwin Press, 1994.

Levy, Lital. "Historicizing the Concept of Arab Jews in the *Mashriq*." *Jewish Quarterly Review* 98, no. 4 (2008): 452–469.

_______. "From Baghdad to Bialik with Love": A Reappropriation of Modern Hebrew Poetry, 1933." *Comparative Literature Studies* 42, no. 3 (2005): 125–154.

_______. "Jewish Writers in the Arab East: Literature, History, and the Politics of Enlightenment, 1863–1914." Berkeley: University of California, 2007. Unpublished PhD Dissertation.

Majd, Gholi. *Iraq in World War I: From Ottoman Rule to British Conquest.* Lanham, MD: University Press of America, 2006.

Malino, Frances. "L'émancipation des femmes." In *Histoire de l'Alliance Israélite Universelle de 1860 à nos jours*: Edited by D'André Kaspi, 263–294. Paris: Armand Colin, 2010.

_______. "Institutrices" in the Metropole and the Maghreb: A Comparative Perspective. *Historical Reflections* 32, no. 1 (2006): 129–142.

_______. "Prophets in Their Own Land? Mothers and Daughters of the Alliance Israélite Universelle." *Nashim* 3 (2000): 56–73.

_______. "The Women Teachers of the Alliance Israélite Universelle, 1872–1940." In *Jewish Women in Historical Perspective*, 2nd edition: Edited by Judith Baskin, 248–269. Detroit: Wayne State University Press, 1998.

Masters, Bruce. *Christians and Jews in the Ottoman Arab World: The Roots of Sectarianism.* Cambridge: Cambridge University Press, 2001.

Matthee, Rudi, and Beth Baron (eds.) *Iran and beyond: Essays in Middle Eastern History in Honor of Nikki R. Keddie.* Costa Mesa, CA: Mazda Publishers, 2000.

Meddeb, Abdelwahab, and Benjamin Stora (eds.) *A History of Jewish-Muslim Relations: From the Origins to the Present Day.* Princeton, NJ: Princeton University Press, 2013.

Meir, Yosef. *Socio-Cultural Development of Iraqi Jews, 1830 to the present.* Tel Aviv: Naharayim, 1989. In Hebrew.

Melman, Billie. *Women's Orients: English Women and the Middle East, 1718–1918.* Ann Arbor: University of Michigan Press, 1992.

Meriwether, Margaret L., and Judith E. Tucker (eds.) *Social History of Women and Gender in the Modern Middle East.* Boulder, CO: Westview Press, 1999.

Miccoli, Dario. *Histories of the Jews of Egypt: An Imagined Bourgeoisie, 1882–1950s.* London: Routledge, 2015.

Miller, Susan G. "Gender and the Poetics of Emancipation: *The Alliance Israélite Universelle* in Northern Morocco, 1890–1912." In *Franco-Arab encounters: Studies in Memory of David C. Gordon*: Edited by L. Carl Brown and Matthew S. Gordon, 229–252. Beirut: American University of Beirut Press, 1996.

Mills, Sara. *Discourses of Difference: An Analysis of Women's Travel Writing and Colonialism.* London: Routledge, 1991.

Molho, Rena. "Female Jewish Education in Salonica at the End of the 19th Century. In *Salonica and Istanbul: Social, Political and Cultural Aspects of Jewish Life*: Edited by Rena Molho, 139–150. Istanbul: Isis Press, 2005.

Munslow, Alan. *Deconstructing History*, 2nd edition. New York: Routledge, 2006.

Murre-van den Berg, Heleen. "The Study of Western Missions in the Middle East (1820–1920): An Annotated Bibliography." In *The Social Dimension of Christian Missions in the Middle East: Historical Studies of the 19th and 20th Centuries*: Edited by Norbert Friedrich, Uwe Kaminsky, and Roland Löffler, 35–54. Stuttgart: Franz Steiner Verlag, 2010.

_______. "The Middle East: Western Missions and the Eastern Churches, Islam and Judaism." In *The Cambridge History of Christianity Volume 9: World Christianities C. 1815– C. 1914*: Edited by Sheridan Gilley and Brian Stanley, 458–472. Cambridge: Cambridge University Press, 2006.

_______. "Nineteenth-Century Protestant Missions and Middle-Eastern Women: An Overview." In *Gender, Religion, and Change in the Middle East: Two Hundred Years of History*: Edited by Inger Marie Okkenhaug and Ingvild Flaskerud, 103–122. New York: Berg, 2005.

Nahon, Monique. *Hussards de l'Alliance: Rachel & David Sasson*. Paris: Éditions du Palio, 2010.

Najmabadi, Afsaneh. "Crafting an Educated Housewife in Iran." In *Remaking Women: Feminism and Modernity in the Middle East*: Edited by Lila Abu-Lughod, 91–125. Princeton, NJ: Princeton University Press, 1998.

Nashat, Guity, and Judith Tucker. *Women in the Middle East and North Africa*. Bloomington: Indiana University Press, 1998.

Newman, Neville H. "Shapes and Spaces: Inside Joseph Lancaster's Monitorial "Laboratory." *The Journal of Educational Thought* 32, no. 2 (1998): 139–168.

Nicault, Catherine. "Face au sionisme (1897–1940)." In *Histoire de l'Alliance Israélite Universelle de 1860 à nos jours*: Edited by D'André Kaspi, 189–226. Paris: Armand Colin, 2010.

Okkenhaug, Inger Marie. *The Quality of Heroic Living, of High Endeavour and Adventure: Anglican Mission, Women and Education in Palestine, 1888–1948*. Leiden: Brill, 2002.

Plüss, Caroline. "Baghdadi Jews in Hong Kong: Converting Cultural, Social and Economic Capital among Three Transregional Networks." *Global Networks* 11, no. 1 (2011): 82–96.

_______. "Assimilation versus Idiosyncrasy: Strategic Constructions of Sephardic Identities in Hong Kong." *Jewish Culture and History* 5, no. 2 (2002): 48–69.

Pollard, Lisa. "Learning Gendered Modernity: The home, the Family, and the Classroom in the Construction of Egyptian National Identity (1885–1919)." In *Beyond the Exotic: Women's Histories in Islamic Societies*: Edited by Amira El-Azhary Sonbol, 249–269. Syracuse, NY: Syracuse University Press, 2005.

Popiel, Jennifer J. *Rousseau's Daughters: Domesticity, Education, and Autonomy in Modern France*. Durham: University of New Hampshire Press, 2008.

Quartararo, Anne T. *Women Teachers and Popular Education in Nineteenth-Century France*. Newark: University of Delaware Press, 1995.

Quataert, Donald. *The Ottoman Empire: 1700–1922*, 2nd edition. Cambridge: Cambridge University Press, 2005.

_______. "Ottoman Women, Households, and Textile Manufacturing, 1800–1914." In *Women in Middle Eastern History: Shifting Boundaries in Sex and Gender*: Edited by Nikki R. Keddie and Beth Baron, 161–176. New Haven, CT: Yale University Press, 1991.

Reeves-Ellington, Barbara. "Embracing Domesticity: Women, Mission, and Nation Building in Ottoman Europe, 1832–1872." In *Competing Kingdoms: Women, Mission, Nation, and the American Protestant Empire, 1812–1960*: Edited by Barbara Reeves-Ellington, Kathryn Kish Sklar, and Connie A. Shemo, 269–292. Durham, NC and London: Duke University Press, 2010.

Reguer, Sara. "The World of Women." In *The Jews of the Middle East and North Africa in Modern Times*: Edited by Reeva Spector Simon, Michael Menachem Laskier, and Sara Reguer, 235–250. New York: Columbia University Press, 2003.

Rejwan, Nissim. *The Jews of Iraq: 3000 Years of History and Culture*. Boulder, CO: Westview Press, 1985.

Rodrigue, Aron. *Jews and Muslims: Images of Sephardi and Eastern Jewries in Modern Times*. Seattle: University of Washington Press, 2003.

_______. *French Jews, Turkish Jews: The Alliance Israélite Universelle and the Politics of Jewish Schooling in Turkey, 1860–1925*. Bloomington: Indiana University Press, 1990.

Rogers, Rebecca. *A Frenchwoman's Imperial Story: Madame Luce in Nineteenth-Century Algeria*. Stanford, CA: Stanford University Press, 2013.

_______. "Learning to be Good Girls and Women: Education, Training and Schools." In *The Routledge History of Women in Europe since 1700*: Edited by Deborah Simonton, 93–133. New York: Routledge, 2006.

_______. "Schools, Discipline and Community: Diary-Writing and Schoolgirl Culture in Late Nineteenth-Century France." *Women's History Review* 4, no. 4 (1995): 525–555.

Sagiv, David. *The Jewish Community in Basra, 1914–1952*. Jerusalem: Karmel, 2004. In Hebrew.

Sassoon, David Solomon. *The History of the Jews in Baghdad*. Letchworth, UK: The Alcuin Press, 1949.

_______. "The History of the Jews in Basra." *Jewish Quarterly Review* 17, no. 4 (1927): 407–469.

Sawdayee, Maurice. *The Baghdad Connection*. Locust Valley, NY: Self-published, 1991.

Schor, Laura S. *The Best School in Jerusalem: Annie Landau's School for Girls, 1900–1960*. Waltham, MA: Brandeis University Press, 2013.

Schulze, Kristen E. *The Jews of Lebanon: Between Coexistence and Conflict*. Brighton, England: Sussex Academic Press, 2001.

Schroeter, Daniel J. "The Changing Relationship between the Jews of the Arab Middle East and the Ottoman state in the Nineteenth Century." In *Jews, Turks, Ottomans: A Shared History, Fifteenth through the Twentieth Century*: Edited by Avigdor Levy, 88–107. Syracuse, NY: Syracuse University Press, 2002.

Sciarcon, Jonathan. "Expanding the Mission: The Alliance Israélite Universelle, the Anglo-Jewish Association, and the Jewish Boys' School in Basra, 1890–1903." *International Journal of Contemporary Iraqi Studies* 9, no. 3. (2015): 191–207.

_______. "Unfulfilled Promises: Ottomanism, the 1908 Revolution and Baghdadi Jews. *International Journal of Contemporary Iraqi Studies* 3, no. 2 (2009): 155–168.

Scott, Joan Wallach. *Gender and the Politics of History*. New York: Columbia University Press, 1999.

Sehayek, Shaul. "Changes in the Status of Urban Jewish Women in Iraq as the Nineteenth Century Turned." *Women in Judaism* 3, no. 2 (Winter, 2003): 1–24. Translated by Dina Ripsman Eylon and Dalia Maishlish.

Seyf, Ahmed. "Iran and Cholera in the Nineteenth Century." *Middle East Studies* 38, no. 1(2002): 169–178.

Sezgin, Paméla Dorn. "Jewish Women in the Ottoman Empire." In *Sephardic and Mizrahi Jews: From the Golden Age Spain to Modern Times*: Edited by Zion Zohar, 216–238. New York: New York University Press, 2005.

Shiblak, Abbas. *Iraqi Jews: A History*. London: Saqi, 2005.

Shields, Sarah D. *Mosul before Iraq: Like Bees Making Five-Sided Cells*. Albany: State University of New York Press, 2000.

Shilo, Margalit. *Princess or Prisoner? Jewish Women in Jerusalem, 1840–1914*. Waltham, MA: Brandeis University Press, 2005.

Silberman, Paul. "An Investigation of the Schools of the Alliance Israélite Universelle from 1862–1940." New York: New York University, 1973. Unpublished PhD dissertation.

Simon, Rachel. "Between Two Worlds: Education and Acculturation of Ottoman Jewish Women." In *Social History of Late Ottoman Women*: Edited by Duygu Köksal and Anastasia Falierou, 109–132. Leiden, Brill, 2013.

_______. "Education." In *The Jews of the Middle East and North Africa in Modern Times*: Edited by Reeva Spector Simon, Michael Menachem Laskier, and Sara Reguer, 142–164. New York: Colombia University Press, 2003.

_______. "Jewish Female Education in the Ottoman Empire." In *Jews, Turks, Ottomans: A Shared History, Fifteenth through the Twentieth Century*: Edited by Avigdor Levy, 127–152. Syracuse, NY: Syracuse University Press, 2002.

_______. "Between the Family and the Outside World: Jewish Girls in the Modern Middle East and North Africa." *Jewish Social Studies* 7, no. 1 (2000): 81–108.

_______. *Change within Tradition among Jewish Women in Libya.* Seattle: University of Washington Press, 1992.

Simon, Reeva. S., Eleanor Tejirian, and Gary Sick. *Creation of Iraq, 1914–1921.* New York: Columbia University Press, 2005.

Simon, Reeva Spector, Michael Menachem Laskier, and Sara Reguer (eds.) *The Jews of the Middle East and North Africa in Modern Times.* New York: Columbia University Press, 2003.

Simon, Reeva Spector. "The View from Baghdad." In *Creation of Iraq, 1914–1921*: Edited by Reeva S. Simon, Eleanor Tejirian, and Gary Sick, 36–49. New York: Columbia University Press, 2005.

_______. "Iraq." In *The Jews of the Middle East and North Africa in Modern Times*: Edited by Reeva Spector Simon, Michael Menachem Laskier, and Sara Reguer, 347–366. New York: Columbia University Press, 2003.

_______. "Education in the Jewish community in Baghdad to 1914." *Pe'amim* 36 (1988), 52–63. In Hebrew.

Sluglett, Peter. *Britain in Iraq: Contriving King and Country, 1914–1932.* New York: Columbia University Press, 2007.

Snir, Reuven. "'My Adherence to the Creed of Moses Has Not Diminished My Love for Muhammad's Nation': The Emergence of Iraqi-Jewish Modern Literary Discourse." *Jewish Quarterly Review* 98, no. 1 (2008): 62–87.

_______. "'We Are Arabs Before We Are Jews': The Emergence and Demise of Arab-Jewish Culture in Modern Times." *Electronic Journal of Oriental Studies VIII* (2005): 1–47.

_______. "'My Heart Beats with Love of the Arabs': Iraqi Jews Writing in Arabic in the Twentieth Century." *Journal of Modern Jewish Studies* 1, no. 2 (2002): 182–203.

Somel, Selcuk Aksin. *The Modernization of Public Education in the Ottoman Empire, 1839–1908: Islamization, Autocracy, and Discipline.* Leiden: Brill, 2001.

Stillman, Norman. *The Jews of Arab Lands in Modern Times.* Philadelphia: The Jewish Publication Society, 2003.

_______. *The Jews of Arab Lands: A History and Source book.* Philadelphia: Jewish Publication Society of America, 1979.

Stockdale, Nancy L. *Colonial Encounters among English and Palestinian women, 1800–1948.* Gainesville: University of Florida Press, 2007.

Szajkowski, Zosa. "Conflicts in the Alliance Israélite Universelle and the Founding of the Anglo-Jewish Association, the Vienna Allianz and the Hilfsverein." *Jewish Social Studies* 19, no. 1–2 (1957): 29–50.

Tilburg, Patricia A. *Colette's Republic: Work, Gender, and Popular Culture in France, 1870–1914.* New York: Bergham Books, 2009.

Tripp, Charles. *A History of Iraq*, 2nd edition. New York: Cambridge University Press, 2005.

Tsadik, Daniel. *Between Foreigners and Shi'is: Nineteenth-Century Iran and its Jewish Minority.* Stanford, CA: Stanford University Press, 2007.

Tucker, Judith. *Women in Nineteenth-Century Egypt.* Cambridge: Cambridge University Press, 1985.

Twena, Abraham. *Jewish Education in Baghdad.* Ramla: Geoula Synagogue Committee, 1975.

Visser, Reidar. "Proto-political conceptions of 'Iraq' in late Ottoman Times. *International Journal of Contemporary Iraqi Studies* 3, no. 2. (2009): 143–154.

Walters, Keith. "Education for Jewish Girls in Late Nineteenth and Early Twentieth Century Tunis and the Spread of French in Tunisia." *Jewish Culture and Society in North Africa*: Edited by Emily Benichou Gottreich and Daniel J. Schroeter, 257–281. Bloomington: Indiana University Press, 2011.

Warzeski, Jeanne-Marie. "'Women's Work for Women': American Presbyterian Missionary Women in Egypt, 1854–1914." In *Women Travellers in the Near East*: Edited by Sarah Searight, 79–91. Cambridge: ASTENE and Oxbow Books, 2005.

Wiesner-Hanks, Merry E. *Gender in History: Global Perspectives*, 2nd edition. Chichester: Wiley Blackwell, 2011.

Yehuda, Zvi. "Iraqi Jewry and Cultural Change in the Educational Activity of the Alliance Israélite Universelle." In *Sephardi and Middle Eastern Jewries*: Edited by Harvey Goldberg, 134–145. Bloomington: Indiana University Press, 1996.

_______. "Toward a Study of a Jewish Community in Iraq in the Period of Change: The Jewish Community in Hilla—Changes in Education (1900–1914)." *Miqqedem Umiyyam* (1986): 187–207. In Hebrew.

Zohar, Zion (ed.). *Sephardic and Mizrahi Jews: From the Golden Age of Spain to Modern Times.* New York: New York University Press, 2005.

INDEX